PLACES IN MIND

Public Archaeology as
Applied Anthropology

CRITICAL PERSPECTIVES IN IDENTITY, MEMORY, AND THE BUILT ENVIRONMENT
HELAINE SILVERMAN, UNIVERSITY OF ILLINOIS AT URBANA-CHAMPAIGN, SERIES EDITOR

Places in Mind: Public Archaeology as Applied Anthropology
edited by Paul A. Shackel and Erve Chambers

Identity and Power in the Ancient Andes:
Tiwanuku and Lukermata
John Wayne Janusek

The Ecology of Power: Culture, Place, and Personhood
in the Southern Amazon, AD 1000–2000
Michael J. Heckeneberger

PLACES IN MIND

Public Archaeology as Applied Anthropology

Edited by

Paul A. Shackel

and

Erve J. Chambers

Routledge
Taylor & Francis Group

NEW YORK AND LONDON

Published in 2004 by
Routledge
29 West 35th Street
New York, New York 10001

Published in Great Britain by
Routledge
11 New Fetter Lane
London EC4P 4EE
www.routledge.co.uk

Routledge is an imprint of the Taylor & Francis Group.
Printed in the United States of America on acid-free paper.

10 9 8 7 6 5 4 3 2 1

Library of Congress Cataloging-in-Publication Data for this book is available from the
Library of Congress

ISBN 0-415-94645-X
ISBN 0-415-94646-8 (pbk.)

Contents

Working with Communities
Heritage Development and Applied Archaeology

PAUL A. SHACKEL

In his introduction to this volume, Paul Shackel reflects upon the extent to which archaeologists are becoming increasingly aware of the importance of involving themselves locally in issues and practices related to the management of heritage resources. He suggests that much of this interest on the part of the archaeological community is motivated by an interest in associating themselves with community-based activities that seek to empower historically subordinated groups. Shackel traces this commitment to the ideologies that helped foster the American Civil Rights movement.

Introduction

About a decade ago Laurajane Smith (1994:300) remarked, "Archaeological theory falls short in addressing heritage management and how archaeological knowledge is used within the management process." Since that time some archaeologists, including the authors in this book, have taken strides to become part of the local decision processes, working with communities and stakeholders in heritage management issues. We are now becoming aware that archaeologists are in a clear position to go beyond what Smith (1994:301) remarked as "archaeologists writing about archaeologists, writing about archaeologists . . . with little engagement with concrete, practical problems posed within heritage management." The discipline is in a good position to understand the role of archaeologist as participant and collaborator working on issues related to cultural identity and heritage development. Barbara Little's (2002b) volume on the *Public*

1

Benefits of Archaeology shows how archaeology is becoming much more broadly perceived by the public and practitioners. Archaeologists are increasingly using the discipline for "purposes of education, community cohesion, entertainment, and economic development" (Little 2002a:1). While archaeologists have come a long way in a short time since Smith described the state of the discipline, it is important to realize that we are still far from fully integrating archaeology into the heritage management of places and communities.

One cause for the development of a new community-based archaeology program is that a growing number of professionals now accept the fact that archaeology is more than implementing scientific methods to collect and interpret data. While the New Archaeology placed academically trained professionals in positions as gatekeepers of archaeological knowledge, archaeologists are increasingly relying on community input for their projects. The volumes by Nina Swidler et al. (1997), Joe Watkins (2001), and Kurt Dongoske et al. (2000) are all timely and groundbreaking approaches that show how archaeologists can work with American Indian communities.

While many American archaeologists have focused their attention on working with American Indian communities, there is a need for more diverse case material related to the public contexts of applied archaeology. There are many other ethnic and social groups that want to participate in the development of their own heritage. The case studies presented in this book are about African Americans, American Indians, Irish Americans, impoverished industrial communities, immigrant communities, and communities in Ireland and Australia. The individual chapters represent a variety of conditions and approaches that advance our knowledge of the field and place these efforts within the larger context of anthropology.

The authors show that an increasing number of archaeologists are committed to the idea that communities have a sense of their own past and they want to be part of the decision-making process regarding their own heritage development. This changing perspective in the discipline is paralleled by changes in anthropology as a whole, and while the discipline has changed significantly, archaeologists are only beginning to realize the importance of community involvement. Community participation means that scientists are no longer the cultural brokers. Practitioners are beginning to recognize that many histories can exist in any one place, and these stories of the past are continually being shaped and reconstructed. Archaeologists are in a good place to address these changing perspectives, and they need to respond effectively to these challenges and opportunities.

There are three main themes in this book, and while these may serve as an organizational structure, several of the chapters could easily fit into more than one section, as many of the ideas are interrelated. The first theme is about recognizing the social and political structures of communities and empowering subordinated groups. Archaeologists work with groups to provide a more inclusive history of the past, and they work with minority groups to create the group's own heritage. The second theme is about making archaeology applicable to nontraditional communities. Often, the official meaning of places no longer addresses the needs of a new and changing community population, and archaeology is one vehicle to make local history relevant to a nontraditional group. The third theme is about how professionals use archaeology to understand and create a sense of heritage. Heritage often means integrity, authenticity, and stability, and it is a way for communities to make a claim to a past and assert themselves in the present political and social landscape.

The contributors are from a variety of backgrounds, working in academia, nonprofit groups, and local governments. The latter groups are underrepresented in the archaeological literature even though they are part of the most rapidly growing sector in the field. The conditions and circumstances faced by these contributors provide an important perspective for understanding the direction of applied archaeology. They provide discussions on how archaeologists can take a role in either a participatory or a collaborative approach. The former develops from the outside, while the latter is part of a shared activity (see Chambers this volume). These approaches need to be developed within the context of their projects, and practitioners need to remain flexible and have the ability to change directions.

All of the authors in this book provide a voice to communities that have been underrepresented in official histories. They are working with these subordinated groups to give them a voice in how their past is created. The authors share their perspectives on and challenges in working with communities and other stakeholder groups who have a special interest in the uses of the past. They have taken great strides to democratize archaeology and allow for a more diverse past to be constructed.

Archaeology and Empowering Subordinated Groups

Historian Eric Hobsbawm (1983:13) writes, "The history which became part of the fund of knowledge or the ideology of nation, state or movement is not what has actually been preserved in popular memory, but what has been selected, written, pictured, popularized and institutionalized by those whose function it is to do so." Traditions, meanings, and memories are invented, and they become legitimate through repetition or a process of formalization and ritualization characterized by reference to the past. By implying continuity with the past—and sometimes that is a matter of forgetting a past—or reinventing a collective memory, these traditions reinforce values and behavior (Hobsbawm 1983:1–5).

Official landscapes, like those designated by preservation groups and local and federal governments, are developed to create a memory of a particular event. These landscapes help to promote and preserve the ideals of cultural leaders and authorities. They are often displayed to the public as though the past they represent is reality. They present the past as abstract and timeless and sacred, and they help to reduce competing interests (Bodner 1992:13).

For example, the exclusion of African Americans from the national consciousness was an active process that was reinforced through written symbols, material symbols, and commemoration. While African Americans were able to become U.S. citizens with the passing of the fourteenth Amendment in 1868, it was close to one hundred years before they could gain inclusion in the collective memory of the United States. While Americans institutionalized racism with Jim Crow legislation and the *Plessy v. Ferguson* decision, these institutions began to falter under the 1964 Civil Rights Act. This act covered many aspects of race relations, including voting, public accommodation, employment, education, and health care. Under Title 2, which referred to public accommodation, segregation in public places like restaurants, hotels, and theaters was eliminated; thus, symbolic displays of exclusion slowly disappeared from the landscape. The Civil Rights Act helped to change the American landscape, not only for African Americans, but also for other minority groups. What was once defined as a white landscape is now becoming a multiracial landscape. It is now easier to incorporate other groups into the official public memory, and it is becoming apparent that some federal, state, and local agencies are taking this opportunity to become more inclusive in their interpretations of the past (Shackel 2001b).

While the nature of U.S. cultural resource management (CRM) and the Federal Archaeology program has been influenced by the beautification movement of the 1960s, I believe that much of the shaping, rethinking, and reinterpretation of modern CRM laws are in some way influenced by the Civil Rights movement. By the 1980s archaeologists began to intensify their discussions on ethics, which included the conservation of archaeological resources (Fowler 1984), and the rights of descendant groups. Initially, archaeologists were concerned with American Indian groups, including the issue of reburial (King 1972; Winter 1980; McManamon 1992), but by the 1980s archaeologists also had to develop a working relationship with non-Indian groups through some trial and error. Such is the case of the African burial ground project in New York City (LaRoche and Blakey 1997; Cantwell and Wall 2001:277–294). Community involvement and public interpretation has become increasingly important in federal legislation related to archaeology.

Many of the articles in this book are about empowering subordinated groups and working with decision makers and stakeholders in communities. For instance, Jeffrey Hantman explains his long-term working relationship with the Monacan Indians of Virginia. Scholars have traditionally dismissed this group as a peripheral entity to the powerful Powhatans. Hantman has struggled to demonstrate to a larger audience the vitality of this tribe. His research indicates that the Monacans were in fact the dominant group in pre-1607 Virginia since they controlled the elite exchange links to the American interior. He proposes that the Monacans had larger ancestral territorial lands than the tribe and scholars had previously thought. This information becomes important when dealing with matters related to the handling of human remains as it gives the Monacans greater input. By collaborating with the Monacans on various projects, including a traveling exhibit and display, Hantman has played an important role in making the history of Monacan people a part of the local and state public memory. By making the Monacan story accessible to a larger audience, it may foster the tribe's ability to gain federal recognition.

Carol McDavid's public interpretation and outreach program at the Levi Jordan Plantation in Texas, a plantation with an enslaved workforce and later African-American tenants, provides a rich source of information of mid- to late-nineteenth-century lifeways. Her project is about decentering the archaeologist as the authoritative source of "the truth" about the past. She believes that the concepts of reflexivity, multivocality, interactivity, and contextuality are important components to a long-term, mutually empowering experience about the past. She reports how the archaeology of enslaved people created an uproar in a community that had sublimated this history. Both African-American and European-American descendant communities were her informants, clients, and collaborators. She has solicited their help, and the communities have asked her to initiate activities and ask research questions that serve the interests of their groups. McDavid has created a collaborative, nonhierarchical public archaeology project, thereby establishing a meaningful, democratic, and socially relevant archaeology.

Paul Mullins discusses his collaborative research project that developed in 1999 between Indiana University-Purdue University Indianapolis (IUPUI) and the university's neighboring African-American community groups. The project focuses on the former community of Near-Westside that the University demolished in the 1960s as part of its expansion and urban renewal program. Parking lots, buildings, the Indiana University Medical Center, and the IUPUI campus now cover the neighborhood. Many African-American members of neighborhood associations have been involved in the research project, and they see archaeology as a way to claim a heritage and develop a community history "that establishes a symbolic proprietorship of spaces that today bear no visible traces of African-American heritage." An oral history project is part of this new collaboration, and the enterprise is seen in the community as something distinct from the university's urban renewal past. The archaeology project directed by Mullins is a unique effort to bring the community and the university together to acknowledge a past that was once deliberately erased from the landscape.

Matthew Reeves reflects on his experiences working on African-Jamaican and African-American archaeology sites. In Jamaica he immersed himself in the local community and used local informants to help him with his research. He struggled to create a more inclusive research program with the local community because the local population had very different values and questions about the archaeological site than he would have proposed. At Manassas National Battlefield Reeves explored how racism helped to erase the memory of a local black family's occupation of a prominent community structure. His later work at Montpelier involves working with James Madison's enslaved descendants. Reeves created a survey to elicit comments and research questions from the African-American descendant community about the excavation of one of the slave quarters. A descendant family has participated in an archaeological excavation, and he is working to make African-American history part of the interpretation at Montpelier.

Archaeology and Nontraditional Communities

Material culture, either in the form of statues, monuments, museums, artifacts, or landscapes, may have some ascribed meanings—past and present—associated with it, and these meanings vary between individuals and interest groups. These meanings can transform an object into something sacred when serving the goals and needs of any group. How an individual or a locale creates a meaning of the past can reshape perceptions of national collective meaning. "Individuals and groups can envision themselves as members of a collective with a common present—and future" (Glassberg 1998:5). Various individuals and groups can transcend barriers to be part of a collective memory, with a common past, present, and future.

Of particular interest is how the National Park Service is trying to overcome some of the barriers created by Congressional mandates that appear to be out of sync with the move toward multicultural expressions. For in-

stance, many early national parks were created to promote national patri-
otic histories, rather than local and multicultural histories. In an attempt
to focus on local histories that are meaningful to communities, the NPS
sponsored a *Community Study Report* (Bowser 2000) that highlights the
organization's recent experience in helping to organize community and
park cooperation celebrating diversity (*www.nps.gov/community/commu-
nity report.htm*). The report contains fifteen stories and shows how the
National Park Service connects with diverse communities and promotes
pluralism. For instance, at Alcatraz the NPS explores the history of the
American Indian take over of the island in the 1960s and relates it to current activism within the Indian population. It is part of a larger program
titled "'Promoting Tolerance,' which brings emerging leaders from Eastern
and Central Europe to the United States to learn about techniques to
strengthen pluralism and respect for diversity" (Bowser 2000:20). Representatives came from Russia, Bosnia, Estonia, Romania, and Bulgaria. In
each of these countries, the practice of democracy is a relatively new concept, and the program demonstrates how differences could be reconciled
and minority groups could become part of the political process. The program at Alcatraz shows how the federal government is trying to reconcile
with a previously disenfranchised group. The American Jewish Committee,
a nonprofit group that works toward strengthening intergroup relations and
respect for democracy, sponsored a follow-up program (Bowser 2000:20).

Another example in the *Community Study Report* (Bowser 2000) is the
story of Lowell National Historical Park. The park was established in 1978 to
tell the story of the American industrial revolution, immigration, and the
labor movement. The park is also committed to making its interpretation
reflective and applicable to the surrounding community. The park asked the
community for input in order to make Lowell relevant to life and culture
today. The curators of the "Working People Exhibits" in the Mogan Cultural
Center invited community members, including the recently arrived immigrant and ethnic communities, to provide input when planning this exhibit.

Community members also made recommendations for the interpretive
directions in the park. Some of these recommendations included (Bowser
2000:10–11):

1. Reexamine, update, and improve the way Lowell tells community
   stories, whether the community is telling its own stories, or the park
   is interpreting the story.
2. Seek out active community involvement in revitalizing permanent
   and temporary exhibits, as well as educational and interpretive programs; initiate and continue meaningful community involvement/
   advisory process in these exhibit projects.

3. Restore an active community-driven temporary exhibits program at the Mogan Cultural Center and elsewhere with funding, technical assistance, and advice by park staff; and start a community exhibits committee.
4. Improve and expand how the park connects with the community, such as an active community outreach program with commitment from staff; park will target underrepresented communities to reach new audiences.
5. Market and promote the park more effectively, both to greater Lowell and outside audiences, but especially to the diverse, underrepresented communities and neighborhoods of Lowell.

What is missing in the NPS community studies is demonstrating how these diverse communities can use archaeology to learn about their cultural heritage. At Lowell there was a long-term archaeology project that included excavations around a boardinghouse and an agent's house, and most of the study centered on the period from the early industrial revolution through the late nineteenth century (Mrozowski et al. 1996). There may seem to be a disconnect between the archaeology performed at the nineteenth-century boardinghouses inhabited by mill girls and European immigrants and the immigrant experience of early twenty-first-century Latinos and Cambodians. There may not be any ethnic associations, but there are undoubtedly many similar experiences. Archaeology shows that the American industrial revolution was not kind to the mill girls or the immigrants. Immigrants faced discrimination and received poor wages and substandard housing for their labor. The material evidence shows that alcohol and drug use appears to be high, and the analysis from privy samples shows that the workers had a high concentration of intestinal parasites. Alcohol and drug addiction and lack of access to proper health care are issues that the Latino and Cambodian communities face in Lowell today.

Can contemporary immigrants identify with their predecessors? Yes, I believe they can if the connections are offered with effective interpretation. A good example is the Lower East Side Tenement Museum, an Affiliated Area of the National Park Service, associated with Ellis Island and Castle Clinton. At the immigrant processing stations visitors learn about who came to America, and the Tenement Museum interprets what happened to them when they settled in New York City. The museum's mission is "to promote tolerance and historical perspective through the presentation and interpretation of the variety of immigrant and migrant experiences on Manhattan's Lower East Side, a gateway to America." More than a dozen community organizations serving immigrant residents have collaborated with the museum on programming that uses history to orient and inspire new immigrant populations (Lower East Side Tenement Museum 2003). The Tenement Museum is making history socially relevant to a traditionally disenfranchised group. So the question is, How can archaeologists help make archaeology socially relevant to groups that have been traditionally underrepresented?

Archaeology can explore a diverse past, and it can be socially relevant. Archaeology can place these issues in a historic context that can show communities that these problems are not new; rather they are historic issues that immigrants have faced for a long time. Archaeologists working in applied settings can address the issues of a diverse past, the social relevance of archaeology, and real-world problem solving (see Bender and Smith 2000). It is important to motivate students and practitioners of archaeology to convince stakeholders and decision makers that they can make these contributions.

In this volume Teresa Moyer's work is related to a neighborhood museum in Flushing, Queens, known as the Bowne House. The house has had a significant presence in the community since the seventeenth century, and it has been preserved as a shrine to John Bowne who is heralded for securing religious tolerance for all of the citizens in Flushing. Moyer explains that the Bowne house history can include more than the story of one man. Other histories of women, Irish immigrants, and children can be added to this traditional story. Many of the issues that the seventeenth-century residents of Flushing faced, like immigration, religious tolerance, and the acceptance of differences, are also issues that the current residents of Flushing confront. While she notes that historians have recently claimed that the Bowne House has lost its relevance to the local community, Moyer developed a new archaeology-based outreach program for school children that addresses the modern conflicts facing residents today and that shows the historical root of these struggles.

Diana diZerega Wall, Nan Rothschild, Cynthia Copeland, and Herbert Seignoret show how they have established a program to understand the community of Seneca Village, an American Irish and African-American community established in antebellum New York city. The former community is now buried under Central Park. Learning from the African-American burial ground project, they formed an advisory committee to help guide their efforts by providing research questions for their program. Wall, Rothschild, Copeland, and Seignoret are working with churches, community and civic groups, and local historians to make Seneca Village part of the official history of New York. The program has a strong educational and commemorative component, and in 2001 a history marker describing Seneca Village was unveiled in Central Park. Members of several community boards and representatives of the New York City Department of Parks and Recreation and the Central Park Conservancy participated in the cere-mony. The archaeology project at Seneca Village is about making the for-gotten histories of Irish Americans and African-Americans a part of the local community's history.

Michael Lucas shows the difficulties of performing applied archaeology and creating coherent and inclusive interpretations of public sites. His work centers on Mount Calvert in Prince Georges County, Maryland, a site that served as the county seat from 1696 to 1721. It was later developed into a plantation with enslaved African Americans. No above-ground structures re-main of the original town. Lucas recognizes that the archaeological record is a public trust and that communicating to the public an understanding of the area's heritage is important. Therefore, he sees the public as the primary stakeholders in the project. High school students and local professional orga-nizations have helped to uncover and understand the past at Mount Calvert. Lucas reminds us that we need to be responsible to all members of a commu-nity, and in Prince Georges County, a municipality that is more than 60 per-cent African American, it is important to make this lost town and plantation history relevant to the local community.

Archaeology Heritage Development

Heritage is based on a shared value system that people have about culture and their past. Heritage is what each one of us individually or collectively wishes to preserve and pass on to the next generation. Communities may have a collective heritage that they may want to preserve—such as farms, a historic district, a slave cabin, or an archaeological site related to an impor-tant local industry. In the same way regions and nations may recognize natural or built environments that they collectively believe are worth rec-ognizing, appreciating, and sharing. On the international level, there are per-sons, traditions, and places that are considered to be part of our common heritage.

Heritage is necessary for sustaining local identity and a sense of place, es-pecially by those communities and locales that are threatened by transfor-mations in the global economy. Massive migrations of the last two hundred years have heightened the need for stability and the search for heritage. Tens of millions of people have sought refuge outside their native lands, fleeing hunger, violence, and hatred; and rural people have increasingly migrated to urban areas. People have been cut off from their past, and they are in-creasingly seeking out their cultural roots (Lowenthal 1997:9). As a result a view of heritage that stresses the relationships between the uses of the past and local cultural expression has emerged, and it has become a significant aspect of material culture research.

Heritage means many things to different people; landscapes, architecture, memorials, artifacts, and ceremonies can invoke it. Heritage is often about memory and the struggle between groups to choose a usable past. It generates a precedent that serves our present needs. Heritage is usually displayed and celebrated by those who control the official history, but there are subordinated views that also find ways to create explicit or implicit forms of heritage. More recently the political uses of heritage have been made very explicit within Western culture. We live in a society that has an unquenchable thirst for heritage, and Michael Kammen (1997:214–19) calls the development of Americans' consciousness for historic preservation since the 1950s the "heritage phenomenon." Heritage connotes integrity, authenticity, venerability, and stability, and it clarifies pasts so that they can be used in the present (Lowenthal 1997:xv).

There is a strong sense among some archaeologists that by including communities in the decision-making process, through the means of either a participatory or a collaborative approach, they are helping to create a sense of heritage for that particular group. By practicing archaeology and recognizing its potential for creating heritage, archaeologists can embrace the various and diverse histories found in any one place or community.

In this volume Mark Warner and Daryl Baldwin work collaboratively on the Myaamia Project. Through many treaties the Miami were removed from their traditional homelands in Indiana, resettled in Kansas, then removed again to Oklahoma, leaving portions of their tribe in three states. Baldwin, a Miami tribal member who ensures that this research project directly serves the tribal community, directs the Myaamia project. Warner, Baldwin, and other members of the project work together to preserve, promote, and research Miami tribal history. Removals, boarding schools, allotments, and community fragmentation have negatively impacted the Miami social and cultural fabric. The Miami believe that the archaeological research project is important to secure the health of the community and provide a sense of history and place. The archaeological research team works in Oklahoma by Miami invitation, and the work is done collaboratively with the tribe. The archaeology helps to contribute to minority group identity and helps to empower a group that has been traditionally subordinated.

Peter Birt demonstrates the powerful cooperative bond that can be created between academic and community partners. Heritage is important to Burra, a small historic town in southern Australia that developed in the mid-nineteenth century as mining became established in the region. Today much of the town is an "open-air museum," with many early domestic and mine buildings still in place. The town of Burra acknowledges its past and uses it to foster tourism. Birt's archaeology must negotiate a partnership between many groups with different goals. While he is interested in information about Burra's heritage, others are interested in promoting and marketing heritage tourism. Those involved in the archaeology project also see that it is necessary to work with community groups in order to negotiate the terrain between tourism and academic pursuits. In this case, it is a small mining town that uses the past by developing heritage tourism to reestablish itself as a viable economic entity.

Charles Orser, working in the Republic of Ireland, concentrates his research on rural townlands in north County Roscommon in the years immediately preceding the Great Famine of the 1840s. How the Potato Famine is perceived and interpreted is controversial, since some school districts teach that the Irish famine was a product of crop failure, while other teachers see the famine as genocide, claiming the British colonizers did nothing to help the Irish. Orser has made his archaeological interpretations known to the local community, and he explained that the wealth of material culture found during the famine era is a product of materials purchased by the tenants from the rent money they withheld for the landlords. An elder told Orser that it was more realistic to think that the Irish were ground down by poverty and that the only way they could obtain these goods was through theft. Theft from the English was honorable.

The Meaning of Applied Archaeology

For a long time applied archaeology has been about traditional cultural resource management, but the discipline is undergoing an enormous transition. The increasingly public roles of archaeologists require new skills and expertise related to working effectively with communities and a variety of stakeholders. All of the authors in this volume work with groups that have been traditionally considered subordinated. They provide insights into the challenges and rewards of working with groups and subject matter that might be considered controversial or counter to the official history. Each of these projects had the potential to fail because of distrust, poor communication, or competition over uses of the past. The case studies provide some advice and guidance on how to avoid these pitfalls. They also provide insight into how the value of heritage resources is continually being negotiated and redefined.

The battle over how collective memories develop a sense of heritage shows some of the more visible conflicts on how we define and redefine ourselves. Scholars (see for instance Nash et al. 1998:103) have noted the explicit role the government played in creating a conservative agenda in U.S. public history during the 1980s and 1990s. For instance, William Bennett and Lynne Cheney served sequentially as chairpersons of the National Endowment for the Humanities from the early 1980s through 1992. They discouraged funding for projects that encouraged a pluralistic view of the past. They sharply curtailed any projects dealing with women, labor, racial groups, or any project that might conflict with the national collective memory. Cheney packed the advisory council with critics of multiculturalism. The council severely limited funding for any project related to women, labor, or ethnicity and rejected proposals if they questioned consensus history (Nash et al. 1998:103). It is interesting to note that many of the multicultural expressions found in public places, like the initiatives found in the NPS *Community Study Report* (Bowser 2000), did not occur a decade earlier. It would have been very difficult for a federal agency to challenge the assumptions and mandates of a conservative political administration that controlled and impeded the development of a multicultural history. Today the conservative agenda is back with the second Bush administration, and some government agencies are once again being directed to support consensus histories, sometimes at the expense of multicultural or other controversial histories. For instance, Secretary of the Interior Gail Norton has temporarily rescinded the National Historic Landmark designation of the Fresno Landfill because of the negative connotations associated with a landfill site (Melosi 2002). But what about historic mills? They were about technological development and entrepreneurship, but they exploited workers. And what about coal mining towns? Coal extraction was about technology and profit, but the process also destroyed landscapes and polluted water. Even worse, what about the Japanese internment camp of Manzanar? (Melosi 2002:34). These are all examples of the American past that are associated with social, political, and environmental tragedies that we choose to remember and use to teach us about the past. They are all stories that are now part of our official history. While the conservative right has challenged the meaning of an inclusive heritage, it is our job to move forward and support the types of archaeologies being proposed in this volume.

Robert Paynter (2000:21) points out that historical archaeology is in a good position to challenge the "dominant American imperialist anthropological archaeology." Barbara Little (1994) also notes that historical archaeology, which grew dramatically in the 1960s and 1970s, often served as a handmaiden to consensus history, even serving to counter radical histories. She remarks that archaeology can be about providing a history to a people who were not traditionally represented in the official history. What will the American landscape look like in a decade if we no longer support a multivocal American heritage as proposed by the authors in this volume? It is important, I believe, that we resist this new call for a consensus history and support a more inclusive past.

The claim for a past is sometimes contentious. Different group agendas will often clash over claiming a role in the official public memory, causing the established collective memories to be continuously in flux. Some subordinated groups can subvert the dominant memory; other groups compromise and become part of a multivocal history, while others fail to have their stories remembered by the wider society. The tensions between and within groups who struggle for control over the collective public memory is often situational and ongoing since the political stakes are high (La Roche and Blakey 1997; Shackel 2000, 2001a, 2001b; McGuire and Reckner 2002; Walker 2000).

Michael Shanks and Randall McGuire (1996) remind us that the act of archaeology is a form of commemoration, and when we do archaeology we create a memory of the past that is rooted in our present-day concerns. The articles in this book are about how we can do public archaeology outside of the traditional academic agenda and how we can make use of a participatory and/or collaborative framework to remember a particular heritage and commemorate a past. The authors are concerned about taking an active role in giving a voice to the "other" and helping to create a shared heritage in communities. They are all looking at diverse viewpoints and power relationships, and they are providing subordinated groups a sense of their place in the past and the present. While some archaeologists may not see the need to make their archaeology socially relevant, I think they are missing a great opportunity to make the discipline an integral part of our everyday lives.

Since the 1980s, and especially in the 1990s, public education has become an important part of many archaeology programs. It is seen as a "means of increasing the public return on federal government-funded archaeology" (Green and Doershuk 1998:140). There is a growing awareness that the informed public can ensure the growth of historic preservation efforts. Some of the most successful projects have merged cultural resource management, public participation, and research (Potter 1994). Public participation means more than just presenting the archaeology to the public. It is now about reaching out to members of the community and making them stakeholders in the archaeological discourse. It is a way of making archaeology an integral part of a community's heritage. The authors in this volume understand the power of the discipline and the importance of making archaeology more accessible to the public and developing a socially relevant discipline. Their work is having a significant impact on communities, and it will lay the groundwork for the next generation of archaeology.

References Cited

Bender, Susan J., and George S. Smith, ed. (2000). *Teaching Archaeology in the Twenty-First Century*. Washington, D.C.: Society for American Archaeology.

Bodner, John. (1992). *Remaking America: Public Memory, Commemoration, and Patriotism in the Twentieth Century*. Princeton, N.J.: Princeton University Press.

Bowser, Gillian. (2000). National Park Service Community Study Report. National Park Service. *www.nps.gov/community/communityreport.htm*. Accessed March 1, 2002.

Cantwell, Anne-Marie and Diana diZerega Wall. (2001). *Unearthing Gotham*. New Haven, CT: Yale University Press.

Dongoske, Kurt E., Mark Aldenderfer, and Karen Doehner. (2000). *Working Together: Native Americans and Archaeologists*. Washington, D.C.: Society for American Archaeology.

Fowler, Donald D. (1984). "Ethics in Contract Archaeology." In *Ethics and Values in Archaeology*, ed. E. L. Green, pp. 108–16. New York: Free Press.

Glassberg, David. (1998). "Presenting History to the Public: The Study of Memory and the Uses of the Past. Understanding the Past." *CRM* 21:4–8.

Green, William, and John F. Doershuk. (1998). "Cultural Resource Management and American Archaeology." *Journal of Archaeological Research* 6:121–67.

Hobsbawm, Eric. (1983). "Introduction: Inventing Tradition." In *The Invention of Tradition*, ed. Eric Hobsbawm and Terrence Ranger, pp. 1–14. Cambridge: Cambridge University Press.

Kammen, Michael. (1997). *In the Past Lane: Historical Perspectives on American Culture*. New York: Oxford University Press.

King, Thomas F. (1972). "Archaeological Law and the American Indian." *Indian Historian* 5:31–35.

LaRoche, Cheryl J., and Michael L. Blakey. (1997). "Seizing Intellectual Power: The Dialogue at the New York African Burial Ground." *Historical Archaeology* 31:84–106.

Little, Barbara J. (1994). "People with History: An Update on Historical Archaeology in the United States." *Journal of Archaeological Method and Theory* 1:5–40.

———. (2002a). "Archaeology as a Shared Vision." In *Public Benefits of Archaeology*, ed. Barbara J. Little, pp. 1–19. Gainesville: University Press of Florida.

Little, Barbara J., ed. (2002b). *Public Benefits of Archaeology*. Gainesville: University Press of Florida.

Lowenthal, David. (1997). "History and Memory." *The Public Historian* 19:31–39.

Lower East Site Tenement Museum. (2003). (www.tenement.org). Accessed January 8, 2003.

McGuire, Randall H. and Paul Reckner. (2002). "The Unromantic West: Labor, Capital and Struggle." *Historical Archaeology* 36(3):44–58.

McManamon, Francis P. (1992). "Managing Repatriation: Implementing the Native American Graves Protection and Repatriation Act." *CRM* 15:9–12.

Melosi, Martin V. (2002). "National Historic Landmarks: Controversies and Definitions. The Fresno Sanitary Landfill in an American Cultural Context." *Public Historian* 24, no. 3:17–35.

Mrozowski, S. A., G. H. Ziesing, and M. C. Beaudry. (1996). *Living on the Boott: Historical Archaeology at the Boott Mills Boardinghouses, Lowell, Massachusetts*. Amherst: University of Massachusetts Press.

Nash, Gary B., Charlotte Crabtree, and Ross E. Dunn. (1998). *History on Trial: Culture Wars and the Teaching of the Past*. New York: Knopf.

Paynter, Robert. (2000). "Historical and Anthropological Archaeology: Forging Alliances." *Journal of Archaeological Research* 8:1–37.

Potter, Parker B., Jr. (1994). "Postprocessual Approaches and Public Archaeology: Putting Critical Archaeology to Work for the Public." In *Cultural Resource Management: Archaeological Research, Preservation Planning, and Public Education in the Northeastern United States*, ed. J. E. Kerber, pp. 65–85. Westport, Conn.: Bergin and Garvey.

Shackel, Paul A. (2000). *Archaeology and Created Memory: Public History in a National Park*. New York: Kluwer Academic/Plenum Publishing.

———. (2001a). "Introduction: Contested Memories and the Making of the American Landscape." In *Myth, Memory and the Making of the American Landscape*, ed. Paul A. Shackel, pp. 1–16. Gainesville: University Press of Florida.

———. (2001b). "Public Memory and the Search for Power in American Historical Archaeology." *American Anthropologist* 102:1–16.

Shanks, Michael, and Randall H. McGuire. (1996). "The Craft of Archaeology." *American Antiquity* 61:75–88.

Smith, Laurajane. (1994). "Heritage Management as Postprocessual Archaeology." *Antiquity* 68: 300–9.

16 • Paul A. Shackel

Swidler, Nina, Kurt Dongoske, Roger Anyon, and Alan Downer. (1997). *Native Americans and Archaeologists: Stepping Stones to Common Ground.* Walnut Creek, Calif.: AltaMira Press.
Walker, Mark. (2000). "Labor History at the Ground Level: Colorado Coalfield War Archaeology Project." *Labor's Heritage* 11(1):58–75.
Watkins, Joe. (2001). *Indigenous Archaeology: American Indian Values and Scientific Practice.* Walnut Creek, Calif.: AltaMira Press.
Winter, J. C. (1980). "Indian Heritage Preservation and Archaeologists." *American Antiquity* 45: 121–31.

PART 1

Archaeology and Empowering Subordinated Groups

CHAPTER **1**

Monacan Meditation

Regional and Individual Archaeologies in the Contemporary Politics of Indian Heritage

JEFFREY L. HANTMAN

In this chapter Jeffrey Hantman describes his decade-long collaboration with the Monacan tribe, located near Virginia's Natural Bridge. It is a history of small steps and unexpected alliances, suggesting that effective collaboration requires no small degree of flexibility and patience on the part of all the parties involved. In this case, for instance, Hantman finds that collaboration can be furthered in interesting and productive ways, even as his own identity as an archaeologist is considered and occasionally redefined by his Monacan collaborators.

Introduction

The conflict of values and the historically problematic relationship between archaeologists and Native Americans in the United States has received much attention in the past decade (see Thomas 2000). This attention is a delayed response among archaeologists to a more general perception that all of anthropology was a domestic colonial science of dubious or negative value to indigenous peoples. More than thirty years ago Dell Hymes (1969) published an important challenge to anthropologists to get beyond their role as colonial scientists and to become engaged actively and politically with the communities with which they worked, both at the local level and the larger national and global levels.

For many years, archaeologists remained aloof to the suggestions articulated by Hymes. We did so in part due to our perception of the distancing effect of time as perceived by a profession of mostly non-Native American archaeologists, wherein we wrote about a different people than those who were around us today (even as in some areas ethnographic analogy was freely used). This lingering colonial approach is most tangible in the scientific tradition of assigning archaeological names to even temporally recent periods with known or demonstrable connections to tribal groups documented in the historic era. In addition, preoccupation with questions which were of little interest to Native American people in the framework of their own sense of history kept archaeologists marginal or out of discussions of community heritage or political issues such as federal recognition.

But the passage of the Native American Graves Protection and Repatriation Act (NAGPRA) has helped, if not forced, a change in attitude and approach. Where an unsolvable conflict of values seemed to emerge early in the post-NAGPRA years, Watkins (2000) and Thomas (2000) among many others have called for and provide evidence of an applied, collaborative archaeology in which archaeologists and Native Americans can find common ground and learn from each other. The impact of this change in attitude and approach has been felt at the local community level in the area of heritage and community identity. This change has been particularly important for many non-federally recognized American Indian communities in the eastern United States. In the East, many Native American groups have long been in the "Catch-22" position of being denied federal recognition because they are no longer land-holding groups and typically do not speak Native American languages. In addition, Indian identity in the East was often subsumed or lost in American race policy, eugenics, and a more general perception that the only "real" Indians survived and live west of the Mississippi. Anthropologists may have rejected the idea of the acculturated native, but the model lives on in the popular cultural politics surrounding Indian identity in the East.

A collaborative and applied archaeology can play a particularly important role where the very social identity and history of Indian communities is challenged. Documenting this identity and history remains a fundamental concern for many non-federally recognized tribes in the East. The process by which tribes receive status as a federally recognized group is at the moment an extremely confused process, a description of which lies beyond the scope of this chapter. The process was controlled until recently by the Bureau of Indian Affairs, and a long queue of tribal peoples sought recognition by trying to prove continuity of place and culture since the point of initial European contact (1607 in Virginia, for example). Today, an alternative path to federal recognition is to seek recognition via an act of Congress, beginning with the support of the tribal group's Congressional delegation. The Monacans, in concert with five other tribes in Virginia, are seeking federal recognition today via their Virginia Congressional delegation. While that today is the single largest issue facing these six tribes in Virginia, over the last decade the first and largest hurdle for non-federally recognized tribes such as the Monacans has been to gain acceptance by the public, as well as legislators, that they are in fact Indian communities with a shared sense of identity and history.

In this chapter I review my own experience working with the Monacan Indians of Virginia over the past decade. The Monacans are a state-recognized but not yet federally recognized Indian community located in the Piedmont/Blue Ridge Mountains region near Lynchburg, Virginia.

The Monacans of Virginia: Tourism and Identity

Hotel lobbies and tourist information stops in Virginia and Maryland include a polished brochure promoting a visit to the Natural Bridge, located in west-central Virginia near a heavily traveled interstate highway and the tourist-frequented Blue Ridge Parkway. The Natural Bridge has long drawn attention for its beauty and unique qualities as a geological phenomenon, but the cultural history of this landmark has been minimal.

Today, the Natural Bridge has been transformed into a place to learn a cultural history, specifically that of the Monacan Indians. The attraction, as the tourism brochures state, is the opportunity to "journey back 300 years" to learn and "participate" in Monacan history. As in most living history museums, a typical array of technological tasks are featured—making canoes, building houses, tanning hides, making pots, fashioning stone tools, and weaving baskets. The Monacan people are full participants in this venture. The new Monacan focus of the park, and the fact that the brochure emphasizes Monacan history as a tourist attraction, is nothing short of remarkable given longstanding popular and scholarly attitudes dismissive of an Indian history in Virginia west of Powhatan's territory around Jamestown, or extending past 1607. The upsurge of attention to Monacan history is a function of explicit efforts by the Monacan people to bring attention to themselves and their history, a dramatic change in attitude from a nearly four-hundred-year-long effort to stay beyond the gaze and interference of colonial and state governments (see Cook 2000, Hantman 1990; Wood and Shields 1999).

Applied archaeology has played a role in this transformation. Since the early 1990s, along with graduate and undergraduate students in the department of anthropology at the University of Virginia, I have been involved in archaeological research which, broadly stated, sought to write a history of the Monacan people from 900 A.D. to the colonial era. Our efforts were not initially designed as applied or community based. It is worth noting that when I began this research program I knew nothing of the contemporary Monacan community located just fifty miles south of the University of Virginia. I was told of a community with "claims" to Indian ancestry, but this did not draw my attention in 1990, nor did I see or presume a link between my archaeological research and the present. Since then, much of my work, and now even more so the work of Virginia doctoral students and undergraduates, has become collaborative with, and sometimes done explicitly for, the Monacan community. We have all gained much from the collaboration.

This chapter is a meditation on both the public presentation of Monacan history and my own ten-year role as an archaeologist working in collaboration with the Monacan tribe. The title is inspired by James Clifford's (1997) essay "Fort Ross Meditation," based on his visits to a historic site in California, which forces the contemplation of colonial global crosscurrents and the history of peoples long ignored in the documentary record. The public exhibit at the Natural Bridge site, as well as the locally developed Monacan Heritage Museum within the main Monacan community center near Lynchburg should also locate the Monacan people in a similarly global and long-term cultural history and geography. It also (ideally) forces meditation on historical considerations of race, racial identity, and eugenics in the region—that is, the acceptance that Indian people/Indian culture survived more than a century after the image of the "vanishing Indian" became dominant in the eastern United States (Trachtenberg 1998).

Ten years ago the Monacans would not have been accorded such public acknowledgment and acceptance, if not celebration, of their history and identity. This transformation has affected non-Monacans and Monacans alike. Meditation on my own interaction and collaboration with the Monacan Indian community considers an experience of some successes and some lessons learned. In the early 1990s when our collaboration began, this was relatively uncharted water in the Middle Atlantic region. We were writing the history of an interior native people long noted on historians' maps simply as among the "poorly known tribes" of the East. Since the early 1990s, of course, many archaeologists have worked collaboratively with diverse Indian communities (Dongoske, Aldenderfer, and Doehner 2000) to help gain recognition for tribal groups in both the legal and vernacular sense in the Eastern United States (Handsman and Richmond 1995). Frank Speck's (1925) earlier work with Eastern U.S. tribal groups should also be noted, though his emphasis was still on the coastal, reservation-based Indian communities, that is, those he felt retained some remnant of their Indian origins. The remainder of this chapter is in two parts: First, I will describe the Monacan tribe followed by a history of my involvement with the Monacan community, touching on thematic issues of including those who have been neglected by history, building community, and multiculturalism and race. In the second and concluding part, I discuss two aspects that I think are especially critical to working with American Indian communities in the Eastern United States—working from the historic regional cultural geography to the present community and thinking about the individual in the past and the present.

The Monacan Tribe and Archaeological Research

The Monacan Indian Nation is one of eight tribes recognized today by the Commonwealth of Virginia. Recognition for the Monacans came only in 1989 following a sixty-five-year-long period in which the Indian ancestry of this community was denied due to the direct application of an earlier applied sociology that we recognize today as misguided eugenics theory. In the 1920s the Monacan community of Virginia was targeted as a test case to prove eugenics-based principles wherein "one drop" of African ancestry was presumed to have erased Indian identity, and that intermarriage across racial lines led to genetically based social and individual pathologies. The painful legacy of the eugenics movement in Virginia resulted in the unwillingness to recognize "Indian" as a race in a biracially segregated Southern state except where reservation land had been retained. This changed in the 1980s, and the Monacans are now the only Indian tribe to be formally acknowledged west of the Tidewater/Coastal Plain region occupied in the past and present by the more widely accepted descendants of the Powhatan chiefdom. As of this writing, none of the Virginia Indian tribes, including the Monacans, are federally recognized. However, as noted previously, the Monacans are part of a current intertribal collective effort to gain Congressional federal recognition.

The term *community*, of course, is fluid and subject to many meanings. Sometimes it refers to all who share a self-identified or state-identified ethnic or racial identity but with variable spatial boundaries. Sometimes it refers to a place. In this chapter the term *Monacan community* means both. There is a center to the Monacan community of Virginia, at a place called Bear Mountain near Lynchburg. Here there is a subdivision where many Monacans live clustered in suburban-style homes, a large and active community center, an Episcopal (former mission) church and school, an historic cemetery, the Monacan Heritage Museum, and the remains in the local landscape of log cabins, corn and tobacco cribs, and projectile points documenting the long-term link of these people to Bear Mountain. There is also an *extended community*, which applies to all those who are of Monacan ancestry—that is, those who are on a tribal roll maintained by the tribe and determined by genealogy. This includes a significant number of Monacans who live in smaller clusters of expatriate communities in Glen Burnie, Maryland, and Johnson City, Tennessee. Both of those expatriate communities were formed in the 1920s and '30s, when Virginia's eugenics laws required the identification of ethnicity/race on any and all legal documents, including birth and marriage certificates, and the Monacans were literally and aggressively forbidden the use of the term *Indian* (see Smith 1992). Those who resisted moved to communities just across state lines where they remain today. Also included are the many others who have for personal and economic reasons moved elsewhere throughout the East. At the central community in Amherst, there is a dormitory built in the 1990s to house all those who return on the first Saturday of each October to Homecoming Day. This, more so than the public Pow-Wow now held principally as a fair and a fundraiser, is the means by which the extended community renews its ties on an annual basis.

My own work is applied in that it may serve the current efforts to receive federal recognition in establishing a continuity of place and community, particularly in my own focus on the seventeenth century. Early colonial documents mention and even map Monacan villages, but their name falls from the colonial records as the English failed to venture into the Virginia piedmont and mountain regions (Hantman 1990). To find archaeological evidence of the presence of Monacans in the Virginia interior would serve to help strengthen the case for the continuity of Monacan presence in Virginia from European contact to the present. However, this type of recognition was not the initial driving force, from my perspective, of my research and collaboration. Instead, I have been involved in seeking recognition of a different kind: simply acknowledging the existence and validity of a group of people as a community. Having been taught and having spent some time in my archaeological writing emphasizing the fluidity of culture, challenging ideas of authenticity, and acknowledging the cultural constructions of so-called facts, the applied archaeology I did created a conundrum for me, since those ideas did not initially serve the needs of the community. However, as a researcher having professional credentials and association with the University of Virginia, I have nevertheless been pleased to help put the Monacans on the historical and contemporary map of Virginia.

The research conducted was scientific in its design and historical in its focus. In the early 1990s I hypothesized and published an argument that Monacan history was a key to understanding the colonial period in Virginia, and I set about to conduct archaeological research to evaluate that hypothesis (Hantman 1990; 1993; 2001). My interaction with the community and the impact of that interaction was not part of my initial research design or intent but has nevertheless been quite real. In a state such as Virginia, where identity and heritage are so intertwined, my effort to write a precolonial and colonial-era Monacan history proved to have significance in ways I did not initially imagine. From nervous first meeting to eventual co-authored publications and conference papers (Hantman, Wood, and Shields 2000), my actual and potential role took on significance in ways I did not foresee. Collaborating with the Monacan tribe over ten years has been an extraordinary experience, and the history of that effort may offer some insights into the nature of collaborative, community-based, Native American public archaeology in the East. It also forced the consideration of the clash between anthropological theory, which I hold to be valid, concerning issues of identity and race and the equally real issues of heritage, community, and the politics of culture for American Indians in the eastern United States today.

A Decade of Collaboration

The first stage of our collaboration began in 1990 with, simply, an introduction. In those years tensions were great between archaeologists and Native American communities as the impact of the passage of NAGPRA took decision-making power and authority regarding treatment of human remains and archaeological collections and placed them in the hands of Native American tribes (see Thomas 2000 for a summary of the impact of this legislation). Many archaeologists resisted this federally mandated transfer of power. The ramifications were not great in the small, isolated community of Monacans in central Virginia, however. At that time and in that place, when I first met with the Monacan community, *archaeologist* was not a bad word or dishonorable profession. Instead, I was welcomed as an archaeologist. The only wariness I felt was that directed at any outsider in a community that had largely been closed to outsiders for decades. Here, archaeology offered the possibility of sanction and validation by the state (the state university in any case) of a rich history deserving of attention equal to that of other Indian people and deserving of a place in Virginia's historical consciousness.

A paper I had published in the *American Anthropologist* in 1990 argued for the importance and centrality of the Monacan tribe in the colonial era despite their relative invisibility in the canonical colonial texts authored by Jamestown colonist Captain John Smith. In an alternative to the textbook story of the Jamestown encounter influenced by John Smith and played out largely in terms of English-Powhatan relations, I argued that the Monacan presence in Virginia had a large impact on the actions of the Powhatans and the English at Jamestown. Further, I argued that the Monacans in the cultural geography of pre-1607 Virginia were in fact the dominant group, with their power built on precontact elite exchange links to the American interior. This version, admittedly hypothetical and not necessarily widely accepted at the time by my colleagues, placed the historic Monacans in a significant and powerful position. Nothing could have been further from their own sense of place in Virginia's history or their own acceptance of the story told in Virginia's textbooks and public parks like Jamestown. In that version, if mentioned at all, the Monacans were a marginal people, dispersed, even "barbarous" according to John Smith (see Hantman 1990; 1993). This image stood in stark contrast to the depictions of the Powhatan people of the Virginia coast, who were said to have a complex and hierarchical society, led by a powerful ruler, reminiscent of the contemporary governments of Europe. The legacy of such colonial depictions, because they were written down, had enormous influence and held sway into the present. My narrative, based more on archaeological data than the colonial era hearsay reported by John Smith, resonated well for obvious reasons with the Monacan people in 1990. My argument was picked up by the popular media—newspapers in Roanoke, Lynchburg, and Richmond—and, hypothetical or not, it added to a sense of Monacan identity and public outreach which had been building in the prior decade's effort to gain state recognition. An earlier text (Houck 1984) had made the historical argument that supported the state recognition effort; my article and continuing research added a distinction to the history, which made my work welcome, if not encouraged, in the Monacan community.

My research was made known to the Monacan people via a connection made possible by the fortunate coincidence that in 1990 I was a fellow with the Virginia Foundation for the Humanities (VFH). The VFH had funds in that year to support initiatives on Virginia Indian history and public policy and education. I was introduced to the tribe by, and as part of, the VFH. Thus, I arrived in an unusual way for an archaeologist. I was not an individual researcher seeking to take anything away from the tribe or permission to dig up ancestral remains. Instead, I was part of a humanities organization that had funds to bring to the community for purposes of heritage education. This, along with my more palatable version of Monacan history, allowed for a probably atypical introduction of archaeologist and Indian community. In short, the leaders of the community welcomed me, though many others kept an understandably cautious distance that most any outsider would have experienced. Academics in particular, still remembered as the proponents of the eugenics-based race theory and practice that hit particularly hard in this community (Cook 2000; Smith 1992), were especially suspect. The positive circumstances of our first meeting, and the message I had to share, laid the foundation for the years of collaboration that ensued. Most importantly, the Monacan tribe had a story to tell of their history. Although they were an Indian people who had already been "validated" by the state, they were not really in the general public consciousness; the archaeological narrative could change that identity from a marginal Indian people to a central one.

The second stage of our collaboration involved grant writing and design of a modest traveling museum exhibit and a video to be produced by the Monacans themselves. The exhibit was made not only to be on regular display in the Monacan Community Center for the benefit of the Monacan people, but also to be portable so that it could travel to the local public schools. Those same schools had denied access to Monacan children until the 1960s; even after admission the Monacan children were subjected to intense discrimination and hurtful slurs. The exhibit extolled a proud and important history of the Monacan people. Funded by the Virginia Foundation for the Humanities, its opening was accompanied by a community-wide celebration, feast, and speeches by tribal leaders and local politicians. I mention this to emphasize the importance of this seemingly modest exhibit. Since the early 1990s we have assisted in the establishment of a permanent museum/heritage center in the Monacan community, now open and containing exhibits I will discuss below. This museum also includes the log cabin schoolhouse run by missionaries in the early twentieth century, when Monacan children were kept from local public schools. As a result of our collaborative research and grant writing, this log cabin is a rare eastern U.S. historic Indian site listed on both the Virginia and the National Register of Historic Places.

A third aspect of our collaboration was the involvement of the Monacan tribe in village excavations that I directed during the 1990s. Admittedly, the members of the tribe did not have the time or inclination to participate in the summer excavations, but they visited on occasion and were kept apprised of the findings. Prior to our most recent excavations at a seventeenth-century village, a blessing ceremony for the ancestors and the archaeologists (who were to disturb the village) was held. Over the past decade a division of labor has emerged in Monacan historical research. In this small community genealogical information and court record searches, most critical to the federal recognition process, are the domain of the Monacan tribe's historians. In brief, this remains sensitive information, and the memory of its misuse by the eugenicists lives on as if the 1920s had just passed. The unwritten record, including the key linkage of the seventeenth century when prehistory meets history in Virginia, is the domain of the archaeologists. While this is not typical for many archaeologists who engage both the written record and the material culture of archaeological sites, this has been a division of labor in our collaboration.

The levels of our collaboration intensified and involved both state and federal agencies when we worked jointly on seeking the repatriation and/or reinterment of human remains. Some of these remains were recovered as part of an emergency excavation of a burial mound endangered by river erosion, which I oversaw; others were collections housed in the state's Department of Historic Resources, deposited there by a local history museum that had held the bones for nearly a century. The state worked through the federal NAGPRA review board. In that federal bureaucratic context giving the Monacans approval for the reinterment of human remains recovered relatively far from their contemporary community center was not an easy task. In addition, as a non-federally recognized tribe, the Monacans had a difficult case to make before the NAGPRA board, a board protective of privilege afforded federally (but not state) recognized tribes. Tribal leaders took the lead in pursuing the repatriation; research conducted at the University of Virginia provided the documentation required by NAGPRA and the state. A decision was made in the late 1990s to return the excavated remains of hundreds of individuals who had been interred in burial mounds throughout the precolonial Monacan territory, and repatriation and reburial ceremonies have now taken place twice in the historic Monacan cemetery near their Virginia community center. The symbolic power of this act, the link to the ancestors, and the acknowledgment by the federal NAGPRA board of the contemporary Monacans as the rightful heirs to these human remains cannot be underestimated. Remarkably, as I imagine such mortuary rites did in the past, these (re)burial rites held in 1998 and 2000 served to bind the dispersed communities together over space and historical distance. The Monacan repatriation and Monacan historian Karenne Wood were featured along with the Pawnee repatriation efforts in the widely distributed documentary "Who Owns the Past?" and this has been a particular point of pride.

Last, our collaboration has resulted in publications in popular archaeology magazines and in conference papers. In 2000 I coauthored a paper with Monacan historians Diane Shields and Karenne Wood that appeared in *Archaeology* magazine. At the 2002 SAA meetings two Virginia doctoral students, Lisa Lauria and Jen Aultman, coauthored a paper with Shields and Wood on the next stage of our collaboration—the return of a once-private artifact collection now owned by the National Park Service to the Monacan ancestral museum. Students from Virginia are helping with the inventory of the collection so that its ownership can be transferred officially to the Monacan Museum.

In sum, the archaeological research conducted by the University of Virginia has helped put a people long neglected onto the contemporary and historical map of Virginia. The Natural Bridge tourist attraction, modeled on the Jamestown and Colonial Williamsburg living history museums, serves as one bit of testimony to that. I also believe that we have helped the community build a sense of its own deep history. Homecoming Day now includes a videotape, made by the tribe, that runs on a loop all day long and focuses in part on the archaeological research and our findings. We have also added to an appreciation of historic and contemporary cultural diversity in the recognition of Indians who did not "vanish" from Virginia and the East. The popularity of the traveling exhibit (now expanded to include a kit with slide show and artifact replicas) makes the link from past to present and reaches school groups of all ages throughout central Virginia.

This last point is not without its difficulties, however. Multiculturalism and the politics of race in America in the 1990s still required individuals to choose one identity. Particularly for Native Americans who had been denied even that right in Virginia for most of the twentieth century, that possibility was a cherished opportunity. Of course, such politics also reifies the idea of race and downplays the diverse or multiple ancestries of so many families. But, I think it is fair to say that the Indian ancestry needed to be acknowledged first—it had been denied for too long. With that established, discussion of the fluidity of ethnic boundaries in Virginia's history may now begin.

Regional Archaeologies, Colonial Names, and Community

The methods of applied archaeology that I engaged reflected the regional approach I was trained in as an anthropological archaeologist, particularly a "prehistorian." Working with contemporary American Indian communities requires an awareness that use of the landscape has changed dramatically over the centuries (see Handsman and Richmond 1995). Unfortunately, this well-known anthropological point is often lost on contemporary policy makers and the general public, particularly in the absence of a well-documented transition. As described earlier, the Monacan community defined today consists of isolated points on a map—a primary community in central Virginia with connected smaller communities in Maryland and Tennessee. The expatriate communities are known to be twentieth-century phenomena, but to focus on just the community in Virginia as the entire record of the Monacans is to miss much of what I believe is Monacan history. Even a look at John Smith's map of Virginia in 1612 shows Monacan territory to be more extensive than the area of the present-day community. In fact, the Monacan were (in 1607) acknowledged as the people of the central James River Valley, and few would dispute this given the power of the ubiquitous document which is Smith's map.

However, another name appearing on Smith's map identifies the Mannahoac in the Rappahannock River to the north as a separate tribal group.

Later maps, derived from colonial-era records, identify other groups including the Saponi, the Nahyssan, and the Tutelo. The plethora of names that appear gives rise to the perception of dispersed, "poorly known" groups in the Virginia interior. This, again, stood in marked contrast to the perception of the neighboring Powhatan as a centralized, hierarchical, cohesive tribal group—organized as a complex paramount chiefdom.

The University of Virginia's regional archaeological research did not reveal a record of material culture and cultural geography that could support the dispersed, disconnected image of the Monacans or one in which *Monacan* appropriately refers only to a small stretch of one river system. Instead, from a regional perspective, the distinctive mortuary ritual of mound burial, the ceramics, and settlement patterns all combine to suggest a compelling connectedness that traversed the Piedmont and Blue Ridge mountain physiographic provinces and linked the people of central and western Virginia. Our archaeological study suggested that this area, not those proscribed by multiple names in colonial-era documents and maps, reflects precolonial Monacan territory.

This interpretation was introduced to the tribe in our collaboration, but it was slow to be accepted. Historical memory did not extend beyond the place called the Bear Mountain community in central Virginia, but as we discussed the uniformity and distinctiveness of mound burial practices and the biases of colonial observers, the idea began to take hold. At first, the Monacan response to our precolonial definition of Monacan territory was that this was too big an area—there remained a hesitation to make historic claims on too much land by such a marginalized people. Over the past ten years such temerity has gone, and the archaeological data is now cited as evidence by the tribe for claims in matters of the repatriation of human remains (land claims have not been a focus). Our collaboration on this issue led to the successful repatriation and reburial of human remains from cemeteries that had been excavated far from the modern-day Bear Mountain community.

These successful efforts at repatriation have had a significant impact on the contemporary community and its sense of identity in Virginia history. Not insignificantly, they have also established a precedent for federal recognition of the continuity of Monacan people from prehistory to the present. The dispersed community of today is thus, interestingly, a new version of an old pattern.

Individual Archaeology and the Community

At the opposite end of the spectrum has been our involvement in an archaeology of the individual that I was not trained in and would not myself have envisioned. Instead, it arose as a desire of the Monacan Tribal Council and has taken on perhaps as much significance as any other archaeology project that we have collaborated on over the past decade.

In brief, in reporting on the analysis and plans for repatriation/reburial which the university had negotiated with the state and the tribal leaders, I made a request to keep samples for possible future analysis. The initial response to that request was negative. The human remains to be reburied had been excavated by nonprofessional archaeologists in the early twentieth century and had been stored in museum boxes since that time. In this case science had to take a back seat to the respect owed to the ancestors. I accepted this perspective, in part, because in an earlier collaboration concerning a different mound excavation and reburial, consent had been given to save other samples (following a blessing ceremony). The decision-making power was in the hands of the tribe, and their current opinion was clear. However, almost as an afterthought, one council member asked if I had ever seen the practice of facial reconstruction as done by forensic anthropologists and artists and prominently featured in museums and television documentaries. This council member had just that week seen a demonstration of the practice on television which showed the reconstruction of the face of a Jamestown colonist.

I did not have the technical expertise to do such work. In fact, as an anthropologist I questioned the very practice, but I was now talking with a community that had no images of itself—as individuals—prior to photographs taken in the 1920s. They sought images of faces, of human beings, of individuals who lived lives that could be (at least in part) reconstructed, as compared to the collective images of mounds, sites, and potsherds. This was in every sense an understandable human desire. The tribal council members all concurred on the desire to see the face of a Monacan who lived in the "heroic" age I had described in the language of political economies. I was asked if I could arrange, prior to reburial, to reconstruct the faces of one or more of those we were about to reinter. I agreed to find out, and with the help of several colleagues with connections to the world of forensic anthropology, the contacts were made. Again, I collaborated with the tribe in a grant proposal to the Virginia Foundation for the Humanities, and funding was approved. This is an expensive process, and we received funds to reconstruct the faces of two individuals. The two individuals chosen were an adult man and an adult woman who had lived in the fifteenth century. We determined what they ate, the (good) condition of their health, and some individual and idiosyncratic aspects of their lives. The artist (Sharon Long) reconstructed the faces, bringing them to life. The research and the faces were featured in *Archaeology* magazine (Hantman, Wood, and Shields 2000). Today, they are the centerpiece of the Monacan heritage museum, and from what I have observed and heard, they make a most powerful and personal connection for the community. They link past to present, from Monacan prehistory to contemporary identity politics. Only in this case, politics is not the issue; instead, it is the desire to see the past on individual terms. Certainly, archaeology today has invested much to regain that sense of the individual in history. In this case the applied anthropology I conducted with the Monacan tribe taught me a new way to approach that perspective.

In conclusion, from the regional polity to the individual, the applied archaeology the University of Virginia has conducted with the Monacan community has been, for the most part, a successful and mutually beneficial experience. We have learned from each other, helped to build a sense of community, helped (but not succeeded) in the effort to gain federal recognition, and have together brought the individual and the collective Monacan past into the present and future.

References Cited

Brown, Kenneth L. (2001). Interwoven Traditions: Archaeology of the Conjurer's Cabins and the African American Cemetery at the Jordan and Frogmore Plantations. In Conference Proceedings for *Places of Cultural Memory: African Reflections on the American Landscape*, held May 9–12, 2001, Atlanta, Georgia. National Park Service, Department of the Interior. Also available on line at http://www.cr.nps.gov/crdi/conferences/AFR_99-114_KBrown.pdf.

Brown, Kenneth L. (2003a). Report to the Texas Parks and Wildlife Department: The Archaeology of Cabin 1-A-1: The Praise House. Texas Parks and Wildlife Department.

Brown, Kenneth L. (2003b). Report to the Texas Parks and Wildlife Department. The Levi Jordan Plantation State Historic Site, Technical Report Series, No. 1: The Levi Jordan Plantation Research Design. Houston, TX.

Brown, Kenneth L. (2003c). Management Summary Report for the Texas Parks and Wildlife Department. The Levi Jordan Plantation State Historic Site, Brazoria County, Texas. Houston, TX.

Clifford, James P. (1997). *Routes: Travel and Translation in the Late Twentieth Century*. Cambridge, Mass.: Harvard University Press.

Cook, Samuel R. (2000). *Monacans and Miners: Native American and Coal Mining Communities in Appalachia*. Lincoln: University of Nebraska Press.

Dongoske, Kurt E., Mark Aldenderfer, and Karen Doehner. (2000). *Working Together: Native Americans and Archaeologists*. Washington, D.C.: Society for American Archaeology.

Handsman, Russell G., and Trudy Lamb Richmond. (1995). "Confronting Colonialism: The Mahican and Schaghticoke Peoples and Us." In *Making Alternative Histories: The Practice of Archaeology and History in Non-Western Settings*, ed. P. R. Schmidt and T. Patterson, pp. 87–118. Santa Fe: School of American Research Press.

Hantman, Jeffrey L. (1990). "Between Powhatan and Quirank: Reconstructing Monacan Culture and History in the Context of Jamestown." *American Anthropologist* 92:660–76.

———. (1993). "Powhatan's Relations with the Piedmont Monacans." In *Powhatan Foreign Relations*, ed. H. Rountree, pp. 94–111. Charlottesville: University of Virginia Press.

———. (2001). "Monacan Archaeology in the Virginia Interior." In *Societies in Eclipse: Archaeology of the Eastern Woodland Indians*, A.D. 1400–1700, ed. D. R. Brose, C. W. Cowan, and R. C. Mainfort, Jr., pp. 107–24. Washington D.C.: Smithsonian Institution Press.

Hantman, Jeffrey L., Karenne Wood, and Diane Shields. (2000). "Writing Collaborative History." *Archaeology* 53, no. 5:56–59.

Houck, Peter. (1984). *Indian Island in Amherst County*. Lynchburg, Va.: Lynchburg Historical Research Company.

Hymes, Dell H. (1969). "The Use of Anthropology: Critical, Political, Personal?" In *Reinventing Anthropology*, ed. Dell Hymes, pp. 1–79. New York: Vintage Books.

Jefferson, Thomas. (1787) *Notes on the State of Virginia*. Ed. William Peden, 1982. New York: W. W. Norton.

Smith, J. David. (1992). *The Eugenic Assault on America: Scenes in Red, White, and Black*. Fairfax, Va.: George Mason University Press.

Speck, Frank. (1925). "The Rappahannock Indians of Virginia." In *Indian Notes and Monographs* 5, no. 3. New York: Museum of the American Indian, Heye Foundation.

Thomas, David H. (2000). *Skull Wars: Archaeology and the Search for Native American Identity*. New York: Basic Books.

Trachtenberg, Alan. (1998). "Wanamaker Indians." *The Yale Review* 86:1–24.

Watkins, Joe. (2000). *Indigenous Archaeology: American Indian Values and Scientific Practice*. Walnut Creek, Calif.: Altamira Press.

Wood, Karenne, and Diane Shields. (1999). *The Monacan Indians: Our Story*. Madison Heights, Va.: Office of Historical Research, Monacan Indian Nation.

CHAPTER 2

From "Traditional" Archaeology to Public Archaeology to Community Action

The Levi Jordan Plantation Project

CAROL MCDAVID

In this chapter, Carol McDavid describes the attempts by herself and her colleagues to place the archaeology of a Texas plantation into the service of an explicit "community action" agenda, the major aim of which is to "use archaeology to create a more democratic society." This endeavor relates closely to anthropological interests in forming "dialogic" relationships with traditional research subjects, and it seeks to move collaboration to a level that involves significant and sincere cooperation between stakeholders. The Levi Jordan Plantation public archaeology project described here is partly conducted on the Internet, a feature that McDavid suggests can provide greater opportunity for equitable exchange among its varied participants.

Introduction

For the past ten years I have been involved with the public archaeology of the Levi Jordan Plantation in Brazoria, Texas, a nineteenth-century sugar plantation located about sixty miles south of Houston. The Jordan archaeology project has evolved, over seventeen years, from a "traditional" archaeology project with little public involvement (Brown 2000) to a public archaeology project controlled by members of ethnically diverse local descendant communities, using archaeologists as consultants/collaborators (McDavid 2000). In this chapter I will first discuss, by way of background, the concepts of "collaboration" and "consultation" in the context of American historical archaeology and anthropology. I will then describe the history of the Jordan public archaeology project, identifying its major players. Next, I will relate the development of the Jordan project's current primary interpretive activity, the Levi Jordan Plantation website.[1] In doing this I will also examine how this project applies and enacts certain aspects of archaeological theory and method. Following this I will discuss the future of the website project, and will close with some additional thoughts on *intra*disciplinary collaboration.

Collaboration and Consultation in Anthropology and Archaeology

Before describing the particulars of the Jordan public archaeological project, I will situate it in terms of other collaborations within both archaeology and anthropology. In the late 1980s, when this archaeological project began, collaboration with descendant and other communities to do archaeology was not a common practice, at least in terms of historical African-American sites such as the Jordan site. This was not as true with regard to prehistoric sites, as evidenced by the passage of the Native American Graves Protection and Repatriation Act (NAGPRA)[2] in 1990, which legally required that archaeologists notify, consult, and obtain consent from appropriate Native American groups during each stage of the research process. Before NAGPRA was implemented, as Native American groups began to lobby for control of their ancestors' remains (and to challenge an extremely resistant[3] archaeological community about who had the right to "own" their pasts), most historical archaeologists did not see their work with African-American sites (or other sites occupied by disempowered minority groups) as being vulnerable to similar challenge (Brown 1997). Even now, there is no "NAGPRA" to protect the interests of these groups—collaboration and formal consultation with the descendants of historic sites are not mandated by any laws other than, perhaps, ethical ones[4] (Lynott 1997; Lynott and Wylie 1995; Messenger 1989; Vitelli 1996).

In cases where ethical guidelines are not enough, and descendant communities of historic sites have had to fight to gain control over research concerning their ancestors, they have succeeded primarily because they were able to deploy local political power and sympathetic archaeologists to achieve their ends. The most famous example is, no doubt, the African Burial Ground project in New York City where, in the mid-1990s, local African-American groups were able to force a U.S. government agency to, first, recognize the importance of the buried human remains on the site and, then, to excavate and analyze these remains in a sensitive, appropriate manner. (For a detailed description of the ways this process played out, see LaRoche and Blakey [1997]; for a more recent overview and discussion of the impact of this on the research itself, see Johnson [1999: 168–170]. See also Blakey [1995] and Blakey [1997]). It is not coincidental that the mayor of New York City at the time was African American, as was a powerful state senator and other key political leaders. In this landmark case local activist and governmental leaders were able to do collectively what the national government and some elements in the archaeological community would not. In terms of archaeopolitics the African Burial Ground project has become an archetype for this type of grassroots community activism within African-American archaeology.

Despite this sort of success, some American historical archaeologists still insist that, as scientists, they should avoid involvement with contemporary social or local political agendas. Even well-intentioned archaeologists, who believe in the value of communicating their work to the public, are sometimes uncomfortable with the messy realities of *sharing control* of their research with people outside of archaeology (Brown 2000; McKee 1994). Others go farther, and disparage so-called relativist, reflexive, or critical public interpretations of archaeology (Moore 1994; South 1997) on the basis that the public will not support archaeology if they cannot rely on it to tell them The Scientific Truth. I, and others (including some of the same archaeologists who acknowledge occasional discomfort) would argue that credibility with diverse publics will only come from a willingness to open our discipline to public input and, even, change (Brown 1997; Brown 2000; Hodder 1999; McKee 1994; Weisman 2000).

Happily, this recent attitude has started to have considerable influence in historical archaeology. In addition, prehistoric and historic archaeologists have started to see commonalities in how they interact with members of descendant groups. Recent archaeological conferences have, for example, featured symposia in which historical archaeologists and prehistoric archaeologists have begun to communicate *with each other* about ways to create better collaborations (McDavid 1999a; McDavid 2001). In general terms, though, it is fair to say that American prehistoric archaeologists came earlier to the idea of actively supporting and creating community-oriented collaborations in archaeology, and many have embraced the post-NAGPRA world with enthusiasm and commitment. Historical archaeologists still have much to learn from the paths that our archaeological siblings have trod.

We also have much to learn from the pathways forged by our siblings within sociocultural anthropology. For the last two decades the idea of dialogue has influenced the work of a growing number of ethnographic projects, many of which derived from the work of James Clifford (Clifford

1988; Clifford and Marcus 1986), Renato Rosaldo (Rosaldo 1989), and Vincent Crapanzano (Crapanzano 1986). More recent projects (Hinson 2000; Lassiter 1998) have sought to extend the dialogic metaphor to work that is more explicitly collaborative (Lassiter 1999). In these projects, "Individual research agendas gave way to agendas negotiated with our consultants; writings began to target multiple publics ... [and we began to conceive of] ethnography as a kind of engaged reciprocity" (Hinson 1999).

It is exactly this sort of reciprocity that was sought in the Jordan *public archaeology* project, even though the original *archaeological* project was not conceived as a collaborative one. This transition will be described in more detail below.

The Levi Jordan Public Archaeology Project: History and Players

I will first describe the context for my entry into what became the Jordan public archaeology project and will then examine in more detail how our collaborations developed.

When first reported in 1990, excavation of the slave and tenant quarters of the Jordan plantation had been underway for four years, under the direction of Kenneth L. Brown at the University of Houston (Brown and Cooper 1990). Even though Brown had always hoped that the project would be of use to the public in general terms, his assumption was that his original research goals (having to do with anthropological comparisons of trade and economic status between urban and rural populations) would be of little interest to most people[5] (Brown 2000). As the research progressed, however, different research agendas emerged, from both African-American and European-American descendant communities, as well as from Brown himself.

Because of a variety of factors (Brown 1994; Brown and Cooper 1990), it was evident by the late 1980s that the Jordan site was going to be an extraordinarily rich source of information about African America during the mid- to late nineteenth-century. As the new data enabled Brown to explore questions about social, spiritual, and religious life—in addition to the somewhat dry topics of trade and economic status—the archaeological questions themselves began to change. At the same time controversial historical data about some of the plantation's early owners began to emerge (Brown 1994; Brown and Cooper 1990). This data indicated that these individuals were involved in a number of violent white supremacist activities (Barnes 1998; Brown 1994) and revealed that the archaeological deposit itself was a direct result of these activities. In short, in the late 1880s the African-American tenants were forced to abandon their homes in the quarters quickly, and, in so doing, they took very few of their possessions with them. The quarters were then locked and abandoned, after which the decaying remains were flooded, silted over, and left essentially undisturbed until excavations began. This had the effect of entombing the artifacts, thus creating and preserving the archaeological deposit (Brown 1994; 2003a, b, c; 2001; Brown and Cooper 1990).

Descendants of Levi Jordan responded in varying ways to this information about their ancestors, as well as to the reasons why the artifacts happened to be there in the first place. One reaction was to question the accuracy of the archaeological data—even to the point of insisting that the quarters area was the site of the plantation's sugar mill instead of the location of housing for enslaved people. One person wrote a letter to the local newspaper, asserting the "primacy of . . . 'lived knowledge' of the plantation and events which had occurred there over our 'research knowledge'" (Brown 2000)—even though this individual had never lived on the plantation (and certainly did not live there in the 1880s). Still others accused archaeologists of libeling their ancestors' memories; one previously supportive descendant resigned his position on the Levi Jordan Plantation Historical Society (LJPHS) board because of family pressure to do so; as he put it, "If I don't quit, my father will never speak to me again" (McDavid 1997c). On the other hand, some family members felt a moral imperative to deal openly and honestly with their ancestors' roles in the racial, social, and political upheavals of the past. As a particularly committed white descendant once put it, "For us to forget what happened here would be like forgetting Dachau" (McDavid 1996).

Both African-American and European-American descendants sometimes felt that a public association with the plantation would be embarrassing or otherwise harmful to them. One African-American descendant was certain that she would be discriminated against at work if the fact that her ancestors had been enslaved on the plantation became known. A young white descendant of the planter was taunted and forced to physically defend himself at school after his ancestor's activities were discussed in a local newspaper article. Sometimes guilt (and anger) about past injustices and pride in the community contributions of their ancestors coexisted in the same people. As the years went on, the project created conflict between family members with different points of view and different tolerances for the expression of multiple truths about the plantation's history. It also, occasionally, created unity where it had not existed before, as members of various descendant groups, many of whom had not previously met, became interested in the archaeological project and began to work on it together (McDavid 1997b).

During the same period that members of different descendant groups were dealing with the public knowledge of their association with the plantation, some African-American descendants also began to generate research agendas of their own, as described in (Brown 2000). These did not, interestingly, have much to do with the archaeology itself. In one case they had to do with one family's tradition that their ancestors had been freedmen "living in eastern North America and yet [later] were held in bondage on the Jordan Plantation" (Brown 2000). They wanted to know how this occurred. (It turned out to be true.) Another question concerned the loss of some land that one family's ancestors had purchased in the mid-1880s. Brown immediately set about trying to provide answers to these questions, on the "grounds that this would help demonstrate that we needed the involvement of all of the descendants, and that we would incorporate their questions into the research" (Brown 2000). Later we all came to realize that this was not enough, that it was also necessary to provide training and tools for people to answer some of these questions themselves. How this might be accomplished at the Jordan site is included in future plans, although I should note that it is part of Brown's more recent work at the Frogmore Manor Plantation on St. Helena Island, South Carolina (Brown 2000).

At the same time, as described above, collaborative public archaeology was in the process of emerging as an accepted topic for historical archaeological research. Therefore, in 1992 I was recruited by Kenneth Brown to work with the public dimensions of the Jordan project. My first project, carried out while I was a graduate student in anthropology at the University of Houston, was to conduct ethnographic research to see if it would be feasible to locate public interpretations of this archaeology within the local community surrounding the plantation. It was unknown at that point whether these interpretations would be in the form of a museum, site tours, or something else. I—we—needed to learn about the "interests and conflicts" (Leone, Potter, and Shackel 1987) that formed the social and political landscape of Brazoria and to determine whether the community would support and participate in this sensitive and politically charged archaeology. That research ([McDavid 1996] summarized in [McDavid 1997b]) led to our current project, a collaboratively developed Internet website, which now comprises the bulk of the plantation's public interpretation activity. The website was also the basis of my doctoral research at the University of Cambridge, where I examined whether the Internet can be used to create more open, democratic, relevant, and multivocal ways to talk about archaeology (McDavid 1999b; McDavid 2000; McDavid 2002a; McDavid 2002b; McDavid 2004). Later in this chapter I will describe some of the strategies we developed to do this in more detail.

Most of the key participants in these ongoing collaborations are members of the historical society, others include various community members, from whom I seek advice and support. After helping to organize this society and recruit members from various descendant groups for its board of directors (McDavid 1997b), I continued (and continue) to function as an advisor/consultant in all matters pertaining to the site's public outreach, education, and mission. Likewise, members of the group are my consultants, as I initiate public projects, such as the website project mentioned above. Kenneth Brown also serves on this board and, at this writing, is in the process of completing excavations at the Jordan site; therefore our own collaboration is ongoing.

My objective from the beginning of my work in Brazoria was to find ways to collaborate in reciprocal, nonhierarchical, mutually empowering ways. By "mutually empowering," I mean that no phase of my individual research, past or present, would have begun without official permission to proceed from the members of the LJPHS; nor would it continue without their ongoing support and participation, as will be illustrated with specific examples later in this chapter. In addition to being research subjects in an ethnographic sense, the individuals in this group are my clients, my collaborators, and have come to be my friends. We see our roles as necessary to each other; as my "bosses," they have asked me to initiate and direct certain activities, involving them in my agendas (and being involved in theirs) according to our mutual needs. My voice in our work together is indeed a strong one; so is Brown's, as the principal investigator, and so are the voices of some of his student researchers. Other voices speak as well, however—not only community and descendant voices, but other voices within academia, all of whom bring different skills and interests to the process.

In summary, during the same period that active public participation was starting to be seen as necessary in historical archaeology generally, it also became necessary at the Jordan site, as people started to find the archaeological information itself more compelling and, in some cases, more difficult to deal with. Concurrently, it became necessary to answer challenges to the research and to expand it past the questions that were part of the original (or even the revised) research design. Because of the formation of the LJPHS and our continued work with them to help them accomplish their objectives,[6] the initial archaeological research has now evolved into an ongoing public archaeological project. The infrastructure to support a long-term and mutually empowering collaboration is in place, and the organization has continued to mature. To conclude this chapter I will return to the discussion of the major players, as I describe future prospects for the site and its public interpretation. Next, however, I will focus on the Jordan website project in some detail because, as mentioned above, it comprises the greater part of current public interpretive activity at the Jordan site.

Public Archaeology as Applied Archaeology: Moving from a Postprocessual Archaeological Project to a Postprocessual Public Archaeology

Kenneth Brown's excavation of the Levi Jordan Plantation represents one of the first times that an explicitly *contextual* postprocessual theoretical and methodological approach (Hodder 1986) was used in American historical archaeology.[7] Following from this, my work with this project as a public enterprise has also attempted to incorporate what has been termed a self-reflexive postprocessual methodology in real-site excavation contexts (Hodder 1997; Hodder, 1999). That is, the website project represents one attempt to consciously apply postprocessual theory to public archaeology; or, to paraphrase a popular text on applied anthropology, it is concerned with the relationships between archaeological knowledge (and theory) and the uses of that knowledge in the world beyond archaeology (Chambers 1985:x). Therefore, I have attempted to incorporate four primary postprocessualist themes—reflexivity, multivocality, interactivity, and contextuality—in various aspects of the website's development and delivery.

I should emphasize that the website does not purport to *be* reflexive, multivocal, and so on, but, rather, to employ some degree of all four elements in varying degrees in different parts of the site. There is material on the site that is decidedly nonreflexive and univocal, although we do attempt to use this material in reflexive, transparent ways. I should also point out that [my varying use of the first person in this chapter—in both its singular and plural forms—reflects the collaborative nature of the work as well as the fact that this project also represents my individual research. I acknowledge, but make no apologies for, any confusion that this departure from commonly accepted academic writing may cause,] although I will deal with the question of independent authorship later in this chapter.

Before going further I should clarify terms (see also [Hodder 1997] and [Hodder 1999]). By *reflexivity* I mean that we aimed for openness about our taken-for-granteds, and that we attempted to be self-critical of these assumptions as we decided what sorts of content to include. Being reflexive also required that we be aware of, and open about, what our individual assumptions revealed about our own ideologies; assumptions we made as scientists, descendants, community members, and so on were on the table during the process of creating the site. By *multivocality* I mean simply that we wanted to ensure that a diversity of people had the opportunity to participate in the conversation of the website—in both the content development and online phases of the project. This includes people who do not own and do not intend to use computers, as will be discussed later. By *interactive* I mean that we wanted to provide ways for people to question the archaeological interpretations and ways for them to approach the material from a variety of angles—using different disciplines and different ways of evaluating truth claims. Being interactive also means that we had to provide ways for us to respond to their questions and challenges and to approach those challenges in a democratic way. Finally, by being *contextual* we wanted to communicate how archaeological knowledge depends on history, ethnography, genealogy, and understanding the continuities and conflicts between past and present.

These four elements, which came to operate as both structuring principles and as internal goals for the website, overlap and occasionally merge. For example, sometimes strategies designed to achieve multivocality were the same as those aimed at achieving contextuality; these concepts frequently cross-cut each other and are difficult to compartmentalize. Therefore, while I describe the process of designing some aspects of the Jordan website in a linear fashion, the process itself was only linear in the sense that my systematic evaluation of the site took place *after* the site was designed and published. The design process itself, and the data that emerged from it, operated in a recursive, reflexive, and circular fashion (Hodder 1999:98) analogous to the hermeneutic processes that excavators and other specialists experience as they move back and forth between excavation and interpretation (Hodder 1999).

Developing the Website: Process

Continuing my ongoing work with the Jordan project, in the summer of 1997 I began the process of creating the website. I first met with the LJPHS to obtain their support and initial input. They approved the original website proposal, began to contribute content, and made the final decisions about some of the more sensitive materials that were included from other sources. Working with these people and others, including Ken Brown and some of his students, I began to assemble the various content components—data, texts, images, and so on. By the end of the summer of 1997, we had published a prototype website, so I then asked my collaborators—community and professional—to comment on this version. I spent the spring and summer of 1998 revising the prototype site based on the critiques received and including more archaeological, anthropological, and historical data (as well as content material from members of the various descendant communities). At this point I added online interactive elements to the website, including an online discussion forum, feedback forms, and questionnaires. The systematic evaluation of the site mentioned above (McDavid 2002b) will include qualitative analysis of the ways these interactive mechanisms operated.

Aiming for the Four Principles: Successes and Challenges

Reflexivity Our aim to be reflexive and to reveal our taken-for-granteds operates in a very overt way. The website contains several mission-type statements; these statements are up front, on the home page of the site and in several other places. We state, among other things, that we want to present alternate interpretations of the data *alongside*, not subsumed to, academic interpretations—that is, to present the scientific voice as an important voice, but not the only voice, in interpreting the past.

But stating this is not doing it, so we obviously needed to find ways for local people to add their own material to the site—family stories, pictures, genealogical information, alternate or additional explanations of the data, and so on. A major impediment to doing this was that many people in the community do not use computers. So we met with key people in these descendant communities (usually the elders) and conducted oral history interviews. These interviews were transcribed, and portions of the transcripts were included on the website, with links to other parts of the website that were discussed during these offline conversations. I and usually at least one other family member conducted the interviews. Frequently, the family members were the ones asking most of the questions, and these interviews sometimes led to more intrafamilial discussion about history, genealogy, and so on. Transcripts of the interviews were given to the family members involved, and subsequent meetings were held to clarify information, approve the interview segments used for the website, obtain pictures, and the like.

Another strategy we employed had to do with asking permission. Much of the material we wanted to put on the website was from public records: genealogical information, in particular, came from census records and public birth, death, and marriage records. While we had the legal right to put this sort of material on the website, we decided not to include genealogies or pictures of any named individual without permission from at least some of the family descendants. This had two positive results. First, it assured descendants that we respected their privacy and their families' privacy, and it reinforced our position as collaborators rather than gatekeepers. Second, it opened avenues for additional information and conversation. It was during one of these asking permission interviews, for example, that a relative of George Holmes (who had been enslaved on the plantation) told us about how one of the owners, McWillie Martin, had expressed regret for participating in white supremacist activities in his youth. As he put it, Martin "repented" before his death. This was information about which Martin's descendants were completely unaware. So far, only one descendant family has asked that their family name not be associated with the website, and this was due to a private legal situation, not to the material we proposed to present or to their lack of support for the project.

Despite the success of these strategies, other challenges prevented us from being fully reflexive or multivocal. One important impediment was that much of the website content comes from previously published scholarly articles and conference papers. These materials are important in themselves, not only because they are artifacts of a situated time, place, and mode of production, but also because they represent a legitimate voice—the scientific scholarly voice. However, they do present certain problems when trying to apply them to a forum that aims to be open and reflexive.

Not only is the language usually too technical, certain essentializing words appear throughout these documents. Some collaborators pointed out, for example, that the word *cabin* is problematic (unless there is evidence that the plantation's residents themselves used it, which there is not) because it communicates a certain mental image to contemporary audiences—a certain ideological conception of what an enslaved person's house must be. The word *slave* is even more difficult; the people who lived on this plantation may have been slaves, but they also had other roles, both inside and outside the plantation community (Brown 1994). The word *slave* defines a person according to a condition that someone else has imposed upon him or her. The phrase *enslaved person* was suggested as a possible replacement.

Even though we could have attempted to translate all previously published texts into more appropriate (some might say more "politically correct") language, doing this would likely have been frustrating, given the fluid, dynamic nature of cultural debates about language, and given that replacement language is frequently cumbersome and awkward (as *enslaved person* is more awkward than *slave*; see LaRoche and Blakey 1997). However, taking advantage of the linking capabilities of hypertext, the textual form with which people are able to read websites, we decided to present the previously published materials as-is. We created hypertext links from problematic words to discussions about language and about how words have the power to create and reinforce the categories and vocabularies that we use to describe and understand each other (Rorty 1989; Rorty 1991). These links were then linked to the online discussion forum (helping us to meet our aim of interactivity) to further situate the conversation about language itself within a specific historical context. In this way we attempted to turn a weakness into an interpretive strength, still providing a legitimate place for scientific/authoritative texts within the conversation of the website (Rorty 1989; Rorty 1991). By discussing how our own taken-for-granteds are revealed in the words *we* use, we hoped to encourage the site's visitors to question the words *they* use in everyday talk. This may also help people to see both science and history writing as situated and contingent, rather than as never-changing, authoritative Truth. Obviously, a considerable amount of new text still needed to be written, and in these new texts we attempted to use more appropriate, accessible language. These new texts were usually written by me and vetted by key collaborators before being included on the website.

In order to reveal more about the archaeological taken-for-granteds, I also conducted interviews with Brown and his research students. During these interviews we discussed what had informed their interpretations—the ethnographic and historical data they used, the artifact and artifact context data they had gathered, and the like. After being taped and transcribed, portions of these interviews (reviewed and edited by the archaeologists) were included on the website. The interview segments now include links to the materials discussed during the interviews (diaries, ethnographic material, photos of artifacts, tables, historical records, and so on).

Multivocality   One early decision was to develop a section of the website for participants. This section includes short biographies of academics, students, family members, and others, as well as links to information they wish to put on the site under their own names. Whenever possible, these biographies are written by the individuals. These participant pages are *not* organized according to roles that each individual has; community members are listed alongside archaeologists, for example. Our hope was that this would reinforce our effort to decenter my authority as the website project leader and Kenneth Brown's as the lead archaeologist.

Sometimes project participants have used these pages to publicize information about their own agendas. Our collaborators provide certain information, and the website provides them with publicity for certain individual causes and activities. This highlights our aim for contextuality as well as our collaborative approach. Our agendas merge in mutually empowering, reciprocal ways, and the website project is firmly situated within the social context of the local community, even though it is accessible to people all over the world.

Interactivity   We conceive of interactivity as a part of the *process* of website content development: all of the above strategies illustrate this approach, especially those that focus on ways to get people without computers (especially descendants) involved in this project. We also worked with local schools and libraries to have online workshops with both children and adults, many of whom do not have computers at home. I was present at the workshops to help people who had never used computers and to collect data about how they interact with the website, with me, and with each other while the workshop is going on.

We also included some interactive elements on the website itself. These include a discussion forum, feedback forms, and a questionnaire (the design and content of which was vetted by key collaborators and critiqued by colleagues before publication). However, we did not include many of the features that are usually regarded as pathways to so-called interactivity (Java applets, video clips, sound bites, clickable maps, and the like) because of software and hardware requirements and download times—in a word, because of *access*. We also avoided large pictures and the use of frames for the same reason (although we did add larger pictures that can be optionally viewed in a photo gallery). Our priority was to enable people to see and enjoy the site with a minimum of frustration—even people with older computers and slower modems. Most of our time and effort has been aimed at developing *content* interactively, rather than relying on the technology to create an interactive environment.

Contextuality   Hypertext links have been the most effective way to reinforce the contextual nature of the website, and of the data itself. Internal links from individual participant pages are linked to other sections of the site that individuals have written or provided. In addition, each primary entry point into the material contains numerous internal links to other sections. On the main archaeology page, for example, there are links to history pages, ethnography pages, and links back to oral histories written by family members. These in turn link to family genealogies, church histories, and other documents. There are excerpts from a diary written during and after the Civil War by the plantation owner's granddaughter, linked to an analysis of the diary by a linguistic anthropologist. There are links from this diary to information about people who lived and worked on the plantation, along with links to archaeological interpretations that have been informed by material in the diary. There is oral history information from the African-American descendant community, linked to church histories and to genealogical information about individual families. This is linked to and from archaeological data concerning religious and healing practices that African-American residents used to cope with the difficulties of their lives—linked to information about burial traditions within the community, linked back to the oral history data that discusses those traditions. There is also information about the social and political contexts in which the people on this plantation lived (and in which their descendants continue to live) linked to archaeological data that resulted from those contexts.

Website Project: Summary

The Jordan website project is a work in progress. We do not know how much it will be able to provide meaningful, open, and democratic ways for archaeologists, members of the community, and other people to discuss the "hurtful" (Gero 1995:175) histories of the Jordan plantation. It is certainly true that what we have learned about collaborative content development could apply as easily to any other communicative environment. We could have employed many of the same strategies to plan a museum exhibit, for example.

As the project continues—as it certainly will, even though my doctoral research is complete—we will continue to make changes to the site and will encourage members of the local community to continue to add and change content. One change may provide the means to enhance a part of the site that is currently very underdeveloped: a local computer-literacy teacher is interested in having her students (aged thirteen to fifteen) create the *Kids* section of the website, using material from other parts of the site to write new texts more suited to younger audiences. Archaeologists will do talks and real-site tours, review and discuss texts, and so on to insure that the new texts accurately represent the material presented elsewhere in the website (most of which is now designed for somewhat older audiences). We are hopeful that other similar projects will develop over time, and that they will continue to enhance what visitors from other parts of the world see on their computer screens. Before this happens, however, the character and management of the Jordan archaeology project overall will change, as the following section will describe.

The Future

The board of the LJPHS has evolved, over time, to become a group in which the shared power between members of different descendant groups, and between academics and local citizens, is commonly recognized—both within the community and outside it. This public recognition has recently allowed the *possibility* of realizing some of the society's major goals: restoring the plantation house, constructing a visitor center on the property, and creating regular programming on the grounds of the site, in addition to maintain existing activities such as the website project. This is because recently a public state agency, the Texas Parks and Wildlife Department (TPWD), has purchased the property from its current owners (descendants of the founder), with the written understanding that they will implement the above goals, among others. To do this, TPWD convinced the Texas legislature to appropriate more than $4 million, and a bond sale to provide these funds was approved by Texas voters in November 2001. This sale was finalized in March 2002.

Even though the house and quarters, as well as excavated artifacts and associated archaeological data, are obviously of great importance to this agency, the diverse composition of the LJPHS is just as important. Members of the TPWD staff have made it clear that they want that aspect of the project to continue, although how that will be accomplished is still being negotiated. This agency is aware that the project's current diverse leadership will increase its legitimacy with statewide African-American constituencies; they are also aware that these constituencies are currently underrepresented at state parks and other facilities, and that the political advantages offered by a public interpretation of the Jordan site would be considerable. The coming year (2003) will be critical, not only in terms of making sure that the collaboratively developed goals of the local community are carried through in the new project, but also in terms of insuring that the nonhierarchical power relationships developed so far are translated to the new management scheme. In addition, it will be necessary to deal with serious questions of intellectual property, with regard to the academic research already undertaken.

It is obvious to all participants—even the new ones from TPWD—that sharing power in the context of a state bureaucracy, no matter how well intentioned some of its employees are, will be different than it has been on a local, grassroots level. TPWD staff have said that the agency wants the LJPHS to continue operating in an advisory capacity, with all of its current players, including the archaeologists. Even so, this purchase will mean that primary management authority will shift, and the LJPHS is now in a position in which it must *trust* that a state agency will continue to want decisions about the plantation to be, as one of their staff members put it, "made by consensus" between TPWD and LJPHS. Therefore, we approach the future with both eagerness and some degree of trepidation. Whether this project can continue as a *community* archaeology project is very much in question, even though it does appear likely that it will continue in some other form.

A Final Word on Collaboration—*Within* the Discipline

In this chapter I have not only discussed my own work in public archaeology, but have also alluded rather liberally to that of my colleague and former teacher, Kenneth L. Brown. I want to talk about two things in this chapter with regard to the collaboration we have developed over the past several years: authorship and ownership.

One of our goals for this website project was to decenter the archaeologist as the authoritative source of The Truth about the history of this plantation; that is, as discussed above, we wanted to create a website that was multivocal, and we wanted to provide different lenses through which people could see the past. One issue playing into this was that I see his data differently than Brown himself does, and I tend to write about it differently. Brown tends to write in a traditional scholarly style and, in public talks and the like, usually presents a very scientific, authoritative account of the Jordan archaeology (Brown 1994; Brown 2002; Brown and Cooper 1990). He also frames his data—despite his postprocessualist leanings—in terms of ideas like *evolution, origins,* and *adaptation.* I see the same data in terms of ideas like *multiple identities, fluidity, empowerment,* and *agency,* as I have discussed elsewhere (McDavid 1997a). Obviously, these are not just different words, they reflect alternate ways of understanding, and this chapter is not the forum to discuss the differences in philosophical approach that these words represent. Suffice it to say that *multivocal,* in our case, includes our own different voices insofar as the data itself is concerned.

Even so, while working together to plan website content, we agreed that the Jordan archaeological data provided fresh, radically different ways of looking at the individual and collective lives of the people who lived on this plantation. We also agreed that presenting the data in more fluid, conversational, and contingent terms would help to create a communicative environment that could open the discourse about the data and encourage people to challenge and even elaborate on the original interpretations. So, as discussed above, we decided to write new texts to introduce the more academic ones, and I was the person who rewrote these texts. In doing this I sometimes, in effect, reinterpreted his original interpretations; a multiple hermeneutic (Shanks and Tilley 1987:107–10) was at work as I recontextualized Brown's original data in order to create an open, reflexive conversation with multiple publics. Even though we are both reasonably happy with these new texts, this process tended to blur the traditional lines of authorship. It also had another effect that has not been as easy to cope with.

Because I am the leader of the website project, because I have been the one publicizing it—and because my own voice is such a strong element—I have become, in effect, a primary public spokesperson for the Jordan archaeological project. This is true even though I take great pains to refer to Brown's role as the principal investigator every time I discuss either the website or the archaeological site (whether that discussion is in public venues or in professional forums such as this one). Because of my role as a very *public* public archaeologist, collaborating with a more private, research-oriented archaeologist, we have found that sometimes people misidentify us. They sometimes think that the Jordan project is mine, and Brown's role as the originator and leader of the archaeological research is masked.

This has obviously caused tensions, and it is fair to say that it is only because of constant communication, as well as a basic trust in each other's skills and integrity—added to a shared belief in the importance of this project—that our collaboration has been as successful as it has. To paraphrase Alma Gottlieb, who expressed some thoughts about intradisciplinary collaboration in the *American Anthropologist* a few years ago, we both, sometimes unconsciously but usually *very* consciously, tend to see ourselves in a typically Western way: as individual authors, singular creations, standing alone in our academic achievement (Gottlieb 1997:21). When our achievements become blurred because of perceptions about ownership—of the data, of the discourse, of the entire process—the sort of collaboration we have attempted to develop becomes, at times, very difficult.

These sorts of difficulties were also apparent where other archaeologist team members were concerned. Most of these were Brown's graduate students in the anthropology program at the University of Houston who were analyzing specific components of the Jordan archaeology (as is typical with large, long-term projects of this sort). In a few cases Brown had to exercise his professorial authority to persuade them to contribute their own data to a website being put together by someone they perceived to be competing with them—namely, me, an ex-student conducting Ph.D. research elsewhere. Most eventually came on board and became fully participatory team members; over time, they bought in to the collaborative spirit of the project. Others, despite attributed credit (including copyrights) on their pages, clearly saw the entire project as mine and continued to resist my efforts to engage them in a reciprocal way. Obviously, there are legitimate data protection and copyright issues associated with putting unpublished data on the Internet, but in these cases the main resistance had to do with the collaborative nature of the project and the apparent feeling that somehow sharing the stage with others diluted individual scholarly authority.

Also playing into this, our primary professional agendas (Brown's and my own) are somewhat different. His are, I think it is fair to say, more oriented toward the basic research itself: that is, the process of discovery and exploration that are the hallmarks of both professional and popular perceptions of archaeology. My focus is on what happens after these discoveries take place. In this sort of collaboration, we depend on each other, not only to feed our individual personal and professional agendas, but also to accomplish something we both believe in: to share the stories of the Levi Jordan plantation in ways that are meaningful to everyday people in contemporary life today.

But what is the point of sharing this rather personal narrative about the collaborative tensions in one public archaeology project? First, in terms of the website project, if archaeologists want to use the Internet as a forum to publicly discuss our work, we must become comfortable with its open, contingent environment where, by definition, we live outside the protected shelter of traditional rules about academic ownership and authorship. Through hyperlinks to and from our sites, as well as discussion forums and the like, our arguments will become linked to others. This is not to say that we should not speak loudly, and forcefully, as individuals—only that our voices will not be the only ones telling the story. But if we are willing to see this decentering process as an opportunity rather than a threat, perhaps we can also begin to relate insights from each other—and our publics—more productively. In doing this, our data, and our arguments, will benefit.

As media philosophers Mark Taylor and Esa Saarinen put it,

> The net displaces the notion of the solitary creative genius that has governed our understanding of authorship for over two centuries. Letting go of the isolated author threatens the very foundation of individual identity. This threat must be embraced, for it provides remarkable opportunities for creative renewal. (Taylor and Saarinen 1994:7)

Second, in order to be seen as credible collaborators with our publics, we have to learn how to collaborate with each other more comfortably. I would suspect that the tensions I have described would apply to collaborative endeavors in any communicative or interpretive environment; however, they are not usually addressed openly and explicitly, especially in forums such as this volume. If we say that we want to be open with our publics, but we are not willing to be open with each other, our hypocrisy will be evident to those publics.

Third, by revealing our "hidden sources of discomfort, accommodation, and compromise" (Gottlieb 1997:23), we can help to create the intellectual space for our publics to reveal their assumptions about us, each other, and even, perhaps, about the past. We can, as different types of archaeologists with different skills and talents, begin to learn to trust each other more and begin to come to terms with the tensions between our personal and professional agendas.

Conclusion

The stated intent of the Levi Jordan public archaeology project has been, so far, to help create a more meaningful, democratic, socially relevant archaeology. Indeed, that is probably a major objective for any public archaeology, as the rest of this volume will no doubt demonstrate. It is important, however, to take that project further, past the concerns of a democratic archaeology into a larger arena, where citizens can actively attempt to use archaeology to create a more democratic society (Jeppson 2001).

By helping to create a truly collaborative, diverse, nonhierarchical public archaeological project, what I frequently refer to as a conversation (McDavid 1997a) about the past, we are not only working toward our first objective, but, we hope, the second one as well. When the LJPHS became active, it represented one of the first times that members of both African-American and European-American descendant communities came together with archaeologists, in a setting of shared power and responsibility, to decide how to tell the stories of plantation life in the American South. There are, of course, many plantation interpretations across the South; most of them, until perhaps the last decade, have been tours of fancy houses—that is, they have tended to focus just on the lives of the plantation owner's family. This project is different not only because the objective is to talk about the African Americans who lived at the Jordan plantation, but also because a collaborative effort is being made, by descendants of both enslavers and enslaved, to talk about the lives of both African Americans and European Americans, without doing either at the expense of the other.

As I write this, one year after the terrorist attacks in the United States on September 11, 2001, my belief that human beings can work together to determine, and improve upon, their own fates is even more profound than it was before the attacks. I believe that humans can and will be able to discover—from current crises and their interactions with fellow beings, but also from archaeology and history—which truths about past *and* present are most meaningful and useful. I believe that we can learn, from past and present cruelties, which truths will help our futures to become less cruel (Rorty 1991). That may be the best role for public archaeology: to provide ways for archaeology's fresh view of the past—with all its provisionality and contingency—to create new collaborations, conversations, and "paradigms of imagination" (Rorty 1991:94). This may, in turn, help us to build alternative visions (West 1993:30) to understand and critique our social, moral, and political lives, and to use these critiques to build the future. This may be how archaeology can begin to create a more relevant, democratic society.

References Cited

Barnes, Mary K. (1998). "Everything They Owned." Paper presented at the annual meeting of the Society for Historical Archaeology, Atlanta, Ga.

Blakey, Michael L. (1995). "Race, Nationalism and the Afrocentric Past." In *Making Alternative Histories: The Practice of Archaeology and History in Non-Western Settings*, ed. P. R. Schmidt and T. C. Patterson, pp. 213–28. Santa Fe, N.M.: School of American Research Press.

———. (1997). "Commentary: Past Is Present." In *In the Realm of Politics: Prospects for Public Participation in African-American Archaeology*, special issue of *Historical Archaeology* 31, no. 3: 140–45.

Brown, Kenneth L. (1994). "Material Culture and Community Structure: The Slave and Tenant Community at Levi Jordan's Plantation, 1848–1892." In *Working Toward Freedom: Slave Society and Domestic Economy in the American South*, ed. Larry E. Hudson, Jr., pp. 95–118. Rochester, N.Y.: University of Rochester Press.

———. (1997). "Some Thoughts on Archaeology and Public Responsibility." *African American Archaeology: Newsletter of the African-American Archaeology Network* 18 (Fall):6–7.

———. (2000). "From Archaeological Interpretation to Public Interpretation: Collaboration within the Discipline for a Better Public Archaeology (Phase One)." Paper presented at the 65th annual meeting of the Society for American Archaeology, Philadelphia, Penn.

Brown, Kenneth L., and Doreen C. Cooper. (1990). "Structural Continuity in an African-American Slave and Tenant Community." In *Historical Archaeology on Southern Plantations and Farms*, special issue of *Historical Archaeology* 24, no. 4:7–19.

Chambers, Erve. (1985). *Applied Anthropology: A Practical Guide*. Prospect Heights, Ill.: Waveland Press.

Clark, G. A. (1996). "Letter to the Editor." *SAA Bulletin* 14, no. 5:3.

Clifford, James. (1988). *The Predicament of Culture*. Cambridge, Mass.: Harvard University Press.

Clifford, James, and George E. Marcus, eds. (1986). *Writing Culture: The Poetics and Politics of Ethnography.* Berkeley: University of California Press.

Crapanzano, Vincent. (1986). *Tuhami: Portrait of a Moroccan.* Chicago, Ill.: University of Chicago Press.

Gero, Joan. (1995). "Railroading Epistemology: Paleoindians and Women." In *Interpreting Archaeology: Finding Meaning in the Past,* ed. I. Hodder, M. Shanks, A. Alexandri, V. Buchli, J. Carman, J. Last, and G. Lucas, pp. 175–78. London and New York: Routledge.

Gottlieb, Alma. (1997). "Beyond the Lonely Anthropologist: Collaboration in Research and Writing." *American Anthropologist* 97, no. 1:21–23.

Hinson, Glenn. (1999). " 'You've Got to Include an Invitation': Engaged Reciprocity and Negotiated Purpose in Collaborative Ethnography." Paper presented at the annual meeting of the American Anthropological Association, Chicago, Ill.

———. (2000). *Fire in My Bones: Transcendence and the Holy Spirit in African American Gospel.* Philadelphia: University of Pennsylvania Press.

Hodder, Ian. (1986). *Reading the Past: Current Approaches to Interpretation in Archaeology.* Cambridge: Cambridge University Press.

———. (1997). "Towards a Reflexive Excavation Methodology." *Antiquity* 71, no. 273:691–700.

———. (1999). *The Archaeological Process: An Introduction.* Oxford: Blackwell.

Howell, Wayne. (1997). "The Bay in Place of a Glacier." *Common Ground: Archeology and Ethnography in the Public Interest* 2, no. 3/4:58–63.

Hutt, Sherry. (1997). "Sound Decisions, Respectful Results." *Common Ground: Archeology and Ethnography in the Public Interest* 2, no. 3/4:28–29.

Jeppson, Patrice L. (2001). "Pitfalls, Pratfalls, and Pragmatism in Public Archaeology." Paper presented at the annual meeting of the Society for Historical and Underwater Archaeology, Long Beach, Calif.

Johnson, Matthew. (1999). *Archaeological Theory: An Introduction.* Oxford: Blackwell.

LaRoche, Cheryl, and Michael Blakey. (1997). "Seizing Intellectual Power: The Dialogue at the New York African Burial Ground." In *In the Realm of Politics: Prospects for Public Participation in African-American Archaeology,* special issue of *Historical Archaeology* 31, no. 3:84–106.

Lassiter, Luke Eric. (1998). *The Power of Kiowa Song: A Collaborative Ethnography.* Tucson: University of Arizona Press.

———. (1999). "From 'Reading over the Shoulders of Natives' to 'Reading alongside Natives': Literality, Text, Dialogue, and Collaborative Ethnography." Paper presented at the annual meeting of the American Anthropological Association, Chicago, Ill.

Leone, Mark P., Parker B. Potter, Jr., and Paul A. Shackel. (1987). "Toward a Critical Archaeology." *Current Anthropology* 28, no. 3:283–302.

Lynott, Mark J. (1997). "Ethical Principles and Archaeological Practice: Development of an Ethics Policy." *American Antiquity* 62, no. 45:88–99.

Lynott, Mark J., and Alison Wylie, eds. (1995). *Ethics in American Archaeology.* Washington, D.C.: Society for American Archaeology.

Mason, R. J. (1997). "Letter to the Editor." *SAA Bulletin* 15, no. 1:3.

McDavid, Carol. (1996). *The Levi Jordan Plantation: From Archaeological Interpretation to Public Interpretation.* Master of Arts thesis, University of Houston, University Microfilms.

———. (1997a). "Archaeology as Cultural Critique: A Pragmatic Framework for Community Collaboration in the Public Interpretation of the Archaeology of a Southern Plantation." Paper presented at the annual meeting of the American Anthropology Association, Washington, D.C.

———. (1997b). "Descendants, Decisions, and Power: The Public Interpretation of the Archaeology of the Levi Jordan Plantation." In *In the Realm of Politics: Prospects for Public Participation in African-American Archaeology,* special issue of *Historical Archaeology* 31, no. 3:114–31.

———. (1997c). Research notes in possession of author, recounting conversation with project participant.

———. (1999a). "Collaboration and the Levi Jordan Plantation Web Site Project: Comments for the Collaboration Workshop, a Workshop for Both Prehistoric and Historic Archaeologists." Paper presented at the annual meeting of the Society for American Archaeology, Chicago, Illinois.

———. (1999b). "From Real Space to Cyberspace: Contemporary Conversations about the Archaeology of Slavery and Tenancy." *Internet Archaeology* 6. Special Theme: Digital Publication. http://intarch.ac.uk/journal/issue6/mcdavid_toc.html.

———. (2000). "Archaeology as Cultural Critique: Pragmatism and the Archaeology of a Southern United States Plantation." In *Philosophy and Archaeological Practice: Perspectives for the 21st Century*, ed. C. Holtorf and H. Karlsson, pp. 221–40. Lindome, Sweden: Bricoleur Press.

———. (2001). "Descendant Communities, Archaeologists, and the Internet: A Tool for the Powerful, or a Tool for Empowerment." Paper presented at the annual meeting of the Society for American Archaeology, New Orleans, La.

———. (2004). "Towards a More Democratic Archaeology? The Internet and Public Archaeological Practice." In *Public Archaeology*, ed. N. Merriman and T. Shadla-Hall. London: Routledge.

———. (2002a). "Archaeologies That Hurt; Descendants That Matter: A Pragmatic Approach to Collaboration in the Public Interpretation of African-American Archaeology." In *Community Archaeology*, special issue of *World Archaeology* 34, no. 2:303–14.

———. (2002b). "From Real Space to Cyberspace: The Internet and Public Archaeological Practice." Doctoral dissertation, Department of Archaeology, University of Cambridge.

McKee, Larry. (1994). "Commentary: Is It Futile to Try and Be Useful? Historical Archaeology and the African-American Experience." *Northeast Historical Archaeology* 23:1–7.

McKeown, C. Timothy. (1997). "The Meaning of Consultation." *Common Ground: Archeology and Ethnography in the Public Interest* 2, no. 3/4:16–19.

McManamon, Francis P. (1997). "Why Consult?" *Common Ground: Archeology and Ethnography in the Public Interest* 2, no. 3/4:2.

Messenger, Phyllis Mauch, ed. (1989). *The Ethics of Collecting Cultural Property: Whose Culture? Whose Property?* Albuquerque: University of New Mexico Press.

Moore, Lawrence E. (1994). "The Ironies of Self-Reflection in Archaeology." In *Archaeological Theory: Progress or Posture?*, ed. Ian M. Mackenzie, pp. 43–65. Avebury, U.K.: Aldershot.

Parker, Patricia L., and Emogene Bevit. (1997). "Consultation with American Indian Sovereign Nations." *Common Ground: Archeology and Ethnography in the Public Interest* 2, no. 3/4:22–27.

Preucel, Robert W., and Ian Hodder, eds. (1996). *Contemporary Archaeology in Theory*. Oxford: Blackwell.

Roberts, Alexa, and James E. Bradford. (1997). "A Common Cause on Common Ground." *Common Ground: Archeology and Ethnography in the Public Interest* 2, no. 3/4:30–35.

Rorty, Richard. (1989). *Contingency, Irony and Solidarity*. Cambridge: Cambridge University Press.

———. (1991). *Objectivity, Relativism, and Truth: Philosophical Papers Volume 1*. Cambridge: Cambridge University Press.

Rosaldo, Renato. (1989). *Culture and Truth: The Remaking of Social Analysis*. Boston: Beacon.

Ruppert, Dave. (1997). "New Language for a New Partnership." *Common Ground: Archeology and Ethnography in the Public Interest* 2, no. 3/4:36–38.

Scheopfle, Mark. (1997). "Due Process and Dialogue." *Common Ground: Archeology and Ethnography in the Public Interest* 2, no. 3/4:40–45.

Shanks, Michael, and Christopher Tilley. (1987). *Re-Constructing Archaeology: Theory and Practice*. London: Routledge.

South, Stanley. (1997). "Generalized versus Literal Interpretation." In *Presenting Archaeology to the Public: Digging for Truths*, ed. J. John H. Jameson, pp. 54–62. Walnut Creek, Calif., London, New Delhi: Altamira Press.

Sucec, Rosemary. (1997). "Telling the Whole Story." *Common Ground: Archeology and Ethnography in the Public Interest* 2, no. 3/4:52–57.

Swidler, Nina, Kurt Donoske, Roger Anyon, and Alan Downer, eds. (1997). *Native Americans and Archaeologists: Stepping Stones to Common Ground*. Walnut Creek, Calif., London, New Delhi: Altamira Press.

Taylor, Mark C., and Esa Saarinen. (1994). "Pedagogies." In *Imagologies: Media Philosophy*. London: Routledge.

Vitelli, Karen D., ed. (1996). *Archaeological Ethics*. Walnut Creek, Calif., London, New Delhi: Altamira Press.

Watkins, Joe, and Tom Parry. (1997). "Archeology's First Steps in Moccasins." *Common Ground: Archeology and Ethnography in the Public Interest* 2, no. 3/4:47–49.

Weisman, Brent R. (2000). "Local Politics and Archaeology." *Anthropology News* 41, no. 9:17.

West, Cornel. (1993). *Keeping Faith: Philosophy and Race in America*. New York, London: Routledge.

Notes

I would like to thank Kenneth L. Brown for his comments on this chapter, for helping me to recollect certain incidents that occurred during our ongoing collaborative work in the Brazoria community, and for his willingness for me refer to his work so liberally and to discuss our collaboration so openly. I am grateful to Patrice Jeppson for helping me to see past the narrow focus of one project to the ways it can be a part of larger societal objectives. I also want to thank the members of the Levi Jordan Plantation Historical Society and their ancestors. Without these people this work would not be possible. Finally, as always, thanks go to my husband, Herman Kluge, for countless hours of proofreading and editing, as well as his ongoing patience, humor, and support.

1. See http://www.webarchaeology.com.
2. The legislation legally empowered Native American groups to have control over the process by which their ancestors' lives are researched and presented, and to have control over the results (artefactual and otherwise) of that research. See http://www.cr.nps.gov/nagpra/NACD/nacd3.htm.
3. It should be noted that when NAGPRA was passed, most prehistoric archaeologists did (and in some cases still do) resist the idea of sharing control of their research with members of Native American groups. However, a full discussion of the history of consultation in prehistoric archaeology, with regard to NAGPRA in particular, is outside the scope of this paper. See Clark (1996) and Mason (1997) for examples of the resistant view. See Howell (1997), Hutt (1997), McKeown (1997), McManamon (1997), Parker and Bevit (1997), Roberts and Bradford (1997), Ruppert (1997), Scheopfle (1997), Sucec (1997), Swidler et al. (1997), and Watkins and Parry (1997) for discussions of ways that consultation and collaboration with Native American groups is necessary to, and can benefit, archaeology.
4. See www.sha.org and www.saa.org for the ethics statements for the Society for Historical Archaeology and the Society of American Archaeology.
5. The project has been privately funded—by Brown, the property owner, and field school tuitions—from its inception. Although the usual professional and ethical mandates to publish site reports, and so on, apply here, as they would to any archaeological site, it has not been subject to the same reporting requirements that, for example, a cultural resource management project would have been.
6. See http://www.webarchaeology.com/html/about.htm.
7. See Preucel and Hodder (1996) and Johnson (1999) for overviews of the various threads that have developed in postprocessual writing over the last two decades, of which so-called contextual archaeology is one.

CHAPTER 3

African-American Heritage in a Multicultural Community
An Archaeology of Race, Culture, and Consumption

PAUL R. MULLINS

This chapter provides a strong argument for the importance of understanding the needs and aspirations of the communities in which archaeologists work. Mullins's public archaeology project on Indianapolis's near-Westside has involved close collaboration with the community's predominantly African-American neighborhood association, a relationship that has proven to be of major benefit in many instances, but that is also subject to misunderstandings related to different goals. Whereas the neighborhood association's principal interest has been in using archaeology to promote African-American achievement, the archaeologists see a somewhat more complex pattern of multicultural influence and racial and class inequality. That these goals are different does not mean that they are entirely incompatible. Recognizing that such different goals do exist might well be a necessary first step toward reconciliation and increased collaboration.

Introduction

Perhaps the two most striking buildings in Indianapolis, Indiana's near-Westside opened in 1927. At the corner of Indiana Avenue and West Street stood the Walker Theatre, an Afrocentric Art Deco commemoration of Madam C. J. Walker. Madam Walker's near-Westside beauty firm began modestly enough just a few hundred yards from the new theater, and from those origins Walker's enterprise became one of America's great business success stories. Completed eight years after Walker's death, the theater center featured a stage festooned with African cultural symbols, and it housed the Walker Manufacturing Company as well as African-American businesses and professional offices.

A few blocks to the north sat Crispus Attucks High School. In 1922 postwar racists and xenophobic civic organizations spurred the city school board to segregate Indianapolis's high schools. Attucks opened five years later, consolidating all Black high school students in one school and providing a generation of Black residents a common social and educational experience. The school gained fame for its rigorous academic programs, became a meeting place for local community organizations, sponsored night classes for adults, and assembled widely renowned basketball teams that won three state championships in the 1950s.

Sitting just a few blocks apart, the Walker Theatre and Crispus Attucks were the social and material heart of Black Indianapolis. Today, though, the Walker and Attucks are among only a handful of near-Westside buildings more than a half-century old; thousands of homes, businesses, and institutions that once stood near the two have been leveled by a complex mix of neglect, gentrification, and a host of urban "renewal" projects. The Walker and Attucks are powerful testaments to the contradictions of life across the color line, but now they often pass unnoticed or are painted as reminders of an unpleasant but distant past. As in many other communities, some local visions of Indianapolis's near-Westside are transparent populism, and many other local histories simply overlook or ignore these neighborhoods. It is easy to disregard the near-Westside's past today because it is mostly hidden underneath parking lots, undistinguished apartment complexes, and drab university architecture.

Archaeology certainly suggests a much more complex community history than the barren urban cityscape suggests today, and it is a history that in turn says a great deal about the city and the region. In fall 1999 Indiana University-Purdue University Indianapolis (IUPUI), the Ransom Place Neighborhood Association, and the Indianapolis Urban League began a collaborative research project that uses excavation, oral history, and documentary research to investigate identity in Indianapolis's past and present alike. At the heart of this project is the question of just what race and racism "look like" in the material world: that is, how can we see the effects of racial ideology in consumption patterns and material culture, and how do our contemporary assumptions about race and sociocultural identity impact the way contemporary people—archaeologists included—interpret objects? This question of how material culture reflects, creates, or reinforces sociocultural identity and lines of difference is certainly well examined by archaeologists (Delle et al. 2000; Franklin 2001; Mullins 1999; Orser 1996). In some ways this research on the complexities of identity also serves the community's interests very well in Indianapolis. Many African Americans, for instance, view archaeology as one mechanism to reclaim a heritage concealed by urban transformation: various African-American constituencies are now either physically dispersed from the near-Westside, defending a small residential foothold, or simply feeling ignored by scholars and city fathers. Many of these people have seen that archaeology can demonstrate their physical, social, and historical connection to spaces in which they now seem invisible. However, archaeology paints a picture of very complex lines of difference and an intricate political mosaic that created the contemporary cityscape, and some community constituents seem to desire something less equivocal. Many community constituencies hope archaeology will reveal a longstanding and unique ethnic experience: that is, some contemporary city residents hope German, Irish, or African-American identities will be clearly signaled in the material world and will look as unique as they conceive this heritage to be today. Yet when marshaled alongside oral memory and textual research, material culture tells a much more ambiguous and complex story.

Indianapolis's near-Westside was home to a vast range of newcomers migrating to the heartland from Europe, the South, and the Indiana countryside; this swath of neighborhoods included some rather affluent householders as well as profoundly impoverished neighbors. Today, most of these neighborhoods have been erased by an urban transformation that conceals a much different social and physical landscape. However, this social and cultural complexity either passes unnoticed or is painted in simplistic terms now. An essential goal of our project is to produce rigorous, academically relevant scholarship, so it certainly is not enough to provide a comfortable illusion of the city's historical and contemporary inequalities. Yet inequality took many different forms in the lives of near-Westside residents, who included men and women, Europeans and African Americans, and rich and poor alike: is it possible to say something coherent about life across the color line in this community or to hope that archaeology can produce a genuine political consciousness to change these conditions? It is unclear how effectively archaeology can fan such a consciousness, however, archaeology certainly can contribute to a public discussion about race: Historically, such a discussion has failed Americans, even though race has been at the heart of American life (Blakey 1997). Our goal is to use archaeological objects and sites as a mechanism to discuss racial inequality's imprint on apparently mundane objects and commonplace landscapes, and the most interesting insights of our project will likely emerge from that discussion.

Illuminating Invisible Histories

Indianapolis's near-Westside is today characterized by quite forgettable expanses of parking lots punctuated by chain businesses, apartments and condominiums, and, most visibly, the Indiana University Medical Center and IUPUI campus. This landscape effectively masks most near-Westside history, and the attention paid to the most visible material remnants of the African-American past is often superficial. The Walker Theatre, for example, memorializes Madam C. J. Walker, whose biography might well provide the prototypical American Dream story (Bundles 2001). Walker is often locally celebrated as the model for the self-made entrepreneur, and her life is definitely a testament to the power of perseverance and ambition. Nevertheless, the real power of her life story may be its resounding commentary on the standard Horatio Alger tale: American Dream ideology did not acknowledge that Black women aspired to secure the same social and material self-determination that was taken for granted by White men and often considered exclusively male even in African America. A daughter of slaves and a former laundress, Walker had come to Indianapolis in 1910 to expand her business selling hair and beauty products. Scores of African-American women much like Walker herself became agents selling company products and training women in the "Walker system." Walker left Indianapolis in 1916 and died in New York three years later, never to see the Theatre Center that her daughter saw to completion in 1927.

Sitting at the corner of Indiana Avenue and West Street in the heart of the city's most significant African-American commercial and leisure district, the Walker Theatre was perhaps African-American Indianapolis's most prominent social space. Businesses of all sorts lined Indiana Avenue around the Theatre and stressed how Walker's entrepreneurial, social, and civic aspirations were shared by vast numbers of African Americans. Crispus Attucks High School also provided countless examples of African-American ambition in a city and nation hostile to African-American citizen privileges. In the face of dehumanizing everyday injustice, African Americans made Attucks and education a focus of community identity. Attucks's segregation, though, is often historically attributed to a Ku Klux Klan–led school board that came to power in Indianapolis in 1925 (Moore 1991). The Klan-dominated city government was quick to throw its support behind all forms of racial and ethnic segregation, which included an existing plan to segregate the city's Black students. The Klan's emergence as an accepted civic voice encouraged particularly bold public expressions of racist sentiments in the mid-1920s. Nevertheless, support for the Klan clearly reflected Indianapolis's dominant White nativism, and their violent heritage makes them an easy foil today (Moore 1991:149–50). Blaming segregation on the Klan itself evades deep-seated xenophobia that was common in many communities, including Indianapolis. Yet most local accounts of Attucks and the Walker Theatre alike tend to romanticize them as aesthetic reminders of a time that bears little or no relationship to the contemporary city.

Our project's interest has been to bridge the comfortable but contrived distance between past and present. The most significant element of this project—and the space in which these issues probably can be most productively raised—is the archaeology site itself. Two of our three excavations have been conducted in the Ransom Place district, a six-block neighborhood that today is the only surviving above-ground remnant of the thousands of homes that once dotted the near-Westside. Urban "renewal" in the near-Westside has been championed by broad, shifting coalitions for more than seventy-five years, so the vast expanses of asphalt bordering Ransom Place provide a powerful but often-overlooked commentary on urban transformation. Among the parties advocating varying scales of demolition, resettlement, and rebuilding, the Indiana University Medical Center and IUPUI figure most prominently, and the joint medical and undergraduate campus today covers nearly three hundred acres of the near-Westside. In the early twentieth century Indiana University located its medical school adjoining the 1859 City Hospital; the medical school began to slowly buy up surrounding lots and residential properties. By World War I an African-American neighborhood ringed the hospital, which employed many African Americans but was itself segregated (Thornbrough 2000: 64). Much of the neighborhood declined during the Depression, and in 1947 the university medical center's historian concluded that it "would be impossible to envision an uglier site for a great institution. The area was partially a dump and entirely a revolting slum. Scores of houses must be torn down" (Rice 1947:164).

IUPUI moved to the near-Westside in the 1960s, just to the southeast of the medical campus, and IUPUI quickly began to purchase properties throughout the by-then deteriorated near-Westside. Most of these were vernacular homes built since the Civil War; most had become African-American homes by the 1960s, when many were quite neglected. Ransom Place had been part of this community, but it escaped the wrecking ball as the university focused on areas to the south and west. In 1984 the city prepared to host the 1987 Pan American Games, and it launched an urban renewal project that took aim at neighborhoods along and around Indiana

Avenue. Among the targets of the 1980s transformation was Lockefield Gardens, a 1937 Black public housing project that was a key social space in the near-Westside (Darbee 1994:926–27; Thornbrough 2000:85). Lockefield Gardens had fallen into disrepair by the 1980s, and more than half of the units were torn down in 1983 to make way for a more streamlined campus road. By that point only a few residences or businesses tenaciously remained on campus; soon they were all gone.

This is not a unique history among city governments and urban universities, but it did not seem to be a particularly sound foundation for a cooperative community project. Our ability to negotiate this heritage is due in large part to working through an existing neighborhood association and focusing on oral history as one of the project's initial research steps. The Ransom Place Neighborhood Association provided an existing collective, which eliminated the need to identify appropriate individuals who could represent the community. Working within the association's channels provided an easy forum to present archaeology; it allowed neighbors to collectively discuss the research project, and attending association meetings made me a familiar figure in the neighborhood and gave me ongoing insight into every sort of community concern ranging from preservation policy to yard sale organization. Neighborhood associations cover Indianapolis and carry varying degrees of social and material clout; most cater to residents' practical concerns, which can range from scheduling garbage pickups to publicizing neighborhood histories. Some of these associations have embraced historic preservation and articulately championed community histories, as Ransom Place itself did when it was placed on the National Register in 1992. Consequently, the association grasped the potential utility of a public archaeology project, though they may not have had a concrete sense of exactly what it would produce.

A central methodological step in the project was to design an oral history component with clearly focused research goals. Over two years I attended meetings of the association and other local African-American groups, and from that experience I began to work with the Indiana African-American Genealogy Group. The group's members were interested in conducting an oral history project and had strong community links and a number of group members who wanted to conduct interviews. Their interest was in community members born before or around 1920, and their research interests extended beyond mere genealogical descent questions. With the university providing support for interview transcription, we have begun a project in which ten different interviewers are each conducting two interviews with African-American elders. At the genealogists' behest, some of the questioning directed to elders focuses on family histories and migration patterns, since the genealogists are particularly interested in how and why African Americans made their way to Indianapolis. Archaeologically, we are interested in the African-American material world, ranging from where people obtained goods to what sorts of things we would have found in their homes. Initial discussions have revealed that different memoirists see different elements of that material world as significant; many have discussed food or dining goods, while others focus on decorative goods or their homes. Our interest is in painting a picture of everyday life that stresses apparently mundane details; archaeological material culture clearly illustrates such experiences, and in the context of interviews we can begin to connect those prosaic things to concrete social practices ranging from food preparation to shopping in White consumer spaces.

Some of my academic colleagues are uncomfortable with IUPUI's historical role resettling a very broad swath of the near-Westside, but I am convinced that almost all of the community elders I work with see the archaeology project as something distinct from the university's urban renewal past. The reasons for this are complex and certainly differ from one individual to the next, but some of it may be this African-American community's particularly strong generational dedication to education. African Americans in the near-Westside share a very powerful commitment to education, particularly those generations who went to Crispus Attucks. Attucks was renowned for its academic rigor, and the stunning number of African Americans who went on to advanced degrees reflects a widely shared commitment to education. Educators are celebrated in many elders' memories, and scholars from elementary to university levels still receive genuine respect, so many community members view our project with pride.

Some community members concede that much of the space now covered by the IUPUI campus had become quite neglected by the 1960s, and some families were eager to accept the resettlement payments from the university. Community members do not paint the university as the sole villain in urban renewal, which was instigated by a complex patchwork of city, state, and business forces whose social interests remain somewhat unclear even today. Ultimately, it is difficult to find a clearly identified villain because of the bureaucratic tangle concealing most urban renewal strategies, but elders certainly acknowledge that anti-Black racism figured significantly in all of these projects.

African-American history—if not all history in general—has been widely effaced from the near-Westside, so one of our first moves was to ask how archaeology might address the historical invisibility of a community that had a rich heritage. Our public program has focused on developing a community history that establishes symbolic proprietorship of spaces that today bear no visible traces of African-American heritage. For our partners in the Neighborhood Association, archaeology sites provide a stark contrast to most of the near-Westside's contemporary landscapes: architectural features, dense artifact assemblages, and landfilling episodes provide graphic illustrations of the near-Westside's complex history, a complexity that is hidden in the modern landscape. Simply having archaeologists in public space displaying a steady stream of artifacts affirms the neighborhood's connection to spaces that today are not associated with the city's complex but poorly understood African-American community. The people who live in Indianapolis's near-Westside today (or feel some connection to it) respect archaeological scholarship, but archaeology is probably most significant as a public stage that stresses African-American Indianapolis's heritage.

For many of our African-American constituents, archaeology is important primarily for this public stage, and the actual interpretation of excavated material culture is somewhat less important: that is, the practice of excavating risks being more consequential than the insights derived from it. However, the community clearly does value those times when we can use artifacts to spark discussion in spaces beyond archaeological sites. In summer 2002, for example, I and my colleagues Elizabeth Kryder-Reid and Owen Dwyer installed an exhibit on race and material culture at the new Indiana State Museum. The exhibit focused on excavated material culture and the question of how we "see" race in commonplace things. We selected apparently mundane things that all harbored powerful symbolism. For example, the exhibit included excavated milk caps and examined their relationship to the city's most prominent amusement park, Riverside Amusement Park. Riverside admitted Whites only, but the park allowed African Americans entrance to the park one day each year if they brought a milk cap. This was known by the park as "Colored Frolic Day," and African Americans often refer to it as "Milk Cap Day"; many people of color view milk caps as indications of public racism, not simply as a quaint reminder of the days when milk was delivered to the door.

In summer 2001 we conducted our first excavation on the IUPUI campus at the Evans-Deschler site, a German-American home and meat-packing shop that sat just three feet away from an African-American boardinghouse. In large part this excavation was significant simply to establish that a community archaeology project could be productively conducted between the university and its neighbors. This project unites an African-American constituency with the institution that spearheaded hundreds of property purchases that uprooted thousands of residents. The university has not subsequently made any systematic effort to recognize the residents who had lived for more than a century on what became the campus, even though literally thousands of archaeological features dot the campus and are routinely destroyed for pipe trenches and parking decks. Despite this past relationship, many campus administrators are interested in documenting the community's history. For instance, administrators developed a proposal to name some newly built dormitories after community historical figures. The association expressed its interest in helping to generate such a list, and research for that project was conducted under my direction. Initially, this may seem like a hollow gesture, but it met with considerable support and pride from the Neighborhood Association. The vast number of university buildings standing today include only one named after an African American, a teacher named Mary Cable who was a teacher and principal at a Black school on campus. Cable taught and knew many community elders and is highly regarded in community memory; however, that building is slated to be razed. Simply introducing African-American names to the campus establishes a meaningful working relationship between the university and its neighbors, while it recognizes the space's history in a tangible material form.

The Evans-Deschler site is probably typical of many on the campus: in the middle of a nondescript gravel parking lot slated for construction, the space had been home to a series of working-class migrants from the South and Europe for more than a century. The excavation revealed several deep cellar fills that were aesthetically impressive deposits of glass bottles and architectural elements. Like many urban sites, these deposits were stratigraphically complex and often partially disturbed, many units included dense deposits from the Depression and the 1940s that relatively few archaeologists would rush to preserve. Nevertheless, both the African-American and German-American communities considered the material culture important. University administrators recognized this was a more critical measure of significance than state regulations, which permitted the site's wholesale removal. There is certainly reason to be hopeful that this partnership can continue to provide rigorous archaeological research and responsible community history. A thorough campus survey is now being conducted that collects oral histories, documents the campus's demography over more than a century, and establishes an archaeological management plan that will reflect the Neighborhood Association's specific research interests.

The Evans-Deschler site provided an opportunity to examine how racial caricatures of German Americans and African Americans are not particularly clearly reflected in material culture. Our project has attempted to stress the complexity of life in near-Westside neighborhoods and to demonstrate that easy social caricatures are inadequate explanatory mechanisms rarely clearly reflected in the material world. For instance, Ransom

Place is composed of vernacular homes built since the 1870s. The neighborhood became predominantly African American in the first decade of the twentieth century, when the Great Migration delivered scores of African Americans to the urban Midwest. Today, Ransom Place is depicted by city officials and realtors alike as a charming neighborhood that represented the foothold of one of the city's most important ethnic communities. The panoply of colorful vernacular homes, narrow streets, and modest well-groomed yards seems to underscore that Ransom Place was an idyllic walking neighborhood for aspiring Black bourgeois who were pursuing a dream with which many of us can identify. One of Ransom Place's central avenues, California Street, has even been locally dubbed the "Negro Meridian," a reference to Indianapolis's prestigious, exclusively White Meridian Street neighborhood. Some quite influential families did in fact make their homes along California Street, but Ransom Place was a cross-class neighborhood because of racist codes. As in much of segregated America, wealthy and working-class African Americans were compelled to live alongside each other because of legal and informal segregation, and very strict anti-Black segregation by realtors profoundly shaped neighborhood formation and class identity in Indianapolis.

Painting a heroic Black bourgeoisie may in some measure compensate for long-term misrepresentation of the near-Westside as a scene of universal poverty, decadence, and languor. In 2002, for instance, a state legislator wondered why IUPUI had been built on the site of a "black ghetto," voicing a common long-term caricature among racist ideologues, the city government, and urban planners. Typically, such exaggerations have been used to rationalize denying basic services, and eventually these caricatures legitimized razing the neighborhoods. Residents are eager to refute such exaggerations, but portraying these residents as countless Black Horatio Algers in Madam Walker's mold does not provide an especially critical historical vision of the near-Westside. It certainly is meaningful that many African-American residents labored to secure citizen rights that were otherwise taken for granted among White Indianapolis residents; however, anti-Black racism meant that this was not just another city neighborhood pursuing its share of the American Dream.

Dispelling contemporary misconceptions has been key to developing a meaningful archaeological history of the near-Westside. Public perceptions of the near-Westside associate it most closely with the city's African-American community, which did in fact become numerically predominant throughout the whole area by the Depression. The near-Westside's central thoroughfare, Indiana Avenue, was the heart of Black Indianapolis from the early twentieth century, and it was home to a legion of African-American saloons, theaters, and clubs that hosted almost every business and leisure activity. Because these neighborhoods were overwhelmingly African American in contemporary residents' memories, there has been a tendency to assume this was always the case. Yet thousands of homes once covered Indianapolis's near-Westside, and the residents included white Indiana-born residents (known as Hoosiers) as well as a vast range of European immigrants. Many Irish immigrants, for instance, lived in near-Westside neighborhoods and typically worked at Kingan and Company's pork-packing plant, which was on the opposite side of the White River (Donnelly 1994:870–71). Kingan's, a massive meat-packing company that originated in Belfast in 1845, came to Indianapolis in 1862 and continued to advertise in Ireland for immigrating laborers. Germans were likewise common in these neighborhoods, and in 1900 they accounted for 23 percent of the city's population (Hoyt 1996). Some German Americans worked in one of Indianapolis's hundreds of German stores, and others worked in industries along the White River. These newcomers' neighbors included every possible European immigrant group: Russians, Poles, Swedes, Italians, Welsh, French, and Greeks lived in the near-Westside by the early twentieth century.

As in many communities, though, Indianapolis history has become atomized into Black, White, and various ethnic experiences, and particular areas in the city today tend to be associated with a particular cultural group (for example, the German Southside). These identifications have some genuine basis in historic settlement patterns, but they typically oversimplify the city's multicultural character and evade the complex social and labor relations between groups throughout Indianapolis. Ransom Place and Indianapolis neighborhood histories suffer from a commonplace romanticization that tends to view urban neighborhoods in isolation, reduce each to a distinct demographic, and focus on a particular period in the neighborhood's past. In Indianapolis much of this has to do with the sway of neighborhood associations. Many of these associations have articulately championed an ethnic history, which lends a neighborhood some shared spatial past and often figures in real estate advertising. Indianapolis's Fountain Square Historic District, for instance, focuses on its historically German community, and Fletcher Place is associated with Irish and German residents alike. A few neighborhoods have a clearer class focus, such as the Old Northside, which was an affluent nineteenth-century neighborhood.

In a similar fashion Ransom Place has focused on its African-American community and stressed that the area now called Ransom Place was a prestigious neighborhood in Black Indianapolis. There is some demographic truth to this characterization, but in 1900 85.8 percent of the neighborhood's residents were white (Brady 1996). By 1910, though, two-thirds of

Ransom Place's residents were Black or mulatto, most arriving from the South. In contrast, other areas in the near-Westside remained white Hoosier or European into the Depression; clearly the near-Westside has complex demographic patterns, but it was certainly not always African American. While this might seem a forgivable misconception, ignoring Ransom Place's quick transition from white to Black evades how such a profound shift became possible at the turn of the century. Ransom Place's African-American heritage distinguishes it today; however, its multicultural heritage tells an equally significant story about turn-of-the-century racial ideology and its impression on many urban landscapes. Today, most of Indianapolis is carved into ethnic and class enclaves indebted to racism's effect a century ago, but no neighborhood association has tackled this commonplace but uncomfortable past.

In contrast to most of the city's other historic neighborhoods that claim particular ethnic pasts, Ransom Place remains home to a significant number of African Americans, and many of them are long-term residents with an articulated interest in preserving the neighborhood's African-American heritage. Nevertheless, defining these communities in monolithic cultural and racial terms risks reproducing the very ideologies that made segregation possible in the first place. Consequently, much of our project's energy has been spent examining how Ransom Place in particular and the near-Westside in general provide some distinctive cultural heritage while also illustrating the common but unpleasant mechanisms of racial and class inequality.

Historicizing the Racialized Landscape

For our community partners in the Neighborhood Association, archaeology's key contribution is to draw attention to the historical dimensions of an otherwise mundane or ignored cityscape. That attention comes in the form of site tours, local news coverage, and scholarship that each paint the near-Westside and its residents as rather typical Americans laboring under the quite un-American social conditions fostered by racial ideology. There is a risk to creating a self-celebratory history that is simply melting-pot ideology or transparent real estate boosterism; however, placing race and racism at the heart of the project makes it difficult to ignore the profound inequalities that shaped residents' lives and transformed this community over more than a century. Our central goal has been to demonstrate that in various ways race lurks within any space or object, whether it is a mass-produced good or a contemporary landscape. We believe applied archaeology is an ideal mechanism to historicize the landscape, identify the color line's complex impact on that landscape, and make that racial landscape more difficult to ignore or overlook. The university and city's own trans-formations of this community are unfortunate in many ways, but this is certainly not a unique history, and many more communities were like-wise razed in complex patchworks of racism, xenophobia, and classism that remain stamped on the modern landscape and in present community formations. We hope Ransom Place residents and visitors alike will ac-knowledge that similar commonplace processes have left very visible land-scapes all around us should we choose to see them.

Acknowledgments

Oral history and most primary documentary research for this project was conducted with the support of an Indiana University Arts and Humanities Grant. The public program at the Evans-De-schler site was supported by a grant from the Indiana Humanities Council. Thanks to the Ransom Place Neighborhood Association, particularly Daisy Borel, for their commitment to the project. Jeanette Dickerson-Putman, Herman Saatkamp, Bob Martin, and Karen Whitney have all lent important university support to the project. Jody Hester conducted much of the background historical research. Glenn Irwin, Elizabeth Van Allen, and Miriam Langsam shared their research and thoughts with me. Thanks to the numerous faculty colleagues and students who have discussed many of these thoughts.

References Cited

Blakey, Michael L. (1997). "Past Is Present: Comments on 'In the Realm of Politics: Prospects for Public Participation in African-American and Plantation Archaeology,' " In *In the Realm of Politics: Prospects for Public Participation in African-American Archaeology*, special issue of *Historical Archaeology* 31, no. 3:140–45.

Brady, Carolyn M. (1996). *The Transformation of a Neighborhood: Ransom Place Historic District, Indianapolis, 1900–1920*. Unpublished Master of Arts thesis, Department of History, Indiana University, Indianapolis.

Bundles, A'Lelia. (2001). *On Her Own Ground: The Life and Times of Madam C. J. Walker*. New York: Scribner.

Darbee, Leigh. (1994). "Lockefield Gardens." In *Encyclopedia of Indianapolis*, ed. David J. Bodenhamer and Robert G. Barrows, pp. 926–27. Bloomington: Indiana University Press.

Delle, James A., Stephen A. Mrozowski, and Robert Paynter, eds. (2000). *Lines That Divide: Historical Archaeologies of Race, Class, and Gender*. Knoxville: University of Tennessee Press.

Donnelly, Cathleen F. (1994). "Kingan and Company." In *Encyclopedia of Indianapolis*, ed. David J. Bodenhamer and Robert G. Barrows, pp. 870–71. Bloomington: Indiana University Press.

Franklin, Maria. (2001). "A Black Feminist-Inspired Archaeology?" *Journal of Social Archaeology* 1, no. 1:108–25.

Hoyt, Giles R. (1996). "Germans." In *Peopling Indiana: The Ethnic Experience*, ed. Robert M. Taylor, Jr. and Connie A. McBirney, pp. 146–81. Indianapolis: Indiana Historical Society.

Moore, Leonard J. (1991). *Citizen Klansmen: The Ku Klux Klan in Indiana, 1921–1928*. Chapel Hill: University of North Carolina Press.

Mullins, Paul R. (1999). *Race and Affluence: An Archaeology of African America and Consumer Culture*. New York: Kluwer/Plenum.

Orser, Charles E., Jr. (1996). *A Historical Archaeology of the Modern World*. New York: Kluwer/Plenum.

Potter, Parker B., Jr. (1994). *Public Archaeology in Annapolis: A Critical Approach to History in Maryland's Ancient City*. Washington, D.C.: Smithsonian Institution Press.

Rice, Thurman B., Jr. (1947). "History of the Medical Campus: The Romance of Riley Hospital." *Indiana State Board of Health Monthly Bulletin* (July):163–67.

Thornbrough, Emma Lou. (2000). *Indiana Blacks in the Twentieth Century*. Bloomington: Indiana University Press.

CHAPTER **4**

Asking the "Right" Questions
Archaeologists and Descendant Communities

MATTHEW B. REEVES

Matthew Reeves has worked with communities of African descent in Jamaica and the United States. In this chapter he discusses ways in which descendant communities can be encouraged to become involved in both research and planning activities related to heritage resource management and archaeological inquiry. Familiarity with the ethnography of existing descent communities can also contribute to the formulation of new research questions.

Introduction

My exposure to descendant groups through archaeological research has led to some wonderful experiences both in the field and in interpreting the archaeological and historical record. An integral part of this journey is how my interactions with descendant groups have informed the questions that I have directed toward the archaeological record. All of these experiences have involved the study of either African-Jamaican or African-American groups. Descendant involvement is of particular importance among groups of African descent due to their exclusion from much of the formal history of this country (Franklin 1997; Potter 1991). Not only has written history bypassed these descendant groups, but the process of archaeological research has also left these groups by the wayside. More often than not, the cause of this exclusion lies in the nature of the research questions. When archaeology has turned its attention toward African-American sites, archaeologists have unintentionally devised research questions that have further marginalized these groups by excluding them from the research process (Blakey 1997:143).

This exclusionary process has as its most blatant expression the positivist science of archaeology and as its more subtle expression—but just as damaging—the selective inclusion of African Americans who Euro-American scholars feel are appropriate informants (Blakey 1997:142–45). The end effect is the creation of research questions that have little relevance for the descendant communities: the research agenda rests more in the rhetoric of the researcher than the descendant groups. The interpretation of marginalized and indigenous groups necessitates a diverse perspective that goes beyond the research paradigms of the archaeologist. Involving descendant groups in the research process is one means of accomplishing this goal (Horton and Crew 1989:227).

Most African-American archaeologists have advocated involving the descendant community (LaRoche and Blakey 1997; Franklin 1997; Singleton 1997), as have many Euro-American archaeologists (McDavid 1997; Potter 1991). What they have argued for is a more inclusive research program in which local community members are informed and involved in the research process. However, making the interaction between community members and archaeologists into a meaningful shared research process is often difficult. Too often, local community members are mined for their information about site location, family history, and past lifeways, while their viewpoints regarding their own history are not accessed or even seen as relevant to the data or research process. My approaches to the problem of meaningfully involving descendant groups in the research process—while always enriching and meaningful for myself—have too often not fully engaged these groups in the research process. In order to more fully understand some of the interactions between archaeologists and descendant groups, I will describe my experiences in the relationship between descendants, sites, and interpretation. My focus in describing my journeys in this area is to devise a means of creating an engagement between descendant groups and the archaeological record: in other words, asking the right questions.

In my field experiences, I have encountered three categories of experiences in working with descendant groups: (1) immersion within a descendant group by living within the community being studied, (2) interpreting the finds from the archaeological record from the context of community members' social relations, and (3) actively engaging descendant groups in a structured manner to conceptualize research questions. In all three of these interactions with descendant communities, what has become very apparent is the importance of engaging descendant groups in defining the research questions.

Immersion Within the Community

One of my first experiences working with descendant communities came during my dissertation fieldwork in Jamaica. I was conducting excavations on several slave settlements associated with an early-nineteenth-century plantation located in the rural interior district of St. Catherines Parish. My fieldwork was funded through a Fulbright Fellowship and was conducted in conjunction with the Jamaican National Heritage Trust.

One of the slave settlements was associated with a coffee plantation known as Juan de Bolas. The owner, Samuel Queneborough, ran the plantation with close to 250 slaves from 1799 until his death in 1815. From 1815 to emancipation, the size of the enslaved population dwindled to 125, and after emancipation in 1838, many of the slaves purchased land from Queneborough's descendants and became independent farmers producing food crops for the urban markets of Jamaica (Reeves 1997). What makes Juan de Bolas unique is that many of these same families still live in the Juan de Bolas district today. During my fieldwork at Juan de Bolas, one of the first things that struck me was the presence that the plantation-era history still had within the descendant community.

Many elderly residents recalled their grandparents talking about Samuel Queneborough and overseers on the property. One descendant in particular recalled that his great, great, great-grandmother, Mary, had several children by Queneborough and, upon emancipation, was given the land they live on today. This same plot of land, encompassing the barbeques of the coffee plantation, has been passed down through the family to the present day. Interestingly, research in the Jamaica archives bore testimony to this oral legend in the form of Samuel Queneborough's will, whereby he freed a slave named Mary and provided her an annual sum of £40. Other older residents recalled more extraordinary tales of emancipation day—celebrated every August 1 before its incorporation into Jamaican Independence Day in 1969—when spirits of slaves, known locally as duppies, could be heard rattling chains, playing fife and drum, and lighting fires in the bush. All of these stories demonstrated to me that while slavery was a distant memory in the community, its presence was still felt through the ties with enslaved ancestors.

For my own research, I relied heavily on the descendant community for locating the slave settlements associated with Juan de Bolas and for oral traditions regarding slavery in the area. In my research I was fortunate to obtain the assistance of two residents of Juan de Bolas, both of whom were descendants of the enslaved population of the district. Within a short time of beginning work at Juan de Bolas, the entire district knew of my research and often paid visits to the sites where we were working. This was rather unique in comparison with other archaeological studies conducted on plantations, as most are in locations where descendant groups have left the area, and even if contact is made, oral history relating to plantation life is spotty at best. Such a connection between the residents of Juan de Bolas and their ancestors was fortuitous as it allowed for a high degree of interaction between the archaeological research process and the descendants.

During my initial surveys at Juan de Bolas in 1992 and 1993, I frequently asked residents what information they would like to have addressed through archaeology of the slave settlement at Juan de Bolas. More often than not, such requests would be answered by remarks concerning finding "Spanish jars full of gold." Such response was informed by the fact that the only researchers of non-African descent who visited the area were geologists looking for gold and copper deposits combined with local legends of former slave owners burying jars of gold coins. Other responses, however, were more relevant to my research agenda. My key informant wanted to know how his ancestors survived the rigors of slavery. This response became firmly lodged in my list of "burning questions" and served as the seed for my research proposal.

This comment was further nurtured through my months of living within the community at Juan de Bolas. Through my discussions with community members, which ranged from the history of the area to aspects of their daily lives, I was able to formulate an idea of the ethos of the community. One of the most noticeable aspects was the pride that community members held in not working for the local sugar estate, which drew workers from surrounding districts. The incentive for working at the local sugar estate was that it provided one of the few means of obtaining cash. The disincentive was the harsh labor conditions and the economic dependence of families who worked at the estate, forcing them to return year after year. Most residents in Juan de Bolas held firm in supporting their households through small-scale production of garden crops that were sold at local markets, going to the United States for wage labor on farms, and running small shops in the community. In these activities the descendant community at Juan de Bolas maintains continuity to their ancestors' ways of surviving as independent peasant farmers after emancipation and with their enslaved ancestor's means of survival through their provision grounds.

This theme of economic independence provided me with the framework that inspired my research questions: looking at the market activities of enslaved Jamaicans in the early nineteenth-century. The marketing activities of enslaved Jamaicans were based on the long-established institution of provision grounds begun in the late seventeenth century. Within this system the enslaved population grew their own provisions and sold the excess at weekly markets. These markets not only fed the urban population of Jamaica, but also entrenched the enslaved population in the informal market economy of the island and served as the basis for the enslaved to obtain their household possessions (Mintz and Hall 1991). I hypothesized that by comparing the quantity and diversity of artifacts present in individual household assemblages, an idea could be formulated regarding the complexity of access to market goods. In the end, comparisons of household goods provided very tangible information, as a wide range of materials were recovered from excavations at various house areas, thus suggesting a complex interplay between slaves' roles on the plantation and their roles as independent producers and consumers. Inspiring me further was the connection this had to current residents of the Juan de Bolas community in terms of their present-day market activities (Reeves 1997). Seeking the expression of this survival tactic in the archaeological record was the key to creating a research program that I felt had depth and larger meaning. While my research certainly has not drastically changed the lives of Juan de Bolas residents, I feel that my interest in their past has placed their present-day activities within a broader context grounded in the history of their people.

Descendant Involvement through Intensive Study

In the work that I carried out in the American South, I did not have the fortune of living as closely with descendant communities on a day-to-day basis as I did in Jamaica. However, the work that I conducted in Jamaica convinced me of the value of making research inclusive of direct and indirect descendant groups. One case in point came during archaeological research and excavation I was conducting at Manassas National Battlefield. Work at Manassas Battlefield was conducted through a cooperative agreement between the National Park Service and the University of Maryland. Projects conducted by the University of Maryland were compliance driven but were provided sufficient funds to allow for substantive research to be carried out. The first project I conducted at Manassas was at a site known as Sudley Post Office (see Reeves 1998). Locally, the site is best known for its use as a hospital during the Civil War and as a post office afterwards.

In conducting excavations there, done in preparation for the stabilization of the structure, we expected to find deposits relating to the nineteenth-century past at Sudley. However, once in the field, it became abundantly clear that most deposits encountered related to the early twentieth-century occupation of the structure. Following the history of the structure into this time period through the documentary record led us to a dead end with a chunk of unknown occupation stretching from 1900 to the 1930s. Clearly, however, given the quantities of artifacts and presence of items such as marbles, harmonicas, and toys, not only was the site intensively used during this time period, it was likely occupied by a household that included children.

During the second month of excavations at Sudley, a site visit from an elderly white gentleman one day changed this absence of information. He recalled a black family by the name of Davis occupying the structure when he was a boy in the 1920s. Before this time inquiries among local community members did not yield any response with regard to the early twentieth-century history of the structure. Most recalled the use of the structure as a post office and not much else. The quantity of materials we were finding from the early twentieth-century, combined with the surname of the family that might have left these deposits, led me to do more probing about the community for the history of the Davises.

When I presented the name *Davis* to members of the local white community, many of the same people who failed to mention the Davis's occupation at Sudley Post Office began to recall this family's presence. One older resident recalled that during the Davises' tenure at Sudley, everyone knew they were there, but the informant never remembered approaching the structure. Other residents remembered rumors from their parents that the Davises were involved in bootlegging. Despite the large amount of domestic debris that related to the Davis family, very few alcohol-related bottles were recovered. Unfortunately, no descendants of the Davises that lived at Sudley Post Office during the Davis occupation could be located.

In the process of interviewing local residents, I began to come to a better understanding of the place of the Davis family, adjacent to a white community church during the Jim Crow Era. While the white community tended to view the Davises at a distance, they still kept a critical eye directed at the family. The question that arose from the Davises' locale was, How did an African-American family live under the intensive scrutiny and maintain any sense of social vitality? In looking at how this stress might manifest itself in the archaeological record of the Davis household, a clue came from interpreting the spatial arrangement of the Davis living space. First, all the deposits relating to the Davis occupation were confined to the eastern side of the structure, out of view of Sudley Church and the local crossroads. Among these remains was evidence of recycling activities, such as large amounts of iron, quantities of buttons—possibly from selling rags—and numerous pieces of hardware that might have been stripped from items being recycled. There, too, in the eastern yard were the artifacts of socializing such as harmonica parts, children's toys, and smoking implements. All these activities might be seen as unacceptable to the local white community in a space so close to the local church. However, by keeping the activities confined from view of the church and crossroads, the Davises managed to disappear from the eye of the white community. Such a strategy for the use of space was quite different from earlier households who arranged their space to be as visible as possible to the local community.

What my work at Sudley revealed was the importance of involving all portions of the descendant community in the research process. It was only through the questions directed at the Euro-Americans within the community that some of the overt racism of the early twentieth-century was given specific form.

In both my Jamaican and National Park Service experiences with descendant communities, a critical analysis of my involvement of community members would deem me guilty of many of the limitations African-American scholars have directed toward Euro-American archaeologists. First, my research questions, while being informed by the local community, were formulated and given authority by my own research and educational background (Franklin 1997:40). Second, when the descendant community was involved in the formulation of research questions, the selection of which questions were most appropriate and the degree to which the descendant community was pursued was devised by my own conceptions of what was appropriate. This is not to say, for example, that my research in Jamaica should have been guided by the search for "Spanish jars full of gold," but having a more structured manner of involving the descendant community would have been beneficial. This critical self-reflection is not meant to serve as a catharsis by self-flagellation; rather, it is simply to state that when the involvement of a descendant community in the intellectual process is not possible or is weak, the structure of the research process should be questioned to see how the involvement could be improved.

Descendant Involvement through Larger Organizations

In light of this critical analysis of my own research experiences, I would like to present my next venture in archaeology and descendant communities. In my work at Montpelier, home of James and Dolley Madison, I had the good fortune to participate in the first gathering of Madison slave descendants, which occurred on April 27–29, 2001. An important organizing force behind the descendant gathering was the newly formed Orange County African-American Historical Society (OCAAHS). The secretary of this group, a descendant of slaves from a neighboring estate to Montpelier, was hired by the Montpelier Foundation to organize the event.

Termed "Re-Membering Montpelier," the gathering was intended to spark interest in organizing the descendants of Montpelier slaves in order to gather family information, create ties between descendant families, and to eventually promote a joint Madison family and Montpelier slave descendant gathering—hence the title of the project, re-membering Montpelier. As part of this event, I prepared a handout on archaeology at Montpelier and a questionnaire in which descendants were asked what questions they thought were relevant in regards to archaeology of their families at Madison plantation.

I had hoped this would be a successful technique in reaching the community, as my materials were meant to show what the potential for archaeology of the African-American experience at Montpelier was and the kinds of questions that had been asked of the archaeological record. Upon reviewing the materials I hoped they would come up with questions they felt would be appropriate to ask of their ancestors' homesites, household goods, and landscape. The response to this survey was less than satisfactory; no surveys were returned.

Despite this lack of response, there was one very close set of descendant contacts that emerged from the gathering. One group of family members who attended the event was descended from George Gilmore, a former slave of James Madison. Following emancipation, George Gilmore built a small log structure that, today, is on the lands making up Montpelier. George Gilmore eventually bought the land in 1901 and passed it on to his son upon his death in 1905. In January 2001 the Montpelier Foundation stabilized the structure, and archaeological excavations were carried out during this process. The majority of these excavations focused on the deposits below the structure, where incredibly dense arrays of artifacts were recovered, including beads, straight pins, buttons, and other artifacts relating to sewing and leather working.

Following the April gathering, several members of the Gilmore family visited the archaeology lab, and I showed them the artifacts recovered from the excavations. The family members were extremely interested in the results of the excavations, and over the next several months, photos and ideas were exchanged by e-mail. What finally came of these discussions was a plan to have the family members come down in October 2001 for a week of excavations at the cabin prior to the replacement of the floorboards at the structure.

In October 2001, four family members came out for a week of archaeological excavations at the Gilmore cabin. Family members were given an introduction to archaeological excavation technique and were assigned units to excavate under the supervision of staff and volunteer archaeologists. During the process family members were quite excited not only to locate artifacts used by their great-grandparents, but also to be part of the research process into their family's home.

During the week of archaeological investigations, family members were invited to take part in developing the interpretive plan for the cabin. They were very interested in being part of a panel of archaeologists, historians, architects, and interpretive staff involved in the development process. In this forum they were given an equal voice with the "experts" in determining what time period would be interpreted and the content of the interpretive material. What came of this meeting was the need to gather more information on the cabin and the family's role within the local community. In addition, particular issues of terminology were addressed and corrected. In all future work involving the site, the family will be consulted and involved in any formal decision-making process.

In addition to the contact made with the Gilmore descendants, the Montpelier archaeology department is also using the OCAAHS as a means to reach the larger local community. Tours of sites at Montpelier are planned, and the group is kept up to date on archaeological research at Montpelier. It is hoped that through this contact, the wider community can be reached and brought into the research process.

Conclusions

In looking back on my experiences with descendant groups, what I have come to recognize as being extremely important in making the past, especially the archaeological past, relevant to these groups is involving them in two areas: (1) the research process, and (2) the planning process for presenting the results to the public. Involvement in the research process necessitates that descendants have some understanding of how archaeology is carried out, what archaeological data consists of, and finally how archaeologists interpret the data. Involving descendant groups in this process goes far beyond a static presentation of information. Active involvement in the archaeological process allows community members to see more tangible aspects of the past and gives them ownership over a portion of their ancestors' history by making them a part of the discovery process.

In motivating individuals to take an interest in the research process, archaeology has incredible potential. Not only does the lay public pick up the methods quickly, but research also usually provides instantaneous rewards. These rewards consist of the process of discovering artifacts or analyzing materials. This reward is heightened for descendants, as this process of discovery brings them in closer connection with their ancestors. This interest can then be channeled into including descendants in devising research questions and involving them in a meaningful interaction with the past.

The involvement of descendant groups in the planning process is another means to bridge the gap between archaeologists and descendant groups. The key to descendant involvement in the planning process is to provide a means for their voices to be heard. A powerful example of such involvement can be seen in the case described by Carol McDavid of the Levi Jordan Historical Society located in Brazoria, Texas (1997:114–29). In this example the descendants were elected to the board of directors for the society and were an integral part of planning interpretive themes derived from historical and archaeological research. Once descendants held an active role in the direction of the research and interpretation, their interaction with the project changed from passive interest to active involvement. While most archaeologists do not have the opportunity to get descendant groups involved at such a high level of power (due to previously existing boards or control by state or federal powers), devising a structure so that descendant groups have a voice in the decision-making process is a necessary and effective means of gaining the group's confidence and ensuring their involvement in all aspects of the research and interpretive endeavor.

Getting descendant groups, and the public in general, interested in archaeology and involving them in the research and planning process necessitates meaningful interaction with them as a group. This involves making them part of the planning, research, and interpretation processes so they have an investment in the information. As is the case for most group activities, it is only once a group has a vested interest in an activity that a meaningful dialogue and set of actions will emerge.

References Cited

Blakey, Michael L. (1997). "Commentary: Past Is Present: Comments on 'In the Realm of Politics: Prospects for Public Interpretation in African American and Plantation Archaeology.'" In *In the Realm of Politics: Prospects for Public Participation in African-American Archaeology*, special issue of *Historical Archaeology* 31, no. 3:140–45.

Franklin, Maria. (1997). "Power to the People": Sociopolitics and the Archaeology of Black Americans." In *In the Realm of Politics: Prospects for Public Participation in African-American Archaeology*, special issue of *Historical Archaeology* 31, no. 3:36–50.

Horton, James O., and Spencer R. Crew. (1989). "Afro Americans and Museums: Towards a Policy of Inclusion." In *History Museums in the United States: A Critical Assessment*, ed. Warren Leon and Roy Rosenzweig, pp.215–36. Urbana: University of Illinois Press.

LeRoche, Cheryl J., and Michael L. Blakey (1997). "Seizing Intellectual Power: The Dialogue at the New York African American Burial Ground." In *In the Realm of Politics: Prospects for Public Participation in African-American and Plantation Archaeology*, Special Issue of *Historical Archaeology*, 31, no. 3:84–106.

McDavid, Carol. (1997). "Descendants, Decisions, and Power: The Public Interpretation of the Archaeology of the Levi Jordan Plantation." In *In the Realm of Politics: Prospects for Public Participation in African-American Archaeology*, special issue of *Historical Archaeology* 31, no. 3:114–31.

Mintz, Sidney W., and Douglas Hall. (1991). "The Origins of the Jamaican Internal Marketing System." In *Caribbean Slave Society and Economy: A Student Reader*, ed. Hilary Beckles and Verene Shepherd. Kingston, Jamaica: Ian Randle Publishers.

Potter, Parker B., Jr. (1991). "What Is the Use of Plantation Archaeology?" *Historical Archaeology* 25, no. 3:94–107.

Reeves, Matthew B. (1997). *"By Their Own Labor"—Slaves' Survival Strategies on Two Jamaican Plantations*. Ann Arbor, Mich.: University Microfilms International.

————. (1998). "Views of a Changing Landscape: An Archeological and Historical Investigation of Sudley Post Office (44PW294), Manassas National Battlefield Park, Manassas, Virginia." *Occasional Report* No. 14. Washington, D.C.: Regional Archaeological Program, National Capital Area, National Park Service.

Singleton, Theresa. (1997). "Commentary: Facing the Challenges of a Public African-American Archaeology." In *In the Realm of Politics: Prospects for Public Participation in African-American Archaeology*, special issue of *Historical Archaeology* 31, no. 3:146–52.

PART 2

Archaeology and
Non-Traditional Communities

CHAPTER 5

"To Have and Enjoy the Liberty of Conscience"

Community-Responsive Museum Outreach Education at the Bowne House

TERESA S. MOYER

As many of the chapters in this book suggest, much of the recent effort of public archaeology has centered on establishing relationships with descendent communities and providing public education activities that assist varied public constituencies in understanding aspects of their heritage. In the following chapter, Teresa Moyer describes a case in which archaeology is employed to demonstrate the historical relevance of a 17th century landmark associated with the early American struggle for religious freedom to Flushing, New York's current population, which includes a sizable Asian immigrant population. This is a valuable case study of how narrowly themed heritage institutions such as historic houses might respond to the changing constituencies of the neighborhoods in which they are located.

Introduction

The development of the Bowne House Outreach Education Program consists of a collaborative, interdisciplinary process that explores archaeology, anthropology and museum education as ways to maintain the relevance of local history to a modern population. The program employs historically-based themes of Flushing, Queens in New York City concerning religious tolerance, ethnic diversity and urban change. It aims for a multi-cultural, multi-generational audience to converse about the continuing effects of social difference. Aligning with a contemporary approach by archaeologists and museum educators to include traditionally under-represented populations and address cultural conflict, re-investigation of history at the Bowne House looks toward its application in a modern context. Community involvement in the development process establishes an ongoing relevance for local history while creating a program responsive to its audience. As such, historical archaeology at the Bowne House offers a vehicle for local students, families and teachers to find empowerment for social action by learning about history as a cumulative process in which they participate.

The project came during a period of re-definition for the Bowne House as its history and that of its residents came under review in preparation for restoration and archaeology programs. The Bowne House has been a significant social and historical presence in Flushing since the seventeenth century, but since 1999 a complete structural restoration has largely closed it to the public. The restoration architects and archaeologists peeled back layers of the house and its yard to reveal physical data for comparison to the traditional chronology and history of the property. This work, however, removes the structure from a pool of cultural resources for local schools. The Outreach Education Program responds by maintaining the relationship between local educators and the museum through two primary objectives. One, it sought to take Bowne House into schools through classroom-based investigations of historical maps, documents and artifacts. These materials highlight the process of research in historical archaeology and involve materials from excavations in the Bowne House yard. By doing so, the program integrates archaeology into interpretation of the house for education for the first time. Two, it includes the population in the development as consultants and informants, following the idea that community involvement makes a more effective program. The historical resources available about the Bowne Family, Flushing and historical events offer ideal teaching material for the modern population as they also revise assumptions made about the site. In turn, questions about the construction of history resonate with diverse populations living in the area. Archaeological and anthropological questions about the modern context for the Bowne House thus establish a purpose for its history and deepen the responsibility of its administrators to the community.

Several key ideas inform the project, all drawing from the concept that archaeology offers a means and media for the present to discuss where it has been and the effects on modern life. Applied archaeology can mediate discussion about issues with historic roots that face modernity. From an anthropological standpoint, the traditional telling of history at the Bowne

House is stale to its immediate population. On a local level, Queens is one of the most diverse places in the United States, and several of its cultures represent some of the fastest-growing minority groups in the country. The re-investigation of the Bowne House involves the awareness that political purposes craft history—in this case the empowerment of youth who on a national scale qualify as minorities. Local participation informs the approach to community-responsive programming from cultural and practical standpoints and, ideally, results in more effective programming. For the purposes of this chapter, I generalize the views of informants to the work rather than compromise discussions that in good faith occurred on an informal basis or in confidence. This chapter will outline the process for developing the program and conclude by discussing the Outreach Education Program.

History and Its Application at the Bowne House

Interpretation at the Bowne House traditionally discussed themes of religious tolerance and conflict management by freezing these ideas in seventeenth century Flushing history. The story concentrated on John Bowne and his role in securing religious toleration in Flushing. Soon after issuance of the charter in 1645, even before John Bowne's acts, Flushing colonists and the Dutch authorities disagreed over religious freedom (Kieft 1645; Director to Stuyvesant 1653: 218). In 1657, Flushing asserted its position to the influential and totalitarian Dutch governor Pieter Stuyvesant through a Remonstrance (Trébor n.d.). This social context supported the traditional concentration at the museum on the story of John Bowne. Other heritage monuments along the Flushing Freedom Mile in the neighborhood also espouse themes of American freedoms.

John Bowne (1627–95) emigrated from England to Flushing via Boston in the 1650s. The traditional history assumed from his account book that he built the oldest portion of the existing house by 1661 (Bowne 1661). He married a Quaker preacher after moving to Flushing, supported his family through agriculture and trade, and hosted Quaker Meetings in the house. During this time, Stuyvesant imposed many constrictive policies on colonists. He forbade Quaker Meetings and forced colonists to convert to the Dutch Reformed Church, while also persecuting Lutherans, Catholics and Jews. Bowne, however, stood up for his right to practice religion freely as established by the charter for Flushing and went to jail overseas. He undertook a massive letter writing campaign to plead his case and succeeded in becoming a martyr, in receiving a pardon, and in effectively causing the Dutch to reign in Stuyvesant's control over the colonists (The Bowne House Historical Society 1953; Kupka n.d.). After Bowne died in 1695, the house descended through the family. It became a National Landmark in 1945 as a national shrine to a local hero for symbolizing the American right to religious freedom ("Senator Mead . . . " 1945). By the time the house and remaining yard became a Landmark, it had held several large families, Irish immigrant servants, day laborers, slaves, and suffragist spinsters with stories linking local history at the site to larger societal and national trends. Until recently, the administrators' scope for the Bowne House kept it in low profile, but current members of the Board envision it becoming part of national and international networks of museums working in socially-oriented themes.

Archaeology and restoration, as forms of primary source research, reveal cracks in the trustworthiness of the traditional story, but teasing apart the myth from the evidence requires significant amounts of further research work. The section supposedly built by Bowne in 1661, for example, now proves much younger and the location for the original site remains a question (Moore, personal communication). Re-investigation in archives into Bowne, the period and his descendants reveals serious evidence as to question the inclusive integrity given to him by the traditional history and family memory. A preliminary investigation into Bowne's position as treasurer to Flushing, for example, reveals negative responses to his work stemming from fiscal improprieties. The perpetuation of Bowne's and the Quakers' traditional story relies on pressing modern values and ethics on the past and, granted, on an assumption that people are predictable and consistent in their actions. Peer review and the issue of slavery offer ways to round out the traditional, positive view of Bowne and social history. Research into census records and other primary sources indicate that Bowne and subsequent generations owned slaves, despite evolving Quaker policy that dismissed slaveowners from the Friends (Minutes 1785; Population schedule 1790). Flushing slaveowners tended to call them "Negres," but still inventoried them as property (Bowne 1661; An Exact . . . 1698). Further, Quakers and their admirers touted a tolerance of diversity, though acceptance poses another matter for research. The character and actions of many Quakers in the colony, such as concerning inconsistencies in slavery policy and practice, thus seem as condemnable today as those of other groups. By not questioning modern assumptions about the traditional history, such as the role of Quakers in Flushing life, personal integrity, or the predominance of English men as historical figures, the traditional approach to the Bowne House freezes the mythology of John Bowne. Controlling the John Bowne story anticipates the public's view of the family and disables visitors from making well-informed decisions about the site. While most visitors do not realize that more happened on the site than just John Bowne, adoption of broader interpretations can aid them in a more historically contextual understanding of tolerance. Further, revealing modern attitudes about change amongst various cultural groups in Flushing indicates that conflict over tolerance continues to exist in the neighborhood.

Thus, Bowne's story poses significant avenues for the Outreach Program. The story of his history teaches about what constitutes fact or perspective and the effect on interpretation. The construction and use of Bowne's story pose important questions for traditionally under-represented students, leading to discussion themes centered around the construction and political uses of history through bias in the historical record, modern imprints on the past, and social and historical context in interpretation. The basic message remains significant for youth: as Bowne's letters to the Dutch authorities underscore arguments for religious tolerance in the colonies, cultural tolerance and confidence in personal ideological beliefs contribute to identity and social action. A main problem for the project then, involves how to involve the community in using historical archaeology to address its social issues.

Involving the Audience

The Outreach Education Program differs from earlier education work at the Bowne House by interpreting with archaeology and by distinguishing between a museum that presents information and a dialogic one that invites participation from the modern community. Prior to restoration, the education program focused on John Bowne's struggle for religious tolerance, but also explored concepts of commerce, social interaction and colonial life during the seventeenth century. On-site programs led by a corps of volunteers included tours for schools, senior citizen groups and tourists, special events and hands-on activities. An off-site outreach program introduced the Bowne House in a slide show and Handling Objects from the collection (School Programs n.d.). During their visit, students walked through arrangements inside the rooms of reproductions, period objects and furnishings and an herb garden beside the house. This stage set-like setting imbued students with the weight of the history made there by contrasting past and modern environments. Unlike the close-set apartment buildings, storefronts and motorized vehicles of modern urban life outside, the property retained a landscaped yard and iconic house. An exhibit featuring archaeological artifacts from excavations in the 1980s seemed to further the historicity of the site. Other than a one-time exhibit about Asian Americans in Flushing, interpretation concentrated on events long ago and did not seek a connection between the past and present, other than advocating for tolerance.

A focus on history as a cumulative process in the new Outreach Program re-establishes a connection between the Bowne House and modern

Flushing. Some historians blame former administrators of the Bowne House for losing its relevance to the community. Queens historian Jeffrey Kroessler states, "For too long the focus has been on quaint old colonial New York, instead of the much greater message that this house has to symbolize" (Olshan 1998). Dan Donahue continues, "Any non-profit organization has to determine what makes it relevant. . . .Without making it relevant to the modern day, they are in danger of losing their constituency. [A tour of the Bowne House] is like visiting Gettysburg and not learning about the battle" (Olshan 1998). Recent Boards of the Bowne House Historical Society represent a range of interests: advisors, family members, local businessmen, an archaeologist and historians. They express different opinions on the future development of the museum and weigh historical accuracy with expanding the potential of the Bowne House to include, for example, restoration to a later period than 1661 or several furnished rooms reflecting different eras. Such thinking responds to theory about the construction history in museum settings, social concerns, widening the marketing to a non-local audience and fiscal maintenance. Ongoing outreach into the community enables it to participate in answering to the challenge of relevance and creates more effective museum programs.

Discussions with people from Flushing and New York City today, particularly residents, social groups, teachers and museum educators, indicate who should hear the stories not told by the traditional interpretation. Key questions for informants include: Who would receive the messages of the Bowne House? How could history provide a perspective for modern life? And how could archaeology and its research methods help the stories resonate with modern youth? The answers to these questions structure the scope of the program, but the process also establishes a collaborative nature for the work. Audience involvement creates a sense of personal investment that aligns with an objective of social historians to make history matter. If locals perceive history as divorced from their lives – as long-past significant events by great men—they care less about it (Giglierano and Overmyer 1992: 179). The issues gathered during these discussions enable a program that responds to the needs of students, teachers and the Bowne House.

Queens and Flushing are extremely diverse, with a long-standing European-descendant community and more recently groups from around the world. Similarly to colonists seeking a break in the seventeenth century, Flushing in the 1970s drew Korean, Japanese and Indian groups who joined Jewish, Italian and Irish populations attracted to cheaper rents and a reputation as a good neighborhood (Freiberg 1976), a characterization that came in part from its tolerance of diversity. The negotiation of cultural space to accommodate many different groups within Flushing creates conflict that museum education programs can address.

The sizable Asian population of Flushing contends with many of the issues confronted by ethnic minority groups across New York City. Queens
houses over seventeen percent of the city's Asian residents and these numbers persuade social agencies to pay attention: to be Asian American in the
city means vulnerability and a lower income, diversity, poor education and
literacy for new immigrants, adjustment issues, and housing quality and
cost problems. Education and political advocacy together offer means for
changing unfavorable conditions. Analysts argue that ethnic representation in political seats, for example, can change the difficult conditions facing their constituents. Ethnicity-oriented representation, however, may
pose other problems by disenfranchising less represented groups, as
through advocacy for redistricting that benefits one cultural group at the
expense of another. Informants to the project also advise that many Asian
families in Flushing consider education as an entry point into American
life, and that stress on civics in education might encourage Asians to register to vote and in turn have their concerns better represented (Representatives from the New York Times, the Asia Society, Queens Public Library,
local Asian American action groups, Asian Americans in NYC). Although
evidence about the voting habits of Bowne House residents is unavailable,
their choices toward social action relates to voting in the sense of exercising
their beliefs to affect the community in positive ways. As a result, the ethic
for social action and the ability to talk about its historical effects can lead
to a larger discussion about how students might contribute their own ideas
and opinions to modern Flushing.

A changing cultural landscape affects the structural appearance of the
neighborhood and creates conflict between some newer and older Flushing populations. From speaking with several people who grew up in Flushing, specifically of European-descendant cultures, I gain the impression
again of the neighborhood's ongoing historical dissonance and conflict between tolerance and acceptance. These individuals speak fondly of the area
before it urbanized and seem to prefer the romanticized version of Flushing history to one involving slaves or labor issues, though they find these
stories interesting. It follows, then, that a significant debate in Flushing involves historic preservation, or, the legal battle to slow change. The press,
specifically older local newspapers, documents neighborhood attitudes towards change, particularly throughout the economic revitalization aided
by Asian and minority businesses and in historic preservation matters. The
Asian population, in particular, receives credit for rebuilding Flushing's
economic base (Gianotti 1978). Yet, older businesses' owners find competition with the newer businesses. The press portrays "immigrant" settlement not as integration into Flushing life, but demonstration of the
neighborhood's flexibility to tolerate new populations. A fear of diversity
throughout the 1970s, "And while Flushing has absorbed thousands of new

Indian, Japanese, Korean, Hispanic and black families over the past decade, there is concern that the departure of too many white residents will 'tip' the area, causing working-class and middle-class minority residents to also leave," is one element in the search for relevance (Freiberg 1980). Non-European cultural groups imprint Flushing with their own churches, to the dismay of historians and preservationists who prefer its traditional look. Community boards, for example, vote against expansion of Korean churches and resent members' use of loopholes in the law to boost congregation size or to construct new structures. "They are changing the character of the neighborhood," said Gene Kelty, chairman of Community Board 7 (Kuriakos 2001). The "relatively small number" of churches of other immigrant groups, as from Jews, Greeks, Indians and Pakistanis, "has not caused much concern." Complaints about parking or other problems may also express anti-immigrant or prejudicial statements (Kuriakos 2001). Such contemporary concerns in the press create debate and conflict in Flushing and affect the social and political climate of the area.

Teachers experience the effects of cultural issues facing Flushing families from the front line of education. Discussions with local teachers from P.S. 20 and P.S. 24 and the school board inform the program on the use of history in the classroom, difficulties facing educators, and practical considerations. Multi-cultural classes mean several languages, different reading and writing levels, and various levels of acculturation, all contextualized within a modern ethic of equal opportunities for all students. Teachers advise aiming the program for fourth and fifth grade students in response to the New York State Standards for Education, which require the introduction of local history those years. Standardized testing at that level evaluates students' ability to use primary sources and the methods of historical archaeology, in addition to its "neat" or "cool" charisma, align well with this objective. Teachers want material that clearly addresses the skills and concepts specified by the state standards and helps students learn them. The trend as quantified in testing in education toward accountability and performance places great stress on teachers and those with seniority may leave the fourth and fifth grade classrooms for lower-pressure grades. As a result, teachers with little experience—and less confidence in teaching the required skills—may end up in charge of preparing students for testing. Teachers and museum educators alike advise creating a program as user-friendly and resource-rich as possible, but not to assume teachers know how to teach with primary source material. They, moreover, require an introduction to the methods and uses of archaeology, but express interest in using it as a teaching tool. In response to these needs, the Outreach program addresses many of the Learning Standards for Social Studies, including History of the United States and New York (Standard 1), Geography

(Standard 3), and Civics, Citizenship and Government (Standard 5). As a result of the information given by informants, the target audience for learning primary source research skills expands to include teachers and an introduction to archaeology accompanies the program. Information on the expectations of teachers structures a program for user-friendliness, self-sufficiency, and with clear links to the standards, but also an experiential, fun way to learn.

Teachers value history museums as opportunities to supplement required work with experiential learning and they connect with museum educators on the need to provide students with personal and mandatory enrichment. New York City has many cultural institutions that support museum education programs responding to community needs. Museum educators at institutions such as New York Unearthed, the Museum of Chinese in the Americas, the Lower East Side Tenement House Museum, and the New-York Historical Society shared their printed materials, permitted observations of class programs, and advised about the climate for such programs in New York. These discussions and materials demonstrate how well local history in New York fits with a trend in museum education toward anthropology-informed, community-responsive and participatory programs with focus on ethnic culture. Involvement of the teaching and local community by museum staff in project development from the beginning is important, since if the community does not help to define the questions, the answers probably will not interest them (Derry 1997: 25). Some museums employ anthropological techniques, such as participant-observation or interviews, to access their communities with the idea that community input builds a more effective experience for students and staff. The assumption of more effective programs through audience involvement presents a difficult standard to measure. Ongoing conversation and feedback with the users of the program will indicate its success or lead to change. The interviews with teachers, locals and museum educators help the program in many ways, from identifying the audience to the themes to carry from historical and modern resource materials and activities.

The materials chosen for the program reflect the themes of the Bowne House and some inform archaeologists' understanding of the site as they provide historical perspective on political issues facing Flushing today. Historical maps document the evolution of Flushing from fields to close-set apartment buildings. Comparison, for example, of an 1852 M. Dripps map of Queens County to a 1999 Metropolitan Transit Authority bus map show Flushing before it became a bedroom community in the first half of the twentieth century and after it urbanized during the second half (O'Connor 1852; Metropolitan Transit Authority 1999). Maps illustrate the process of change that students experience by walking around their neighborhood and indicate the kinds of buildings and property held by the

Bowne family. Historical documents also demonstrate the issue of political representation, as in the charter consolidating Flushing into New York City, an issue discussed as having modern relevance to poorly-represented ethnic groups. The final agreement incorporated residents' requests for localized, rather than generalized, representation in the municipal assembly through incorporation of aldermen from specific places in Queens ("Charter approved . . . " 1898; Kupka n.p.). Learning from the use of the press to publicize urban concerns, the primary sources in the Outreach program direct students to print media to learn about the world around them. In turn, students realize the tools for exercising their beliefs in the future. Archaeology as a result functions as a teaching tool for making history matter when students apply their primary source skills to modern Flushing by using historically-based issues as a springboard for asking contemporary questions.

The interviews widened greatly the audience and shaped discussion topics for student work. Talking with adults in Flushing schools includes teachers and families in the audience for the Outreach Program rather than viewing it only as for fourth and fifth graders. The program helps teachers gain skills in using primary sources and archaeology as teaching tools. Further, parent involvement is a great strength for schools and contributes to students' success. Options in the follow-up activities take the classroom lessons home by encouraging students to talk about culture and the neighborhood with family members and presenting their work to the class. The approach holds that communities believe in different values and rights in response to social, cultural, and historical events and that sharing cultural information fosters a sense of tolerance. Discussion themes reflect opinions from interviews and the press. Resource materials help the audience understand how ideology changes over time and reflects cultural beliefs, such as for religious or ethnic tolerance, women's rights, or even that people should be fair to each other. Many issues relevant to students, such as immigration, peer pressure, and feeling "at home" in their community can be addressed through the theme of tolerance. Students, as a result, can take an active role in their communities for promoting what they think is right.

Resource Material

Development of the Outreach Education Program involved deciding what materials would get the stories of the Bowne House across to students, teachers and families. Archaeology does a good job of illustrating the stories after John Bowne in strata that demonstrate history as cumulative and by relating artifacts to historical documents. The project is indebted to the work of Lynn Ceci and particularly of James Moore, archaeologists from Queens College (Ceci 1985; Moore 2000). Their work responds to cultural resource management mitigation issues and establishes research questions for archaeological approaches to the Bowne House.

Several generations of descendants lived in the house after Bowne's death in 1695. Historical and archaeological research together provide greater depth to the site by illustrating different perspectives on the roles of ordinary people in local history. A 1776 letter between Robert and John Bowne (1742–1804) discusses several issues key to Queens borough residents, such as fever, tobacco, and the war (Bowne to Bowne 1776). Illness came in tides through the colony, sometimes in relationship to weather or overcrowding, often devastating families. Tobacco was a cash crop, a basic element in the American economy at the time, and conflict between America and England coalesced into the Revolutionary War. The letter personalizes significant contemporary concerns in American society by demonstrating that everyone participates in history—it is not just a bland compilation of facts in a textbook. The letter also suggests the national climate into which Bowne's (1742–1804) children were born later in the century. The archaeological record seems to present their activities as the letter did their father's interests. Children constitute an under-represented history at the Bowne House. Archaeologists uncovered doll sections, tea wares and other objects suggesting young children in the late eighteenth century. During that time, John Bowne (1742–1804) and his wife Anne Field (b.?) had four daughters: Mary (1784–1839), Anne (b. 1785), Elizabeth (b. 1787), and Catherine (b. 1789–1830). The artifacts suggest the girls' activities and along with adult items form a story around everyday activities also frequently lost to historians. Adults, presumably, left pipe stems in concentrated patterns around the house and moved the stoneware and creamware plates. Along with these domestic activities during the girls' childhood, important political work codified American rights and freedoms into policy. In September of 1789, Congress proposed a series of ten amendments that became known as the Bill of Rights. The First Amendment concerned personal liberty and freedom of religion, relating to the rights championed by Flushing residents. In 1790, the time of the first federal census, the girls ranged in age from one to six years old, and the census indicated that their parents had two slaves. The girls, their father and uncle represented local interests in national trends and the workings of everyday life usually lost in discussion about the Revolutionary War. The historical record suggests the kind of political climate into which the girls grew and following their lives indicates choices toward social action possibly inspired by national politics.

The Bowne daughters' tenure at the house brings forth the stories of women and immigrants in Flushing not discussed in the narrow interpretation of the Bowne House to the seventeenth century. Women's activism at the Bowne House coincides at one point with the Civil War and demonstrates the contribution of women to a historical period often heard about from the perspective of men, particularly politicians and soldiers. Aspects of the Civil War, though it did not begin until the mid-nineteenth century, conceptually began in the seventeenth century with the question of slavery and national identity. The 1860 census records Anne Bowne (b.1785), her nieces Mary (b.1813) and Jane (1862–62), Sara Lukens, and an illiterate Irish servant named Catherine McCormick (U.S. Government 1860). A woman's Victorian-style boot suggests women in the Bowne House. While the boot is not a direct testament to the societal role of women in Flushing, Quaker women stationed at the Bowne House used it as a base camp for civic work (Ladies Employment Society; Constitution of the Ladies; The Flushing Female Society). The Flushing Female Association began in 1814 and Anne and Catherine Bowne both signed the statement of intent for the organization, along with several other women. The charter members agreed to donate money, their time and labor, to give the poor an education. Black and white children schooled together until the mid-1800s. Lack of funds closed the school for a year and a half circa 1858, and thereafter students were taxed two cents weekly. A color line is not suggested until 1866 with a "colored Sunday school" (Breath 1923). Concentration on men in the Bowne House in the traditional story downplays a significant part of the social history of the nineteenth century—that of the women and their contribution to ideological conflict during the Civil War. Their work continues in a theme of social activism alive in Flushing today, as through social services groups urging their populations to vote.

The Bowne House also supports investigation into the role of ethnic minorities who immigrated and integrated themselves into New York City life so as to become over time major elements in the political constituency. Catherine McCormick appears with the Bownes on the 1860 census and correlates with an influx of nine hundred thousand Irish immigrants to New York City from 1850 to 1860. A Catholic medallion recovered during excavation may have belonged to McCormick, since the Quakers did not keep religious items (Moore 2002, personal communication). If the medallion did belong to McCormick, then archaeology presents students with an item representing personal beliefs. Students might then follow through by discussing the significance of other objects to them, such as the Korean churches so despised by traditionalists. As a result, students understand that the physical world resounds with the ideological convictions of the people who create it.

The historical and archaeological evidence provides a narrative for discussing the role of ethnicity in the area as it also demonstrates difficulties in interpreting from evidence. The identification of African American and Irish ethnicity at the Bowne House through census records and archaeology resonates with the issues of urban change facing modern Flushing minority groups. The idea for students to understand involves the right to political representation and the social implications of it. Modern residents of Flushing continue to add to the history of the area—imbuing such a sense into students may aid them in becoming conscientious community members.

The Bowne House Outreach Education Program

The ideas discussed in this paper coalesce in a box and a binder that make up the Bowne House Outreach Education Program and translate into lesson plans, reproductions and artifacts. Teachers learn the approach to history through an introduction the program, discussion about archaeology, and questions for guiding class discussions. The program itself consists of units of maps, documents, and archaeological artifacts, as well as guides for group work and follow-up activities. Rather than asking teachers to lecture about local history, the program focuses on students' ability to observe primary sources and to make interpretations based on the evidence. To do so, students work individually, in teams, and as a class. They learn about two primary themes, tolerance and social change, as represented in historical developments in Flushing and at the Bowne House. Each section uses themes of civic responsibility and personal investment to tie the past and the present together.

The program starts with a unit about maps. Map analysis provides students with a bird's eye view of how Flushing changed over time and relates urban development to the property holdings of the Bowne Family. The maps chosen for this unit range from the seventeenth to the twentieth century. They document the increasingly urban nature of the area and visually depict by what time utilities, roads, and modern landmarks existed. Follow-up activities encourage students to think about their environments and, by extension, civic matters by creating maps of their own Flushings or to propose urban development changes.

The historical documents section relates the issues faced by the Bowne Family to national concerns. To do so, students will examine a wide range of sources as contextualized within historic events, such as the Revolutionary War or The Flushing Remonstrance. Federal census records, letters and proclamations track population growth in Flushing and what the neighborhood felt was right, often resulting from prolonged conflict between several groups. Together, the documents section indicates some ideological issues faced by Flushing residents since the seventeenth century. Follow-up activities ask students to think about their civic responsibility to their community and what the term "American rights" means to them.

The third section of primary source material involves archaeological artifacts from excavations on the Bowne House Historical Site property. Historical archaeologists research a site using many of the primary source types included in the program. The analysis of artifacts provides students with a hands-on opportunity to work with objects and extrapolate information from them in conjunction with maps and documents. As a result, archaeology acts as a way to link the units together in order to demonstrate their modern applications. Since many teachers and students do not know much about archaeology or what archaeologists do, an explanation introduces the field and discusses how archaeologists gather their interpretations.

Communities change for many reasons and different primary source media illustrate this theme. Maps, for example, document the built environment, but unlike documents or artifacts, they do not teach as well how individual people lived or what they thought and valued. The evolution of Flushing has not stopped, but is an ongoing process in which students take part. The examples given by the Outreach Program, such as women's roles in civic action, Irish immigrants, or slaves, suggest footholds for students to gain perspective on the role of cultural difference in their own lives. Media of the program, and the "learning by doing" approach of archaeology," provide a visual and tactile basis for learning about change in Flushing, but they can further act as a way for students to ask questions about the historical basis for their modern environment.

Conclusion

The Outreach Education Program presents the Bowne House as a dialogic interpretive program that employs archaeology as a teaching tool for learning about historically-based issues in Flushing. The motif of Flushing as a tolerant place is represented today in advertisements, tourist literature, and in the local newspapers. Used in this way, Flushing residents may negotiate their current discomfort with diversity using the historical mantra as a mask. I do not argue that the museum education programs can define a Flushing identity, but it can help students explore their community and decide for themselves what to do about it.

Archaeologists meditate between the past and the present, but an anthropological understanding of modern communities is essential to apply archaeology to contemporary concerns. Ongoing interpretive development at the Bowne House indicates why a mindset toward applied approaches to archaeology and anthropology partners well with local history. Questions heard throughout the course of this project such as, "Who was John Bowne? And why have I never heard of him?," are endemic to local history and challenge archaeologists to find meaning for their work in the populations surrounding them. Expansion of interpretation at the Bowne House to include a historical continuum up to modern life provides greater opportunities to address topics relevant to the community, such as urban change, cultural toleration and social responsibility. Museums enable archaeologists and anthropologists to apply their academic work in educational forums that also offer opportunities for public involvement. The Bowne House Outreach Education program follows a trend in museums today of asking communities for their input, not only on exhibits about their identities, but to increase the capabilities of museums as public resources. Anthropology contributes valuable methodology for approaching and working with modern communities, but it also creates a conceptual framework for interpreting archaeological cultures. Applied archaeologists must understand cultural perspectives throughout time to place cultures today in context and into perspective, a role that, in addition to facilitating the relevance of museums to communities, places responsibility on the discipline to find its own meaning.

References Cited

———. "An Exact List of All Ye Inhabitants . . . [August] 1698," (1850). In *The Documentary History of the State of New York*, comp. Christopher Morgan and E. B. O'Callaghan, vol. 2. Albany: Weed, Parsons.

Bowne, John. *Account book*. (1661). Bowne family papers, Rare Books and Manuscripts Division, New York Public Library.

John Bowne to Robert Bowne. (1776). Letter. Flushing: Bowne House Historical Society.

Bowne House Historical Society, The. (1953). *The Bowne House 1661: A National Shrine to Religious Freedom*. Flushing: The Bowne House Historical Society.

Breath, Anne. (1923). *A Short History of the Ladies Employment Society*. Typewritten copy deposited at Queensborough Public Library, Long Island History Division.

Ceci, Lynn. (1985).Historical Archaeology at the 1661 John Bowne House, Flushing, New York. Paper prepared for department of Anthropology, Queens College Flushing: Queensborough Public Library, Long Island History Division.

———. "Charter approved by Governor of State to consolidate Flushing into New York City, effective January 1, 1898." (1898). In *History of the Town of Flushing, Long Island, NY*, comp. by Henry D. Waller, 1899. Flushing: J.H. Ridenour.

———. *Constitution of the Ladies Employment Society of Flushing 1866*. Parsons Collection, Queensborough Public Library, Long Island History Division.

Derry, Linda. Constitution. (1997). "PreEmancipation Archaeology: Does It Play in Selma, Alabama?" *Historical Archaeology* 31, no. 3: 18–25.

Director to Pieter Stuyvesant. (1653). 4 November 1653, "Negotiations with the Burgomasters for Aid." In *Documents Relating to the Colonial History of the State of New York*, comp. B. Fernow, vol. XI, 1883. Albany: Weed Parsons.

———. *The Flushing Female Society 1914*. Parsons Collection., Queensborough Public Library, Long Island History Division.

Freiberg, Peter. (1976). "Flushing Fighting to Save its Vitality and Identity." *New York Post*, 29 December, n.p. Clipping deposited at the Queens Historical Society.

Gianotti, Peter M. (1978). "Flushing Fights for New Era of Vitality." N.p. Clipping deposited at the Queens Historical Society.

Giglierano, Geoffrey J., and Deborah A. Overmyer. (1992). "Why Are You Studying My Neighborhood? Reaching a General Audience with Local History Projects and the 'New' Social History." In *History Outreach: Programs for Museums, Historical Organizations, and Academic History Departments*, ed. J. D. Britton and Diane F. Britton, pp. 177–90. Malabor: Krieger Publications.

Kieft, Willem. (1645). "The Charter, October 10, 1645." In *History of the Town of Flushing, Long Island, NY*, comp. Henry D. Waller, 1899. Flushing: J. H. Ridenour.

Kupka, August (n.d.) *The Life and Times of John Bowne*. Flushing: Case the Printer [Henry A. Mayer].

Kuriakos, Sajan P (2001). "The Growth of Korean Churches in Flushing Sparks Community Tensions." *Village Voice NYC*, 14 February. N.p. Clipping deposited at the Queens Historical Society.

———. *Ladies Employment Society Ledgers 1866–77 and 1884–90*. Parsons Collection, Queensborough Public Library, Long Island History Division.

Metropolitan Transit Authority. (1999). *MTA Bus Map*. New York: MTA.

———. Minutes of the Manumission Society, 1st Meeting 1785. New-York Historical Society.

Moore, James A. (2000). *Bowne House Stabilization Project, Archaeological Assessment Proposal, 29 April*. Copy courtesy James A. Moore.

Moore, James A. (2002). Personal communication.

O'Connor, R. F. Charter (1852). *Map of Kings and Queens Counties, Long Island NY*. M. Dripps. Queensborough Public Library, Long Island History Division.

Olshan, Jeremy. (1998). "Will the Bowne House Become history?" *Queens Tribune, www.queenstribune. com/archives/featurearchive/feature98/06/*.

———. *School Programs at the Bowne House*. (n.d.). Flushing: The Bowne House.

———. "Senator Mead Dedicates Bowne House As National Shrine for Tolerance." (1945). *Long Island Daily Press* (11 October). 1, 8. Clipping on file at the Queens Historical Society.

Trébor, Haynes. (n.d.) *The Flushing Remonstrance*. New York: Flushing Savings Bank.

U.S. Government. (1860). Population schedule, New York State, 8th Federal Census, NYPL. Population schedule for Township of Flushing, 1790, vol. 3, New York Public Library.

———. "Valuations of Estates at Flushing 1675 [October 9]." (1850). In *The Documentary History of The State of New York*, comp. Christopher Morgan and E. B. O'Callaghan, vol. 1. Albany: Weed, Parsons.

CHAPTER 6

The Seneca Village Project
Working with Modern Communities in Creating the Past

DIANA DIZEREGA WALL, NAN A. ROTHSCHILD,
CYNTHIA COPELAND, AND HERBERT SEIGNORET

Effective collaboration and community participation can occur on many different levels. In this instance the public archaeology of a nineteenth-century African-American and Irish community in what is now New York's Central Park is furthered by collaboration between archaeologists Nan Rothschild and Diana Wall and educators Cynthia Copeland and Herbert Seignoret. One result of this relationship has been the development of an undergraduate internship program, in which the archaeologists learned to appreciate the educators' emphasis on the learning processes associated with planning and doing research, as opposed to their own earlier focus on achieving research results. Additional participatory relationships with descendant communities and city managers are also discussed in the chapter.

Introduction

Over the last few years archaeologists Nan Rothschild (of Barnard College) and Diana Wall (of the City College of New York) have been working with educators Cynthia Copeland (of the New-York Historical Society) and Herbert Seignoret (also of City College) on the Seneca Village Project. In some ways this is a conventional archaeological project, but in other ways it is somewhat unusual. On the conventional side the project includes the archaeological study of Seneca Village, a nineteenth-century African-American and Irish immigrant community that was located on land that today is part of Central Park in New York City. We have conducted historical research on the village and done some geophysical testing there too—both tasks appropriate to the early phases of studying an archaeological site. But the project also has strong educational and commemorative components. We try to ensure that there is an educational facet to all aspects of the study of the village, and we are all deeply committed to its commemoration. We work with local historians, churches, and community and civic groups toward making the village's history part of the "meaning" of the modern park. All in all, the Seneca Village project provides a good case study for the fact that we are now living in an era when the past is not simply the private preserve of scholars like archaeologists and historians but is important to and used by many different contemporary groups in a variety of ways. The village demonstrates some of the multiple though overlapping levels of meaning that an extinct community can have for modern groups of people.

Here, we discuss a few of those levels of meaning and show how we are working together to make our different, though definitely overlapping, aspirations for the village come to fruition. But first, we describe the village and its history; then, we delineate the project's history; next, we describe the village's archaeological potential; after that we discuss some of the relationships we have forged with different groups, including our advisory committee, various groups that make up the public, and undergraduates. Finally, we detail some of the different meanings the project is eliciting from some members of these groups.

Seneca Village

Seneca Village was a nineteenth-century African-American and Irish immigrant community that was located between 81st and 89th Streets and Seventh and Eighth Avenues—an area that later became part of Central Park. The village was established in the 1820s, when some African Americans bought land there to build their homes and institutions. They were probably motivated to purchase land there at least in part because a few years earlier, in 1821, the second New York State constitution imposed a $250 property requirement for suffrage for African-American men in the state, while it gradually removed all such property requirements for men of European descent (Freeman 1994:92). Landownership in Seneca Village guaranteed a right to suffrage and was a source of pride to the black residents who established a self-determined and viable free black settlement. By buying land in Seneca Village, they were also able to circumvent the tacit boycott on selling land to African Americans that existed throughout most of the city's white community. Furthermore, the land they bought and on which they developed Seneca Village was beyond the margins of the city and was thus relatively affordable (Rosenzweig and Blackmar 1992:70). Most of these black landowners lived in the city downtown, but some built their homes in the village. There was a reliable spring in the village, which provided water for the residents, and of course the Hudson River, with its renewable supplies of fish and firewood, was only a few blocks to the west. After a time some Irish families who had recently come to the New World because of the potato famine rented houses in the village. By the 1850s the village had more than 260 residents, two-thirds of whom were of African descent, and one-third European (State of New York 1855).

Although the village was denigrated in the contemporary press as "Nigger Village" and described as being occupied by squatters whose homes were so dirty that "Death himself hesitates to enter such . . . hovels" (The New-York Daily Times 1856), it was in fact a stable community that persisted for more than a generation. Records show that its occupants either owned or rented their homes. At the time it was razed, it was the site of several institutions, including "Colored School #3" and three churches: the African Methodist Episcopal Zion Church Branch Militant and the African Union Methodist Church, as well as the racially integrated All Angels' Church. Each church is thought to have had its own burial ground in the village.

At the time it was first developed, Seneca Village was well outside the city's limits, which were then at about 14th Street. But as the city began to undergo the dramatic growth that accompanied its burgeoning economy after the completion of the Erie Canal, its border rapidly moved north. By the 1850s its limits were approaching Seneca Village, and the city developed plans for the creation of a major park. After a great deal of political wrangling (see Rosenzweig and Blackmar 1992), it chose the area we know today as Central Park for its location. Using the right of eminent domain, the city seized the land to make the park, evicted approximately 1600 residents, and razed their homes and communition. Although landowners were compensated for their property, most felt that the compensation was inadequate, and renters of course got no compensation for losing their homes.

The Seneca Village Project

After Seneca Village was razed, it was nearly forgotten for almost 150 years, when historians Roy Rosenzweig and Betsy Blackmar did substantial research on Central Park for their book *The Park and the People* (1992). The authors featured Seneca Village in a chapter devoted to the communities that had existed in the area that later became the park. The book inspired the New-York Historical Society, which is located near the site of the village, to become interested in it as a teaching tool. Cynthia Copeland, a historical society educator, and her colleagues organized a series of programs for schoolchildren, teachers, and the public that used Seneca Village as a case study for showing the importance of using primary sources for studying history and understanding the past (Copeland et al. 1999). The enormous public interest in these programs led Copeland and her colleague Grady Turner to curate the exhibit, "Before Central Park: The Life and Death of Seneca Village," at the New-York Historical Society. The exhibit was both a critical and popular success; it opened in 1997 and was on display for more than a year.

Diana Wall had heard about the village in an interview with Betsy Blackmar in 1992; she became interested in it as a research project with possible excavation potential because it not only fit in with her own research interests, but also with those of her students at City College, where she had just begun to teach. As planning for the exhibit began, she and City College undergraduate student Herbert Seignoret attended a historical society program on the village that Copeland had organized. They formed an alliance, and City College students began to do internships at the historical society, working with Copeland on background research for the exhibit. Nan Rothschild from Barnard College—with whom Wall had worked for many years—soon joined them, and together they formed the Seneca Village Project in 1997. We have all worked together ever since.

Although we each have our individual plans for the project, there is one notion that we all share: we are all concerned that the deep historical presence of New Yorkers of African descent has been lost to memory and even denied in the city's popular historical consciousness. And we feel that *all* modern-day New Yorkers (whether of European, American, Asian, or African descent) are being diminished by that omission, which we hope that the Seneca Village project can help to remedy.

The Archaeological Potential of the Village

Obviously, the archaeological and historical study of Seneca Village is a very important component of the project. From an archaeological perspective, then, the first question we had to address was whether any intact remains from Seneca Village might have survived the park's creation and still exist in the modern park. We have both positive and negative evidence suggesting that archaeological remains still exist in the park. For example, a late-nineteenth-century newspaper reports that park workers found burials in an area where one of the churches was located (The New-York Herald 1871), and a magazine account suggests that they may have found more in the early twentieth century (The New Yorker 1959). There is also part of a stone wall visible on the ground surface in the location where one of the churches is shown on an 1856 map (Sage 1856), and its alignment matches that of the church. In addition Copeland recovered more than one hundred artifacts dating to the early nineteenth century on the ground in the area where the village once stood after a heavy rain. Both the wall and the artifacts could be related to Seneca Village. Finally, there was a soil study of the park done in the early 1980s; it indicates that much of the soil in the area of the village was undisturbed, either buried under landfill or not. (We discuss this further, below.) Additionally, on the side of negative evidence, there are no indications that there are *not* remains of Seneca Village intact in the park; no records describe construction that would have eliminated the remains of building foundations or other archaeologically significant underground features. These lines of evidence all support the conclusion that there are intact archaeological remains from the village in the modern park, but we do not have substantial scientific evidence to prove that they are there. So the Seneca Village project has of course involved trying to substantiate their presence.

The Advisory Committee

In the early stages of the project, we all felt that we needed to be able to consult with contemporary New Yorkers who had an interest in the village. We formed an advisory committee consisting of scholars who study African-American and Irish history in New York as well as members of descendant communities that have roots in the village. Two of our committee members, for example, belong to churches affiliated with those that were present in the nineteenth-century village, namely the African Methodist Episcopal Zion Church—known as Mother Zion Church—and St. Michael's Episcopal Church, which in 1846 established All Angels' Church in Seneca Village as a mission to serve the poor (Rosenzweig and Blackmar 1992:72). Other committee members had been active in the controversy surrounding the African Burial Ground project and still others had been identified during programming organized by the New-York Historical Society in conjunction with the Seneca Village exhibit. The committee holds meetings once or twice a year and works in partnership with us in planning the direction of the project. We worked closely with committee members in conceptualizing and writing our research design.

Part of the impetus for the creation of the advisory committee was the experience of the African Burial Ground project, which involved the excavation and study of the remains of more than four hundred people, mostly enslaved Africans, who had died in New York City in the eighteenth century. This project, which has been ongoing since 1991, provides an example of a worst-case political scenario in which a descendant community learns about an excavation and archaeological study late in the process, and its wishes are largely ignored at first (see LaRoche and Blakey 1997). Although the descendant community was ultimately mostly successful in its fight to have its demands met for the direction of the study and analysis of the human remains, there is still bad feeling and a lack of trust between many members of the city's African-American community and some of the anthropologists originally involved in the study.

Of course, there are several important *differences* between the African Burial Ground project and the Seneca Village project. We have no time pressure due to development, and we will not disturb any human remains. There are several positive examples of archaeological projects in different parts of this country where archaeologists have worked in partnership with descendant communities (see, for example, Leone 1995, McDavid 1997, and Derry 1997), and we are trying to learn from these examples. In these cases research has been enriched by input from people with different perspectives, especially when this input is sought early in the process, when research questions are being formulated, rather than when archaeologists simply present the results of completed research to the community.

Community Members

Project personnel have done a lot of community outreach. Copeland and Seignoret have designed and presented numerous programs on the village to elementary and middle school children and their teachers and to the general public as well, at libraries, churches, corporate programs, and hospitals. The primary rationale behind these programs is educational—to inform the public about the existence of Seneca Village and its history—but the programs also have other goals. We use them to identify additional interested members of the public for the advisory committee and to solicit ideas for additional research questions. And we have a political agenda for these programs as well: to build grassroots support for the project. If we hope to be able to conduct excavations in Central Park, one of New York City's sacred places, favorable public opinion will be an important asset. As part of the outreach programs, we ask audience members to sign petitions supporting the project, and we recruit people with interest in the program to sign up as volunteers.

Undergraduate Interns

Copeland and Seignoret's emphasis on education has also educated Rothschild and Wall. The latter now use the study of Seneca Village as a way to engage undergraduates, and they are concerned about incorporating students into the research process every step of the way. In fact students have done most of the documentary and archaeological research that has been done on the village to date. The archaeologists do not worry about getting quick results from the research, because they have learned from their educator colleagues that when working in an educational context, the process of doing research and planning a project is just as important as the results. After years of working with individual students in the context of independent studies, they have recently been able to institutionalize undergraduate involvement in the project. During the summers of 2000 and 2001, the project held summer undergraduate internships; a third internship is planned for 2004. The internships are funded by the National Science Foundation through its Research Experience for Undergraduates program; additional funding has been supplied by the Columbia Institute for Social and Economic Theory and Research and the Professional Staff Congress of the City University of New York. So far, the interns have totaled seventeen undergraduate students from colleges and universities in New York City.

The interns have conducted extensive historical research focused on discovering as much as possible about the residents of the village as well as the people buried in its cemeteries. In addition to looking at contemporary newspapers, they have scoured the archives, looking for maps, deeds, engineering reports, and city council, church, census, death, court, and tax records. What continues to amaze the students, the archaeologists, and the educators alike is the enormous amount of information they have been able to find about this community, which was made up of members of groups that many scholars (perhaps through lack of interest) often assume to be undocumented: African Americans and Irish immigrants. They have discovered that although Seneca Village existed for only a generation, its physical layout is covered in great detail on several different maps. One shows the locations of the individual properties, with the outlines, dimensions, and brief descriptions of the structures there, and it also lists the property owners and the names of the people who lived in the houses (Sage 1856). Another is a topographical map showing the natural features of the village area along with the structures (Viele 1856).

The interns have also found the manuscript census returns to contain a wealth of information. For studying Seneca Village, there are the federal decennial censuses for the years 1830, 1840, and 1850 (United States Government, Bureau of the Census), as well as the New York State census for

1855 (State of New York 1855). Information included in the census for the later years includes information on the buildings (including their fabric and their value) as well as on all their occupants: their names, their relationship to the head of the household (including, for example, "wife," "child," "adopted child," "god child," "servant," or "boarder"), their age, their sex, their "color," (whether they were white or black or mulatto), where they were born, their occupations, and the number of years they had lived in New York, as well as their voting status (including whether they were voters or "persons of color not taxed," which means they could not vote because they did not meet the property requirements for suffrage), whether they were literate, whether they had attended school recently, and whether they were charged as a "nuisance" to the city, noting them as "deaf, dumb, blind, or insane."

Other records that the interns found to provide unusually thick detail about the village and those who lived there include court and church records. Although the city compensated the landowners in what would become Central Park for the land it had confiscated, many felt the compensation was not adequate and filed "Affidavits of Petition to the Commissioners of Central Park " in the Supreme Court of the State of New York. Some of the affidavits that were filed by people from Seneca Village give information on what the landowner thought the property was worth and why. Many landowners included descriptions of the property, mentioning such features as outbuildings or wells to help build their cases, and this information is invaluable for research.

The interns have also looked at the parish records from All Angels' Church. The records, which record baptisms, marriages, and funerals at the church after its creation in 1847, often reveal information about practices in the village and the relationships among those who lived there. They mention who sponsored a child for baptism, for example, and where children were born—at home or in the hospital. Unfortunately, the records from the two other churches have not been found.

As we mentioned above, each of the churches located in Seneca Village had a cemetery there. We are interested in commemorating these cemeteries and therefore the interns have tried to find out as much as possible about them and the people who were buried in them. The African Methodist Episcopal Zion Church, which was located downtown, began to buy land in what became Seneca Village in 1825 and ultimately owned eighteen lots there. In 1827 it began to use some of these parcels as its burial ground (Rosenzweig and Blackmar 1992:71). Twenty-five years later, it built a branch of its church there. African Union Church also had a congregation in the lower city as well as in Seneca Village. These churches used the Seneca Village cemeteries after it became illegal to bury people in lower Manhattan.

The interns have also located information about the people who were buried in the cemeteries in the city's death records. The death records give information on each person who died, including names, addresses, ages, and sexes, as well as the dates and causes of death. They also list the names of the cemeteries where people were buried and the names of the sextons responsible for the burials. The information from the death records allowed them to identify the more than seven hundred people who had been buried in the cemeteries in Seneca Village. So all in all, the interns have learned to deal with many different kinds of historical data. They have entered much of the historical data into an access system that Seignoret designed. One of the interns, Iciar Lucena, has continued to work on this data set after her internship, checking the data gathered by all the interns and ensuring that they are entered into the database in a consistent manner. Their discovery of this enormously rich historical record has proved to be a revelation for many of the interns; it has allowed the people of Seneca village to come alive for them. Their identification with the people of the village is reflected in their research papers, which we discuss below.

During the first two summers of the internships, the interns also worked with geophysicist Roelof Vesteeg, formerly of Columbia University, and learned to use remote sensing techniques on the site. Under Versteeg's supervision they conducted a geophysical study of part of the village area. They first laid out grids covering different segments of the site. Then, they used several remote sensing techniques to in effect "peek" under the ground surface to locate subsurface anomalies that might represent archaeological features. The techniques included electrical conductivity, electrical resistivity, and ground-penetrating radar. In all, the students covered approximately 20 percent of the nineteenth-century village area using at least one of these techniques. Since we are still awaiting Versteeg's final report on the geophysical study, his conclusions, if any, are not known to us.

The interns also worked with Versteeg in designing a Geographic Information System (GIS) database to show the different geographical data sets that cover both the nineteenth-century village and the modern park. These include: the low-altitude aerial overview of New York City that the city recently completed, which of course includes the Seneca Village area (City of New York 2000), utility maps showing some of the underground infrastructure in the park, and the historical surveys that record the village, described above. The interns have also entered a grid of longitudinal and latitudinal coordinates (from global positioning system [GPS] readings) into the GIS. Furthermore, former intern Jessica Davis has continued to work on the GIS and has entered data on the soils and their potential for yielding archaeological deposits in the Seneca Village area (adapted from Warner and Hanna 1982).

The GIS allows the research team to use the modern aerial overview base map with an 1856 map superimposed on it, or to see only the structures from the 1856 map superimposed on the modern park. It should ultimately be possible to click on a particular property, study its topography in the present and in the past, find out who lived there in a particular year in the nineteenth century, pinpoint where the house was located on the property, identify the fabric of the building, and then see the archaeological potential that the soils suggest for that area. This coming summer, we hope to get permission from the New York City Department of Parks and Recreation and the Central Parks Conservancy to work with interns in doing auger testing in the soil in the Seneca Village area, to test if in fact the soil study can be used to predict the presence of archaeological deposits there.

Most of the undergraduates in the Seneca Village internship program have backgrounds in the humanities but are somewhat weak in the sciences. The internship exposes them to the scientific method and introduces them to the production and use of data derived from both scientific instruments and historical research to answer questions relevant to the humanities. We hope that this kind of training in a humanities context will allow them to become comfortable with using the scientific method (and with the kinds of technologies and data appropriate to that kind of study) and to see that they can use this kind of approach to address questions that relate to the humanities.

The Meanings of Seneca Village

Seneca Village has different meanings for different people involved in the project. We'll begin with the meanings Seneca Village has as a research project. Working with our advisory committee, we have developed sets of research questions, some of which can be approached by using historical sources and others that we will try to answer should we be able to conduct archaeological excavations there. Some focus on landscapes and the use of space; these can be partially addressed through historical maps. At a large scale, how isolated or separate was Seneca Village from other settlements in what is now the park? How did Seneca Villagers see themselves, and how did others see them? Reviews of nineteenth-century newspapers shed little light on this subject. On a smaller scale, we are interested in the notions of privacy that are expressed by the way in which Seneca Village houses were oriented. How closely clustered were the houses? Were there outhouses associated with residential structures, and if so, did Seneca Village residents behave as their fellow urban dwellers in lower Manhattan did and place their outhouses as far from the house as possible? Were they similar in construction to those elsewhere in the city? What other kinds of structures were located on residential lots? Were there animal sheds and other outbuildings there?

Other questions require excavations to address. Seneca Village may have been a stop on the Underground Railroad. Some of its residents and property owners appear to have been political activists and abolitionists. Can we find any evidence of the presence of the railroad in Seneca Village? Are there unrecorded basements in the houses there? or perhaps large underground storage pits inside the houses? Such pits have been found in the slave quarters of Southern plantations; they were used by the enslaved to store spiritual objects and personal possessions (Brown and Cooper 1990; Kelso 1984; Leone and Fry 1999; McKee 1992; Mouer 1991). Larger pits could of course be used to hide people escaping slavery.

Other important questions relate to diet and cuisine. If we were fortunate enough to recover faunal materials, we would analyze the kinds of meat and fish that were being consumed, the cuts of meat preferred, whether meat was butchered at home or bought at a market. Did Seneca Villagers procure some of their own foods by hunting, fishing, or foraging for wild plants? The kinds of plants and animals exploited for food can answer some of these questions, and artifacts such as fishhooks and sinkers as well as musket balls and gunflints can also reveal evidence about hunting and fishing. Sherds from dishes can also tell us about cuisine. A preference for bowls as opposed to plates would suggest that Seneca Villagers depended more on slowly cooked stews and soups, like their contemporaries of African descent in the plantation South, rather than the roasts and chops that were popular among their white, middle-class neighbors.

Again, depending on what we recover, an excavation might also provide important information on systems of healing used within the village. We already know from church records that childbirth practices were different for the African-American and European-American residents of the community: the latter tended to give birth in hospitals, while the former had their children at home. Were other medical practices different for African-American and European-American residents of Seneca Village? Did residents use drugs produced as patent medicines or those distributed by dispensaries? Did villagers use folk healers, whose presence might be seen through the discovery of "ritual bundles" used in curing rituals (such bundles have been discovered at other sites; see Leone and Fry 1999; Ricciardi et al. 2000)? Did villagers grow or gather medicinal herbs? The remains of such could be discovered through pollen or phytolith samples. Finally, did villagers suffer from parasites? Night soil from outhouse shafts could be analyzed to reveal the answer to this question.

Rothschild and Wall have their own research questions for Seneca Village, questions that are based on their own individual long-term research interests as archaeologists. Rothschild is interested in community formation and the role of ethnicity in structuring communities; from that perspective the ethnic mixture of Seneca Village intrigues her (Rothschild 1985, 1987, 1988, 1990, 1992, 1993). She is also interested in the changes that occurred within the community as it shifted from a semirural or marginal context to one that was more fully part of the city. Wall's research has focused on the negotiation of different aspects of class, race, ethnicity, and gender in nineteenth-century New York (Wall 1991, 1994a, 1994b, 1999, 2000). She has developed a database of artifacts (primarily dishes and glassware) used in the homes of both the American-born white middle-class and working-class immigrant families; some of the differences in china and glassware patterns are provocative. She is interested in comparing these domestic artifacts with those of contemporary African-American families during this period when immigrant groups in New York were in the process of becoming "white" and solidifying their imagined superiority to their African-American neighbors (Ignatiev 1995, Roedigger 1991; Burrows and Wallace 1999). This is the only known African-American site in the city that has the potential for yielding assemblages dating to the relevant time period.

But Seneca Village has meaning aside from its research potential: it has iconic power as a free black community in antebellum New York. Olivia Ng, a Columbia University undergraduate, did her senior honors thesis on Seneca Village. She included an ethnographic component in the thesis and interviewed project leaders and members of the advisory committee about what the village means to them. Cornell Edwards, a member of today's A.M.E. Zion Church, was "fascinated by the establishment's need to denigrate those who stand in its way. . . . [W]hen powerful people want something that less powerful people have, they demonize and dehumanize them. Seneca Villagers were characterized as 'shiftless' folk living in shanties. . . . [T]his process of dehumanization is similar to that used in slavery" (quoted in Ng 1999:84–85). Cheryl LaRoche, a conservator, was impressed at the control Seneca Villagers achieved over their own lives in creating "a *stable* community within an unstable environment where . . . legal processes were stacked against African-Americans," and discrimination was supported legally. Eric Washington, a historian and journalist, saw village residents as "pioneers" who were "the disenfranchised of society, who . . . set out to build a safe haven for themselves in uncharted territory."

He saw them as intelligent in their use of socially legitimate ways to bypass the restrictions imposed on African-American New Yorkers, without alienating the dominant society (quoted in Ng 1999:85).

Many committee members stressed the need to promote the awareness of the African-American experience as a valid part of American history, and some underlined the fact that not only does the study of the African-American experience contribute to the development of African-American history, but it must also be considered in order to write accurate American history. As historian Venus Greene put it, "Seneca Village, African Americans, Irish Americans and their relationships are 'worthy' of scholarly investigation. It is not merely a question of 'losing' African American history; it is a matter of writing an 'accurate' history. If you leave out this story, you are not really writing New York (or even American) history" (quoted in Ng 1999:86).

Copeland and Seignoret both stressed the educational value of correcting the written record. Copeland particularly underlined the importance of studying undocumented histories like the story of Seneca Village to reveal evidence that forces "dominant cultures to re-examine themselves" (quoted in Ng 1999:86). Seignoret elaborated that "people in the African diaspora can learn more about the contribution that their ancestors have made through archaeological investigation, since historical documentation often neglects and even silences what these contributions have been. Findings from such research can inform broader segments of the population and render historical processes more complex" (quoted in Ng 1999:86).

The interns, too, have expressed their thoughts about Seneca Village and its importance. Cornelia Jervis, an undergraduate at Hunter College, felt "that investigation and documentation of the remnants of Seneca Village [are] crucial for the development of a better understanding of the contributions of African American communities." Siobhan Cooke of Barnard mentioned that "the Seneca Village project is . . . an important endeavor because the focus is on people who were not necessarily in positions of power. . . . The investigation of the lives of these individuals fills in much of the complexity of the time and brings to light experiences of people that may have not been previously investigated." Christina Spain of City College echoed her sentiment: "The Seneca Village project will be a vehicle which will allow me to rediscover the past of other African-Americans. . . . I want to obtain the first hand knowledge about a community that will deepen my understanding about American history." To Christine Seeholzer of City College, the project offered "the excitement of 'touching' history by working with original documents and newspapers, the chance of uncovering little known facts, and most of all, the prospect of educating others and consequently making them more aware and appreciative of our [country's] past. . . . To be part of the rediscovery of a vital part of this city's past, to do hands on research in order to heighten the understanding of its cultural diversity, and to bring people long since forgotten back to life, is a goal well worth pursuing," or "priceless." And as Iciar Lucena of Hunter College put it,

> We cannot talk about the history of the United States without including African-Americans and immigrants, as they are all so deeply entwined. It is a history filled with struggle, prejudice and violence that reflects the unfortunate reality we are faced with today. . . . To learn what their lives might have been like can hopefully educate us and help us to understand more about our fascinating and turbulent history. . . . I feel that I owe it to myself and to future generations of minorities to learn about the people of this community so that we can look to our past in order to build a better future. (Seneca Village Project 2000, 2001)

The undergraduate interns also designed research proposals as part of the final component of their internships. While a few of the proposals were somewhat naive in an archaeological sense, some of the questions they raised were quite interesting. Several interns were interested in how the variables of class, race, and ethnicity would affect archaeological remains in Seneca Village. One student wanted to design a project comparing an assemblage from a nuclear family with that from a household headed by a single woman; another was interested in the spatial organization of the village with particular reference to ethnicity. Several wanted to find out if Seneca Village represented a truly integrated community of Irish and African Americans, or simply a coexisting group of spatially mixed but socially isolated neighbors. An earlier research project by a City College undergraduate showed that the Irish residents of the village seemed to be more marginally located, on the village's edge, than its African-American residents (Webb 1998). It is unclear whether any of the projects proposed by the interns would be feasible, but it is clear that the research potential of Seneca Village caught the interns' interest and appealed to their imaginations.

Finally, we must consider the meanings that Seneca Village might have to those who operate the park. Central Park is administered by the New York City Department of Parks and Recreation, and its day-to-day operations are handled by the Central Park Conservancy, a private, nonprofit organization. One aspect of this project that has interested us the most is the fact that both these entities and the municipal government as a whole have expressed an almost complete lack of interest in Seneca Village. For example, the village's location had never been marked with signage in the park—a fact that intern Nyla Manning of Baruch College noticed when she visited the site after first hearing about the village, long before her internship began: "It was disturbing to fathom that the patch of land where we stood was a place where free blacks and Irish immigrants once lived and there was no trace, no indicator of remembrance. . . ." (Seneca Village Project 2001). But this attitude on the part of these entities may be changing.

Over the past few years community groups have been active in trying to influence the Parks Department to commemorate Seneca Village with signage in the park. And in February 2001 they were successful: there was a ceremony in the park where a historical marker commemorating Seneca Village was unveiled. Representatives of the Parks Department, including Commissioner Henry Stern, and of the Central Park Conservancy, as well as members of several community boards spoke at the dedication and were quite positive in describing the history of Seneca Village. We of course hope that this new interest signifies a change of heart and is a sign that we will get permission to do our soil tests in the park next summer. But in any case, it appears that Seneca Village as a distinctive entity is being recreated over and over by many different groups in today's city. It will be fascinating to see how this process develops.

Acknowledgments

We thank the members of the Seneca Village Advisory Committee, for their ongoing advice and encouragement, as well as the Seneca Village interns, without whose enthusiasm and labor the project would not have progressed as far as it has. We also thank the staffs at various New York City archival repositories, including The New-York Historical Society, The New York Public Library, The Municipal Archives, the New York County Clerk's Office—Bureau of Old Records, and those at the AME Zion and All Angels' Churches for providing access to the rich historical records that are helping us reclaim and reconstruct our understanding of our past. Finally we thank the Columbia Institute for Social and Economic Theory and Research, the Professional Staff Congress of the City University of New York, and the National Science Foundation Research Experience for Undergraduates grant programs. All of the above provided essential support.

References Cited

Brown, Kenneth L., and Doreen C. Cooper. (1990). "Structural Continuity in an African-American Slave and Tenant Community." *Historical Archaeology* 24, no. 4:7–19.
Burrows, Edwin G., and Mike Wallace. (1999). *Gotham: A History of New York City to 1898.* New York: Oxford University Press.
City of New York. (2000). "New York City Physical Base Map." New York: New York Department of Environmental Conservation.
Copeland, Cynthia R., et al. (1999). *Seneca Village: A Teacher's Guide to Using Primary Sources in the Classroom.* New York: The New-York Historical Society.
Derry, Linda. (1997). "Pre-Emancipation Archaeology: Does It Play in Selma, Alabama?" In *In the Realm of Politics: Prospects for Public Participation in African-American Archaeology,* special issue of *Historical Archaeology* 31, no. 3:18–26.
Freeman, Rhonda Golden. (1994). *The Free Negro in New York City in the Era Before the Civil War.* New York: Garland.
Ignatiev, Noel. (1995). *How the Irish Became White.* London: Routledge.
Kelso, William. (1984). *Kingsmill Plantation, 1619–1800: An Archaeology of Country Life in Colonial Virginia.* Orlando: Academic Press.

Leone, Mark. (1995). "A Historical Archaeology of Capitalism." *American Anthropologist* 97, no. 2:251–68.

Leone, Mark P., and Gladys-Marie Fry. (1999). "Conjuring in the Big House Kitchen: An Interpretation of African American Belief Systems Based on the Uses of Archaeology and Folklore Sources." *Journal of American Folklore* 112:372–403.

McDavid, Carol. (1997). "Descendants, Decision, and Power: The Public Interpretation of the Archaeology of the Levi Jordan Plantation." In *In the Realm of Politics: Prospects of Public Participation in African-American Archaeology*, special issue of *Historical Archaeology* 31, no. 3:114–31.

LaRoche, Cheryl J., and Michael L. Blakey. (1997). "Seizing Intellectual Power: The Dialogue at the African Burial Ground." In *In the Realm of Politics: Prospects for Public Participation in African-American Archaeology*, special issue of *Historical Archaeology* 31, no. 3:84–106.

McKee, Larry. (1992). "The Ideals and Realities behind the Design and Use of 19th Century Slave Cabins." In *The Art and Mystery of Historical Archaeology*, ed. Anne Elizabeth Yentsch and Mary C. Beaudry, pp. 195–214. Boca Raton: CRC Press.

Mouer, Daniel. (1991). " 'Root Cellars' Revisited." *African-American Archaeology* 5:5–6.

New-York Daily Times, The. (1856). "The Present Look of Our Great Central Park." July 9. Collection of the New-York Historical Society.

New Yorker, The. (1959). "Paddy's Walk." January 10.

New-York Herald, The. (1871). "Yesterday afternoon . . ." August 11. Collection of the New-York Historical Society.

Ng, Olivia. (1999). "Seneca Village Perceptions." Senior thesis, Department of Anthropology, Columbia University.

Ricciardi, Christopher, Alyssa Loorya, and Maura Smale. (2000). "Excavating Brooklyn, New York's Rural Past: The Hendrick I. Lott Farmstead Project." Paper presented at the Society for Historical Archaeology annual meeting.

Roedigger, David R. (1991). *The Wages of Whiteness: Race and the Making of the Working Class.* New York: Verso.

Rosenzweig, Roy, and Elizabeth Blackmar. (1992). *The Park and the People.* Ithaca: Cornell University Press.

Rothschild, Nan A. (1985). "Spatial Aspects of Urbanization." *American Archeology* 5:163–69.

———. (1987). "On the Existence of Neighborhoods in Eighteenth-Century New York City: Maps, Markets, and Churches." *Historical Archaeology Special Publication* 5, ed. Edward Staski, 29–37.

———. (1988). "Food in Early New York City." *Barnard Alumnae Magazine* (Winter):4–6.

———. (1990). *New York City Neighborhoods: The 18th Century.* Orlando: Academic Press.

———. (1992). "Social and Spatial Proximity in Early New York City." *Journal of Anthropological Archaeology* 11:202–18.

———. (1993). "Keeping Up with the Stuyvesants: House Size and Status in 17th Century New Amsterdam." In *Configurations of Power: Holistic Anthropology in Theory and Practice*, ed. John S. Henderson and Patricia J. Netherly, pp. 228–43. Ithaca: Cornell University Press.

———. (1856). "Central Park Condemnation Maps." Collection of the New York City Municipal Archives, Bureau of Old Records.

Seneca Village Project. (2000, 2001). "Internship Applications." Department of Anthropology, the City College of New York.

State of New York. (1855). "New York State Manuscript Census for 1855, Population Census of the 22nd Ward, New York." Collection of the New York City Municipal Archives, Bureau of Old Records.

United States Government, Bureau of the Census. (1830, 1840, 1850). "Population Schedules of the Census of the United States." National Archives, New York City.

Viele, Egbert. (1856). "Topographical Survey for the Grounds of Central Park." Collection of the New-York Historical Society.

———. (1994a). *The Archaeology of Gender: Separating the Spheres in Urban America.* New York: Plenum.

———. (1994b). "Family Dinners and Social Teas: Ceramics and Domestic Rituals." In *Everyday Life in the Early Republic*, ed. Catherine Hutchins, pp. 249–84. Winterthur, Del.: Winterthur Museum.

———. (1999). "Examining Gender, Class, and Ethnicity in 19th-Century New York City." In *Confronting Class*, a special issue of *Historical Archaeology* 33, no. 1:102–17.

———. (2000). "Family Meals and Evening Parties: Constructing Domesticity in 19th-Century Middle-Class New York." In *Lines That Divide: Historical Archaeological Studies in Race, Class, Gender and Ethnicity*, ed. James Delle, Stephen Mrozowski, and Robert Paynter, pp. 109–41. Knoxville: University of Tennessee Press.

Warner, John W., Jr., and Willis E. Hanna. (1982). "Soil Survey of Central Park, New York, New York." Prepared for the Central Park Conservancy by the U.S. Department of Agriculture Soil Conservation Service, in cooperation with Cornell University Agricultural Experiment Station.

Webb, David. (1998). "Methods of Demography of Seneca Village 1855–56: Research 1997." Manuscript on file, Seneca Village Project.

CHAPTER 7

Applied Archaeology and the Construction of Place at Mount Calvert, Prince George's County, Maryland

MICHAEL T. LUCAS

One significant place of employment for archaeologists is in state and local governmental organizations. In this chapter devoted to his work with a county archaeology program in Prince George's County, Maryland, Michael Lucas discusses the challenges that are inherent in representing archaeology to varied local constituencies. He emphasizes the need to relate interpretations of the past to contemporary social and political issues in ways that are flexible enough to permit varied public responses. He also describes how recent scholarship related to place-based consciousness can be useful in developing effective interpretive strategies. A particularly interesting aspect of this chapter is Lucas's discussion of ways in which work with volunteers can help archaeologists test the effectiveness of their interpretive strategies before presenting them to the general public.

Introduction

A central tenet of archaeological practice is determining the relevance or significance of data collected in the field. In legitimizing the practice archaeologists have to sell the results of their research as relevant to contemporary issues. This is especially true of applied work. Applied archaeologists have to convince their constituents or clients that archaeology serves a purpose beyond the often-esoteric goals of archaeological research and is worthy of public funding. These clients frequently include governmental organizations and the general public.

Many archaeologists in the United States work within state and local governmental organizations. Their practice should be closely followed because in many ways it defines the state of applied archaeology as it exists today. In fact, the future of the discipline is dependent on how well archaeologists sell their work to local citizens and legislatures. This chapter provides examples of how the Maryland-National Capital Park and Planning Commission (M-NCPPC) Natural and Historical Resources Division (NHRD) Archaeology Program, as an applied archaeology program within a local governmental organization, serves the citizens of Prince George's County, Maryland. The NHRD Archaeology Program has a dual obligation to the public. First, the program provides public access to the process of archaeology through various hands-on public outreach programs, including a volunteer program. Second, the program works toward building interpretations that are both grounded within the discipline of archaeology and responsive to the citizens of Prince George's County, Maryland. In demonstrating how these two aspects of the public program work, I will use examples from a multiyear public archaeology program at Mount Calvert, an M-NCPPC property located in eastern Prince George's County.

Beyond whatever comparative goals they may have, archaeologists usually begin with the excavation and interpretation of individual sites. The interpretation of sites like Mount Calvert requires archaeologists to critically examine local values attached to a place. Reconciling archaeological evidence from the past with present social and political realities is the challenge of interpretation (Gadamer 1976; Shanks and Tilley 1987). In applied archaeology, there are always individuals, groups, and organizations that have an interest in the end product. The Mount Calvert project has many stakeholders who affect both the process and products of archaeology.

Applied Archaeology in the Maryland-National Capital Park and Planning Commission

The M-NCPPC is a bicounty agency serving two counties in the metropolitan area of Washington, D.C. The M-NCPPC was established in 1927 by the Maryland General Assembly to provide long-term planning and park acquisition for Montgomery and Prince George's County. Funding for the M-NCPPC comes primarily from a surcharge levied on the property taxes of residents and business owners living and operating within the two counties. These revenues are supplemented with a variety of federal and state grants, and institutional and community partnerships. This chapter discusses some of the ways the NHRD Archaeology Program serves the citizens of Prince George's County.

The population of Prince George's County is just over 800,000. The 2000 United States Census statistics summarize the demographics of the county as 62.7 percent Black, 27.0 percent White, 7.1 percent Hispanic (all racial categories), 3.9 percent Asian or Pacific Islander, 0.3 percent American Indian, and 6 percent other (M-NCPPC Prince George's County Planning Department 2001). Less than 3 percent of the total population lists their residence as rural (M-NCPPC Prince George's County Planning Department 2001). Although the county is majority African American, the population is diverse, and the M-NCPPC incorporates multicultural education in its recreation and public archaeology programs.

A subcomponent of the M-NCPPC's mission in Prince George's County is to preserve and interpret the historical and archaeological resources located within the M-NCPPC park system. To this end an M-NCPPC Archaeology Program was established in Prince George's County in 1988 as a public outreach program under the direction of Donald K. Creveling. Since its inception the program has incorporated hands-on public participation into many of its projects, including the Northampton slave quarters and Mount Calvert excavations. I joined the archaeology staff in 1995, shortly after receiving a Master of Applied Anthropology (M.A.A.) degree from the University of Maryland, College Park.

Applied archaeologists are presented with the dual challenge of interpreting the past while making it relevant to their present constituents. This interpretive challenge also involves a realization that such concepts as race, gender, class, ethnicity, and diversity are culturally constructed and historically situated (Scott 1994; Patterson 2001). Therefore, public archaeology benefits from an awareness that these concepts are themselves artifacts of interpretation that change over time. The difficulty that applied archaeologists face is in creating coherent interpretations of public sites that resonate with contemporary definitions of such terms as *ethnicity* and *diversity*.

A Historical and Archaeological Sketch of Mount Calvert

Mount Calvert is a seventy-six-acre property located twelve miles from Washington, D.C., on the Patuxent River in eastern Prince George's County, Maryland. The property was purchased by the M-NCPPC in 1995 to preserve its cultural and natural resources as part of the six-thousand-acre Patuxent River Park. Historical and archaeological research conducted over the past five years indicates the enormous potential for interpreting George's County's cultural heritage to the public via educational programs and exhibits at Mount Calvert. More than sixty thousand historic and prehistoric artifacts have been recovered and analyzed. Through a combination of historical and archaeological research we have identified a prehistoric village site, at least three late-seventeenth- to early-eighteenth-century structures, the probable location of nineteenth-century slave quarters, and a twentieth-century tenant farmhouse. The following is an abbreviated summary of the cultural resources located at the site.

Stone spear points and other implements found through archaeological survey and excavation indicate Native Americans occupied Mount Calvert beginning around eight thousand to nine thousand years ago. For approximately the next four thousand years, Mount Calvert served as a seasonal base camp for Native American groups living in the region. Archaeological data recovered from the site, including pottery and stone tools, indicate that Native Americans began living at the locale year-round beginning around three thousand to four thousand years ago. A Woodland period village existed at Mount Calvert probably until at least 1300 A.D. and possibly as late as the 1600s. In all, the prehistoric occupation of Mount Calvert accounts for about eight thousand years of cultural heritage in Prince George's County.

Mount Calvert gets its name from the one thousand-acre manor established at the confluence of the Western Branch and the Patuxent River in 1658 by Phillip Calvert, son of George Calvert, the first Lord Baltimore of Maryland. This property included the seventy-six acres now owned and administered as parkland by the M-NCPPC. Few Europeans settled in the area around Mount Calvert until the mid-1670s. Fertile tobacco soils located along the upper tidal Patuxent drainage fueled a steady flow of settlers from St. Mary's County to the south. Wealthy planters and merchants traveled up the Patuxent River to secure productive agricultural lands located within the Patuxent River drainage. This migration resulted in a greater concentration of wealthy, landed households along the Patuxent throughout the eighteenth century, as compared to areas farther inland, or along the Potomac River on the western side of what is Prince George's County today (Kulikoff 1986:208).

The first substantial colonial presence at Mount Calvert came with the establishment of a port town at the site in 1684. The town at Mount Calvert was part of a sustained effort by the Virginia and Maryland legislatures during the late seventeenth and early eighteenth centuries to create towns and ports of entry in the colonies where commercial trade could be regulated. Mount Calvert's importance to colonists was underscored when it became the seat of government for Prince George's County in 1696, and the name was changed to Charles Town. Between 1696 and 1721 colonists developed the town at Mount Calvert by constructing a courthouse, a jail, and an Anglican church, in addition to dwellings, taverns, stores, and other accompanying structures (Lucas 1999a).

Like many towns established through legislation in the Chesapeake region, Mount Calvert's history as a town site was short. A new courthouse was constructed at Upper Marlboro, and the court was moved in 1721. Mount Calvert continued to serve as a ferry crossing and transportation link between Prince George's and Anne Arundel County throughout the eighteenth century. A ferrykeeper's house may have stood at the site during the mid-eighteenth century. Significant changes to the landscape were made in the late eighteenth century when a tobacco plantation was established at Mount Calvert.

The landscape at Mount Calvert was altered considerably to accommodate plantation slavery. John Brown purchased the property in 1775, and by 1790 he had constructed a Federal-style dwelling, slave quarters, and other outbuildings associated with the plantation. Mount Calvert existed as a typical southern Maryland tobacco plantation until the 1850s. Preliminary archaeological evidence suggests considerable potential for interpreting the lives of African Americans and European Americans at the site throughout the nineteenth century.

Mount Calvert was a farm from the 1870s until the M-NCPPC purchased the property in 1995. Archaeological and historical research has helped locate numerous outbuildings associated with the farm. An early-twentieth-century tenant farmhouse was also located through archaeological testing. These cultural resources provide a vehicle for interpreting the early-twentieth-century agricultural heritage of Prince George's County.

Public Involvement in Archaeology at Mount Calvert

In 1995 the NHRD Archaeology Program team began planning an archaeological survey and excavation strategy for Mount Calvert. Our initial concern was locating historic and prehistoric archaeological resources and assessing their integrity. After completing our initial historical background research, we realized the potential of the archaeology at Mount Calvert to address research questions related to a wide variety of topics in Maryland and Prince George's County history and prehistory. At the same time we understood the enormous potential of Mount Calvert as a vehicle for sharing our archaeological findings with the public. Therefore, the need to develop Mount Calvert as a center for public education is a driving force in our planning process. Integral to our interpretive program is the determination not to follow a static formula of excavating the site, conducting research and analysis, and then presenting this constructed knowledge to the public. Instead, we have attempted to actively incorporate public involvement throughout all stages of the process, and as a result, the excavation strategy accommodates public participation, site tours, and special events at the site.

Participation of individuals outside of the NHRD Archaeology Program staff serves to guide the interpretive process and at times acts as a check on the viability of our conclusions. We are continually challenged to ask whether our interpretations make sense to nonarchaeologists. Various stakeholders play a part in negotiating the value of archaeology at Mount Calvert. In the following discussion I will identify some key constituents and clients of the NHRD archaeology program and the challenges their involvement presents. In the end the most salient aspect of the project is how the multiple interests of a diverse set of stakeholders affects the process of interpretation at Mount Calvert.

The general public and interorganizational partners continue to be integral to the Mount Calvert project. Both of these groups lend a particular voice to the process. Yet the ways in which these multiple voices affect the archaeological interpretation of Mount Calvert is not always clear. What is clear is the fact that each of these groups has an interest in determining the value of Mount Calvert as a place worthy of public funding. The first step in the process of providing access to the Archaeology Program is involving our nonarchaeologist stakeholders in what we do.

The citizens of Prince George's County are the primary clients of the NHRD Archaeology Program. Archaeological conclusions are certainly presented to this public through a variety of methods including site tours, exhibits, and special events such as school tours. But the Archaeology Program also offers the opportunity for individuals to become active participants in the process of archaeology. Actively involving individuals in this process, of course, also presents its own set of challenges.

Volunteer opportunities are offered to all residents of Prince George's County. Just as in most archaeology volunteer programs, M-NCPPC volunteers assist with daily field and laboratory activities. At first volunteers are involved with tasks such as helping in the field with excavations or washing and labeling artifacts in the laboratory. Eventually, some volunteers become more active in the process of interpretation. This usually involves M-NCPPC archaeologists simply drawing on those skills and experiences volunteers bring with them.

One direct example is volunteer participation in the production and distribution of archaeological research. Several volunteers have been directly involved in the production of archaeological reports. Volunteers have gathered and synthesized historical background research for the project. In the process of conducting research, rather than simply collect information, these individuals become a part of the production of archaeological knowledge, at times suggesting new research avenues or methods. One volunteer, for example, suggested better methods for using census and other historical records to build a more firm economic foundation for the nineteenth-century plantation that stood at Mount Calvert. Other volunteers come with skills that are more practical for public programs.

Mount Calvert's prehistory is a major component of public tours and special events held at the site. One volunteer with a talent for flint knapping, the art of reducing rough stones into tools such as spear points, put his skills to good use through tool-making demonstrations offered to school groups and the general public. These demonstrations were a highlight of our 1998 site tours. Flint-knapping demonstrations are particularly useful for persuading school students to think about the particular ways artifacts may have been used in addition to simply showing them how tools were made.

The M-NCPPC also offers direct volunteer involvement in the NHRD Archaeology Program through formal partnerships with local educational institutions and other organizations. Several Prince George's County high school seniors have completed science fair projects at Mount Calvert through the Digging the Past Program for Prince George's County public school students. These projects have included hands-on participation in the production of data. The science projects present a challenge to both M-NCPPC archaeologists and students. Research practicum guidelines usually call for the development of research questions followed by the collection and interpretation of data. As mentors, the archaeology staff balances the interests of the students with the needs of the NHRD Archaeology Program and time constraints in constructing an appropriate project. Throughout the projects archaeology staff members emphasize the limits of archaeological data to students and stress that making a connection between artifacts and past lives often involves a creative blend of systematically produced data from the field, historical information, artifact collections from other sites, and imagination. Through the Digging the Past Program, we attempt to show that producing archaeological data is only one step in the process of answering increasingly detailed questions about cultural groups who lived at Mount Calvert. The results of some projects have been incorporated into NHRD Archaeology Program reports (Lucas 1999b).

The NHRD Archaeology Program also maintains partnerships with statewide organizations. The primary organizations involved with the archaeology at Mount Calvert are the Archeological Society of Maryland, Inc. (ASM) and the Maryland Historical Trust (MHT). Each of these organizations is committed to the promotion of archaeology and the preservation of cultural resources throughout Maryland. The ASM is an organization of avocational and professional archaeologists interested in archaeological issues. Similarly, the MHT's Office of Archeology is committed to supporting and promoting statewide preservation and public education programs. Both of these organizations have directly influenced the archaeology at Mount Calvert in particular ways.

Between 1997 and 1999 the ASM conducted their Annual Field Session in Maryland Archeology at Mount Calvert. The Field Session began as an informal weekend of field-testing and survey in 1971. Today the Field Session has developed into an eleven-day program that includes excavation, artifact workshops, lectures, and archaeology demonstrations (Lucas and Creveling 1999). The event is cosponsored each year by the MHT, which provides supplies and supervisory personnel. Hundreds of people from around the state participated in the field sessions at Mount Calvert, and much of what we know about the archaeology of the site was gathered during those three years of excavations. ASM members were active on in both the process of excavation and laboratory work, and in the successful planning and implementation of most Field Session activities. Their involvement helped open the site to a statewide public audience that would have otherwise not participated in archaeology through the regular volunteer program. One participant expressed his enthusiasm for the Field Session in an article in the *Washington Post*, entitled "The History Beneath the Surface: Digs at Mount Calvert Yield Bits of Past Glory," by saying, "It's one of those things that catches your interest and then takes over your life" (Meyer 1999). One high school student who participated in the Field Session also summed up her thoughts on the archaeology at Mount Calvert in the same *Washington Post* article, saying, "Finding the artifacts makes it even more believable. It's like you realize you're touching like the past." Active involvement in the hands-on work of archaeology creates an opening where students and the general public can "connect" with the past, and through those physical objects found in the field make it "even more believable." The MHT has also been an important partner in the Mount Calvert archaeology project by providing monetary support.

Over the past five years the MHT has provided $45,000 in noncapital grant funds to the NHRD Archaeology Program. Annual noncapital grants of up to $50,000 are available to qualifying nonprofit organizations and local jurisdictions to complete research and survey work on Maryland's cultural resources. The financial support of the MHT legitimizes Mount Calvert as a valuable cultural resource worthy of archaeological study and preservation. The partnership forged between the MHT and M-NCPPC, however, extends beyond mere financial support. The M-NCPPC and the MHT are cooperative partners in the development of Mount Calvert as a historical place of relevance not only to the citizens of Prince George's County, but also to all citizens of Maryland.

Public involvement in the project, whether it is through the regular volunteer program or through special events like the ASM Field Session, provides access to the process of archaeology, and thus, a stake in determining the value of cultural resources at Mount Calvert. Yet, control over the products of that process still resides largely in the hands of the Archaeology Program. Therefore, as applied archaeologists we need to be good listeners as well as teachers. A barometer for the success of applied archaeology is how well we listen not only to those who have the loudest voices or the most direct access to the Archaeology Program, but also to all residents of Prince George's County.

The Construction of Place and Significance at Mount Calvert

Getting the public actively involved with archaeology is the first step toward fully engaging the citizens of Prince George's County in the process of connecting cultural heritage to the archaeological record, but obviously, not all citizens of the county are able to participate as volunteers. A successful applied archaeology needs to be responsive to all of its stakeholders and balance competing values individuals and groups might attach to a particular locale. A historically valuable landscape to one group may be historically irrelevant to another (Hardesty and Little 2000:7). One responsibility of archaeologists is to set an initial interpretive agenda that untangles as many of these values as possible, always keeping in mind that determining the significance of a place today is largely dependent on precisely how we present its past.

Ellen Herscher and Francis McManamon (2000:50) claim that if the archaeological record is itself a public trust, then "communicating to the public an understanding of its heritage becomes an essential element of the archaeologist's role as steward." Clearly articulating the importance or value of a particular site to a public's heritage, however, often proves difficult. One obvious problem is identifying a target public. As Alexander Ervin (2000:59) puts it, "The reality is that there are many publics with different social, economic, regional, ethnic, and cultural realities." Although Ervin's remarks are directed toward policy analysis, they ring equally true for public archaeology. We need to recognize that "places, like voices, are local and multiple. For each inhabitant, a place has a unique reality" (Rodman 1992:643). Direct involvement in the Mount Calvert archaeology project allows the public to take part in the process through which archaeological knowledge is constructed, but in order to be successful stewards an interpretive framework must be sufficiently broad to include as many voices as possible. Because archaeology has the power to make the past "more believable" to the public, applied archaeologists have the added responsibility not only to introduce multiple historical themes to the public, but also to examine the context in which those themes are created.

Scholars from a variety of disciplines, most notably anthropologists and geographers, have incorporated various definitions of *place* in their work (Tuan 1977; Jackson 1984, 1994; Appadurai 1988; Hiss 1990; Rodman 1992; Duncan and Ley 1993; Ryden 1993; Hayden 1995, 1997; Low 2000; Low and McDonogh 2001). One reason the term has survived so long as a useful interpretive tool is its ability to join spatial and historical information. For Kent Ryden (1993:38), places are not merely points in space but rather are a conglomeration of "meanings which people assign to that landscape through the process of living in it." In this judgment places are distinct local constructions. Novelist Larry McMurtry's (2000:16) assessment that "a thousand McDonald's will not make Boston feel like Tucson" may be true, yet it is also true that individual places are not static and isolated but rather are dynamic and open. Noted landscape historian J. B. Jackson (1994:151) claims, "A sense of place is something we ourselves create over the course of time." Even Jackson would concede that a sense of place is increasingly difficult to define in today's highly mobile society. Values and meanings attached to a place are embedded in continually shifting social and political realities. And archaeological or historical interpretations of a public place like Mount Calvert need to evaluate the political terrain in which they exist.

Mount Calvert was heralded by M-NCPPC historian John Walton in a 1995 *Washington Post* article entitled "State Buying Site of Old P.G. County Seat" as "probably the most significant piece of ground in the county in terms of the cultural heritage, and particularly from the archaeological point of view" (Meyer 1995). Although the property was known to contain an extensive prehistoric site of interest to archaeologists, the site's colonial past was clearly seen as a primary focal point of its cultural significance and an impetus for purchasing the property. Mount Calvert was the site of the original seat of government for Prince George's County, and the property was purchased in anticipation of the county's tricentennial celebration in 1996. Maryland State Archivist Edward Papenfuse commented on the historical significance of the site at an address to a celebration marking the three hundredth anniversary of the formation of the county. In his address delivered at Mount Calvert, Papenfuse highlighted the symbolic place of Mount Calvert within the late-seventeenth-century struggle for control of power in the colony of Maryland between Catholics and Protestants. This event at Mount Calvert was a kickoff of sorts to the tricentennial celebration, and Papenfuse's remarks, entitled "What's in a Name? Why Should We Remember?" spoke primarily to the British colonial origins of the county (Papenfuse 1998). Like any landscape, Mount Calvert's place in history stretches beyond the colonial period and is still emerging. It is this long and dynamic history that makes Mount Calvert part of a larger process of social change within Prince George's County. The interest in Mount Calvert as a colonial town site stems from a general captivation with finding ancient and lost things.

Colonial towns in the Chesapeake region, Maryland and Virginia in particular, have long fascinated scholars and citizens alike. David Lowenthal (2000) would argue that this fascination comes from a tendency to place a primacy on first things. He says, "The first to find a cure or a continent, to detect hidden treasure, to walk on the moon, or to cry 'Bingo!' inherits fame or fortune; no one remembers who came next" (Lowenthal 2000:62). Earliest historic or prehistoric sites carry a seemingly inherent significance. Ancient sites carry a powerful mandate of authenticity and are somehow considered as places "more 'real'" than most we encounter on a daily basis (Comer 1996:278). Certainly, as Donald Hardesty and Barbara Little (2000:6) point out, "Who would deny that the site of the first English settlement in Virginia at Jamestown is important?" Much of the scholarly interest in and debate about colonial Chesapeake towns revolves around issues of why many failed to survive (Reps 1972; Carr 1974; Earle and Hoffman 1977; O'Mara 1982; Thomas 1994, 1999; Shomette 2000). Many archaeological projects and historical studies have capitalized on the public interest in finding these "lost" colonial sites.

For example, a recent *Washington Post* article, entitled "Intrigue Builds Over 'Lost' City: Md.'s Land Deal Revives a Mystery," discussed the excitement surrounding the search for the "lost" seventeenth-century town of Warrington in Calvert County, just southeast of Prince George's County. The fact that the town may have never even been constructed on the ground seems irrelevant when compared to the power of imagination driving the search. The *Post* frames the issue accurately saying, "Perhaps . . . in the end, its not quite so important if the long lost town was to the south— or anywhere, really. What matters is that Warrington firmly exists in many people's minds" (McCaffrey 2000). Another recent article, entitled "Unearthing Past of Towns That Went Under," highlighted the fascination with these places as lost fragments of our colonial past. The article discussed the work of Maryland historian Donald Shomette. Shomette's latest book, *Lost Towns of Tidewater Maryland* (2000), gives a historical account of ten colonial towns in Maryland that failed to survive. Shomette's work, mirroring the more substantial work of John Reps (1972), reviews the history of "failed" town planning efforts first initiated by the seventeenth-century proprietary government under the Lords Baltimore. In a final lament Shomette (2000:298) cautions that "it is up to us to focus upon the preservation of that all but forgotten legacy of our colonial heritage, our early towns and ports. Lord Baltimore would certainly smile upon that."

The colonial town at Mount Calvert is certainly an important element of Prince George's County's heritage. It serves as a focal point for celebrating the existence of the county. But if the site is of value to all of Prince

George's County, then clearly the history of Mount Calvert as a town should be placed in a larger county and regional historical context. The NHRD Archaeology Program is obligated not only to tell the story of the town at Mount Calvert, but also to demonstrate the consequences of the colonial past it represents. For example, the town at Mount Calvert was platted at a time when slavery was beginning to supplant indentured servitude as the primary source of labor in the colony. As applied archaeologists working in a majority African-American county, we need to address a general public interest in colonial towns, but we must place our interpretations of the town at Mount Calvert within a broad interpretive framework that considers the impact of race relations, as well as the contributions of African Americans to the development of Prince George's County and the state of Maryland.

County Executive Wayne Curry countered Edward Papenfuse's remarks on the colonial history of Prince George's County at the Mount Calvert tricentennial event. In a *Washington Post* article, entitled "In Prince George's, a Happy Diversity Party," Curry, an African American who was Prince George's County's top elected official at the time, called Prince George's County "'a jewel in the American crown,' a place that brings 'people together of all races, colors and hues, that brings people together over the troubled past of segregation to this moment that we can celebrate together.'" The contrast between the remarks made by Curry and Papenfuse speak to the contemporary politics embedded in the interpretation of the past. The working subtitle of Papenfuse's speech was "Why Should We Remember?" meaning, Why should we remember Charles Town, the colonial town at Mount Calvert? Papenfuse's lecture answers this question by suggesting that Mount Calvert's significance as a place resides in its relationship to seventeenth-century governmental politics. Curry's address counters this construction of significance by situating Mount Calvert as a place within the larger historical context of race relations leading to the county's present political climate.

As outlined earlier the history and prehistory of Mount Calvert represents an opportunity to explore many elements of Prince George's County's past. The colonial town at Mount Calvert is merely one brief cautionary example of the need for applied archaeologists to critically evaluate and contrast one public's captivation by "firsts" with histories dismantled by those firsts. As public servants the needs of the M-NCPPC as a governmental organization and those of the citizens of the county temper this critical evaluation. As applied anthropologists we realize that the process of making sense of a place like Mount Calvert as significant to our constituents is itself socially and historically situated (Rosenberger and Shackel 2001:16). In the end, "The present is not just the past's inheritor but its active partner, reanimating the sleeping, excavating the buried, and reworking a legacy in line with present needs"(Lowenthal 1998:141). The NHRD Archaeology Program has the opportunity and obligation to interpret multiple and contradictory histories and to encourage direct public involvement in the process of creating archaeological knowledge either through outreach programs or other forums.

Conclusion

Making a connection between mere public participation in archaeology and the construction of responsible archaeological interpretations is the challenge of applied archaeology at Mount Calvert. What Mount Calvert is as a place, its value and significance to Prince George's County residents, will surely change as we prepare more aggressive public outreach programs and develop Mount Calvert as a tourist destination. Much of the interpretive decision making lies in the hands of the NHRD Archaeology Program staff, and our interpretations will change as we respond to the needs of our constituents.

Carol McDavid's assessment of public archaeology's role is instructive. As she explains, public archaeology is

> more than learning how to handle volunteers at the site, making public talks, and presenting archaeological information in interesting ways. It includes those aspects, but also includes a willingness to share fully in both the production and presentation of archaeological knowledge, and to engage in the debates that surround public perceptions of those materials. (McDavid 1997:1)

NHRD Archaeology Program manager Donald Creveling's (2001) work on the Northampton slave quarters project demonstrates how the direct involvement of a community actively shaped the construction and presentation of archaeological knowledge. In this case the NHRD Archaeology Program worked with a descendant community to construct a cooperative interpretation of the site. Engaging in the kinds of public debates McDavid speaks of, however, is at times a difficult task, and we have not yet fully entered into this phase at Mount Calvert. Still, the NHRD Archaeology Program staff as public servants of Prince George's County, are certainly responsive to the social and political realities that exist within the community. As the public archaeology program at Mount Calvert continues to unfold, we will need to reach out to our various constituents in Prince George's County, not only for support, but also for feedback and critique of our interpretations. In the end, interpretations are fluid and will change as political priorities shift.

In his recent popular book *Maryland Lost and Found Again, Washington Post* columnist Eugene L. Meyer claims, "The fact is that many Marylanders have little sense of place about their state outside their own geographical locales. . . . It has, therefore, been my mission to give readers a sense of place—and a connection to the past" (Meyer 2000:5). Meyer's attempt to connect his audience with Maryland's past speaks to the larger issue of expanding the histories of a single locale to include geographical and political realities on a larger scale. The economy of Prince George's County and the Chesapeake region was founded on slave labor. Locating an African-American heritage within the role of Mount Calvert as a town, and the history of town sites in the Chesapeake region in general, is merely one way of evaluating Mount Calvert's significance as a place within the history of Prince George's County and the state of Maryland.

As we attempt to reconstruct a sense of place or heritage for Mount Calvert, we need to think carefully about how to reconstruct that heritage. The people of Prince George's County would be well served by a public archaeology that critically evaluates colonialism and its aftermath, leading to the political realities of today. At Mount Calvert we have the opportunity and an obligation not simply to search for a lost town, but to place at the forefront of our interpretation the consequences of that colonial legacy. If we simply move from today to the colonial town at Mount Calvert in one uncritical interpretive sweep, we fail to capture how the history and archaeology at Mount Calvert could ever relate to all citizens of Prince George's County today.

Acknowledgments

I would like to thank Paul Shackel and Erve Chambers for inviting me to be a part of this volume on applied archaeology. Their suggestions on earlier drafts of this chapter were very helpful. A special thanks goes to NHRD Archaeology Program manager Don Creveling for reviewing the chapter and providing extensive suggestions and critique.

References Cited

Appadurai, Arjun. (1988). "Introduction: Place and Voice in Anthropological Theory." *Cultural Anthropology* 3:16–20.

Carr, Lois Green. (1974). "The Metropolis of Maryland: A Comment on Town Development Along the Tobacco Coast." *Maryland Historical Magazine* 69, no. 2:124–45.

Comer, Douglas C. (1996). *Ritual Ground: Bent's Old Fort, World Formation, and the Annexation of the Southwest.* Berkeley: University of California Press.

Creveling, Donald K. (2001). *It's a Family Thing: Engaging a Community in Their Past.* Paper presented at the Society for Historical Archaeology conference, Long Beach.

Duncan, James, and David Ley. (1993). *Place Culture Representation.* London: Routledge.

Earle, Carville V., and Ronald Hoffman. (1977). "The Urban South: The First Two Centuries." In *The City in Southern History: The Growth of Urban Civilization in the South,* ed. Blaine A. Brownell and David R. Goldfield. Port Washington NY: Kennikat Press.

Ervin, Alexander M. (2000). *Applied Anthropology: Tools and Perspectives for Contemporary Practice.* Boston: Allyn and Bacon.

Gadamer, Hans-Georg. (1976). *Philosophical Hermeneutics.* Berkeley: University of California Press.

Hardesty, Donald L., and Barbara J. Little. (2000). *Assessing Site Significance: A Guide for Archaeologists and Historians.* Walnut Creek, Calif.: Altamira Press.

Hayden, Dolores. (1995). *The Power of Place: Urban Landscapes as Public History.* Cambridge, Mass.: MIT Press.

———. (1997). "Urban Landscape History: The Sense of Place and the Politics of Space." In *Understanding Ordinary Landscapes,* ed. Paul Groth and Todd W. Bressi. New Haven: Yale University Press.

Herscher, Ellen, and Francis P. McManamon. (2000). "Public Education and Outreach: The Obligation to Educate." In *Ethics in American Archaeology,* ed. Mark J. Lynott and Alison Wylie. Washington, D.C.: The Society for American Archaeology.

Hiss, Tony. (1990). *The Experience of Place.* New York: Knopf.

Jackson, John Brinckerhoff. (1984). *Discovering the Vernacular Landscape.* New Haven: Yale University Press.

———. (1994). *A Sense of Place, A Sense of Time.* New Haven: Yale University Press.

Kulikoff, Allan. (1986). *Tobacco and Slaves: The Development of Southern Cultures in the Chesapeake, 1680–1800.* Chapel Hill: University of North Carolina Press.

Low, Setha M. (2000). *On the Plaza: The Politics of Public Space and Culture.* Austin: University of Texas Press.

Low, Setha, and Gary W. McDonogh. (2001). "Introduction to 'Remapping the City: Place, Order, and Ideology.'" *American Anthropologist* 103, no. 1:5–6.

Lowenthal, David. (1998). *The Heritage Crusade and the Spoils of History.* Cambridge: Cambridge University Press.

———. (2000). "Archaeology's Perilous Pleasures." *Archaeology* 53, no. 2:62–66.

Lucas, Michael T. (1999a). *A Rare and Occasional Settlement: An Historical and Archaeological Interpretation of Colonial Town Planning at Mount Calvert, Maryland.* Paper presented at the Society for American City and Regional Planning History conference in Washington, D.C.

———. (1999b). *"att Pig Pointe Upon Mount Colverte": A Phase I Archaeological Survey of Mount Calvert, 18PR6.* Unpublished manuscript on file at the Maryland Historical Trust Library, Crownsville.

Lucas, Michael T., and Donald K. Creveling. (1999). *Partners in Time: Three Archeological Society of Maryland Field Sessions at Mount Calvert.* Paper presented at the annual Council for Northeast Historical Archaeology meetings, St. Mary's City.

McCaffrey, Raymond (2000) "Intrigue Builds Over 'Lost' City; Md.'s Land Deal Revives a Mystery" *The Washington Post,* B01. 5 August. http://www.lexisnexis.com/universe. Accessed 16 December 2002.

McDavid, Carol. (1997). "Introduction." In *In the Realm of Politics: Prospects for Public Participation in African-American Archaeology,* special issue of *Historical Archaeology* 31, no. 3:1–4.

McMurtry, Larry. (2000). *Roads: Driving America's Great Highways.* New York: Touchstone.

Meyer, Eugene L. (1995) "State Buying Site of Old P.G. County Seat; After 3 Years of Negotiations. Md. Acquiring Mount Calvert" *The Washington Post,* M01. 2 February. http://www.lexisnexis.com/universe. Accessed 16 December 2002.

Meyer, Eugene L. (1999) "The History Beneath the Surface; Digs at Mount Calvert Yield Bits of Past Glory" *The Washington Post,* M16. 26 May. http://www.lexisnexis.com/universe. Accessed 16 December 2002.

Meyer, Eugene L. (2000). *Maryland: Lost and Found Again.* Baltimore: Woodholme House.

Meyer, Eugene L. (2001) "Unearthing Past Towns That Went Under" The Washington Post, T02. 15 March. http://www.lexisnexis.com/universe. Accessed 16 December 2002.

Meyer, Eugene L. and Terry M. Neal (1996) "In Pr. George's, a Happy Diversity Party" *The Washington Post,* A01. 24 April. http://www.lexisnexis.com/universe. Accessed 16 December 2002.

M-NCPPC Prince George's County Planning Department. (2001). "Population." 24 September. http://www.mncppc.org/pgco/facts/pop.htm. Accessed 16 December 2002.

O'Mara, James. (1982). "Town Founding in Seventeenth-century North America: Jamestown in Virginia." *Journal of Historical Geography* 8, no. 1:1–11.

Papenfuse, Edward C. (1998). "What's in a Name? Why Should We Remember?: Remarks on the Occasion of the 300th Anniversary of the Commencement of Justice in Prince George's County, April 23, 1996." 8 July. http://www.mdarchives.state.md.us/msa/stagser/s1259/121/7508/html/0002.html. Accessed 16 December 2002.

Patterson, Thomas C. (2001). "Diversity in Archaeology." In *Cultural Diversity in the United States: A Critical Reader*, ed. Ida Susser and Thomas C. Patterson. Malden, Mass.: Blackwell.

Reps, John W. (1972). *Tidewater Towns: City Planning in Colonial Virginia and Maryland*. Williamsburg: The Colonial Williamsburg Foundation.

Rodman, Margaret. (1992). "Empowering Place: Multilocality and Multivocality." *American Anthropologist* 94:640–56.

Rosenberger, Nancy R., and Paul A. Shackel. (2001). "Postmodernism Has a Place in Applied Anthropology." *Society for Applied Anthropology Newsletter* 12, no. 4:15–17.

Ryden, Kent C. (1993). *Mapping the Invisible Landscape: Folklore, Writing, and the Sense of Place*. Iowa City: University of Iowa Press.

Scott, Elizabeth M. (1994). *Those of Little Note: Gender, Race, and Class in Historical Archaeology*. Tucson: University of Arizona Press.

Shanks, Michael, and Christopher Tilley. (1987). *Re-Constructing Archaeology: Theory and Practice*. Cambridge: Cambridge University Press.

Shomette, Donald G. (2000). *Lost Towns of Tidewater Maryland*. Centreville: Tidewater Publishers.

Thomas, Joseph B., Jr. (1994). *Settlement, Community, and Economy: The Development of Towns on Maryland's Lower Eastern Shore, 1660–1775*. Unpublished dissertation on file at the University of Maryland, College Park.

———. (1999). "One Hundred Lots Make It a Town: Four Surveys of Early Oxford." *Maryland Historical Magazine* 94, no. 2:173–91.

Tuan, Yi-fu. (1977). *Space and Place: The Perspective of Experience*. Minneapolis: University of Minnesota Press.

PART 3

Archaeology and Heritage Development

CHAPTER **8**

Building Ties
The Collaboration between the
Miami Nation and Archaeology

MARK S. WARNER AND DARYL BALDWIN

The relationship between archaeologists and Native Americans has a long and not always congenial history. This chapter, coauthored by a representative of the Miami Indian Nation (Daryl Baldwin) and an archaeologist (Mark Warner), describes in detail both the complexity and promise of a collaborative effort that, in effect, aims to renegotiate the relationship from the ground up. Importantly, the terms of this renegotiation extend not only to recognizing the authority of the Miami Nation in regard to their heritage resources, but also to reconsidering the ways in which knowledge of the past might best be gained. The suggestion that knowledge acquisition needs to be linked with local morality is an important point to consider.

Introduction

With the fairly recent passage of federal laws such as the American Indian Religious Freedom Act (1988), the Native American Graves Protection and Repatriation Act (1990), and the Native American Languages Act (1990), the Miami Tribe of Oklahoma finds an increasing desire to begin developing a means of managing tribal cultural resources. These important federal laws not only create the legal framework that protects the cultural and religious rights of the tribe, but also opens the doorway for the Miami to become much more active in the preservation process. With this increased

137

participation arise discussions around ethics, proprietary rights, and a re-defined role that research will play in managing important cultural re-sources for the tribe. There is still much work to be done in understanding the role of research in cultural preservation and the roles tribes play in con-ducting research. The Miami people have not historically had to deal with the many modern issues associated with cultural resource management,[1] and whites have not in the past had to conduct research under the auspices of tribal representatives. With this equilibrium being established, new types of relationships between tribes and researchers are emerging. This chapter looks at the issues around research and how the Miami Tribe of Oklahoma is developing socially and politically in order to handle the contemporary demands needed to manage tribal cultural resources.

Defining Research and the Tribe's Role: Baldwin[2]

The Miami people have historically had their share of researchers enter-ing the community seeking information from individuals in order to fulfill a research agenda. In the past, researchers never considered how their work might benefit the Miami community. Questions like "What are your needs?" or "How can my research be useful to you?" were never asked. This detached perspective has historically been the status quo when academic institutions worked with tribes. Within the academic circle some will argue that good research must be conducted objectively without participation from their subjects. This may be true for some kinds of research, but if the research is intended to benefit more than the researcher and his discipline, then this perspective may be inadequate.

When we use the term *research*, there is an automatic assumption that some higher institutional process is involved. Academia does provide many useful research models based on a methodical approach that leads to the discovery of information on a particular subject. But it should be remembered that the Miami people also have their own more traditional means for seeking knowledge and understanding. Modern research is a tool, but there are many other ways that lead to the discovery of empirical knowledge. Some of the more traditional means are not considered scien-tific by modern standards, but regardless they are equally important to the people in determining an appropriate understanding and what further ac-tions should be taken in any given project. There have been times during individuals' research that intuition or elder advice has halted the process. These more subjective influences are not for public examination and will not be further discussed here, but they are worthy of noting in light of un-derstanding tribal participation in the research process.

The Miami tribe has been actively involved in several different research-related projects over the last ten years. In most cases an academic institu-tion or individual initiated the research, and the Miami were invited to participate. The term *invited* as used here does not imply that the Miami tribe's sole involvement was that of an informant. It means that we had the opportunity to give input on the process, interpret results, and in some cases proofread final drafts of the research document. In order to participate at this level, tribal representatives themselves had to have some authority or knowledge of the materials they were reviewing. When it comes to more traditional or historic knowledge, elders are always consulted. When projects require the technical skills of a linguist or other related fields, we consult with tribal members who are trained in these areas, or we turn to trusted allies who have worked with the tribe previously. Our ability to maneuver through the research process without violating community and cultural ethics is key to a successful and useful research result.

The Miami people remain intimately connected with their past. This connection requires that we conduct ourselves in an appropriate and respectful manner, especially when the material culture of ancestors is involved with the research. Fields like archaeology study cultures through examination of material remains, which traditionally is conducted through an impersonal process. For some Miami, archaeology may more appropriately be defined as the study of material culture from ancestors whom we still maintain relationships with. Allowing someone to dig in a trash pit in the back yard of an old nineteenth-century allotment house is not much different from inviting someone into grandma's house to dig through her closet while she is in the kitchen making lunch. Miami people continue to feel a strong sense of connectedness and thus responsibility toward our ancestors in the present as well as the past. It is due to this contiguous life view that issues of privacy and protection arise when archaeology work is requested.

The role of research in the Miami community requires not only the expertise relative to the field, but the recognition of all that can be affected by the research, including spiritual matters. In order for research to be useful and conducted properly, qualified tribal people must be involved. Long gone are the days of the linguist or archaeologist stumbling into the community to dig holes, ask questions, and then be on his way. Long gone are the days when research results are written with no expectation that they will be read by Miami people. And long gone are the days when the Miami people simply sit and observe while others interpret their history, culture, and language. It is good to see these old ways of doing things disappear. It means the Miami people are recovering from their past and learning how to redefine their role as a responsible nation in a modern context.

Tribal History

Prior to contact with Europeans and in the early post-contact years, the Miami lived in what is today southern Wisconsin, northern Illinois, and

Indiana (Anson 1970:4–9) During the late seventeenth century, conflict
with the Iroquois and developing trade networks with the French led the
Miami to seek refuge elsewhere. By 1700 they had migrated to the south
and east and settled in what is today Illinois, Indiana, and western Ohio.
The Miami initially enjoyed fairly stable relationships with European
traders (Callender 1978:682; Anson 1970:28). When the French withdrew
from the area in the 1760s, the Miami shifted their trade allegiances to the
English. The expanded contact with whites ultimately led to several
changes in the lives of the Miami. Not only did their housing shift from
traditional lodges to log cabins (Rafert 1996:54–55; Callender 1978:682),
but their patterns of dress (Mann 1999:416) and food choices (Anson 1970:
142) also showed the influence of white customs. Scholars disagree as to
the meaning of these material changes in the everyday lives of the tribe.
Some dismiss them as superficial and maintain that Miami culture was
largely unchanged from that of the 1600s (Rafert 1996:40, 55), while others
point to this period as the beginning of the "disintegration" of tribal culture (Callender 1978:682). As Mann (1999:400) and Anson (1970:175–76)
argue, the actual effect on Miami culture probably rests between these ex-
tremes, where Miami life was characterized by tension between substantive
incorporations of Anglo-American lifeways and attempts to maintain past
practices and reject new customs.

Beyond the internal struggles occurring within the tribe, the end of the
eighteenth century marked the beginning of a disastrous century for the
Miami. In 1794 a confederation of Indians attacked the American Army
near present-day Toledo, Ohio, in a battle known as Fallen Timbers. The
Miami were thoroughly defeated and compelled to sign the treaty of
Greenville in 1795, which marked the beginning of a half-century-long
pattern of land secession. From 1795 to 1840 the Miami were forced to sign
at least seventeen treaties with the American government in which they re-
linquished their rights to their tribal homelands (Rafert 1996:67, 82). The
last of these treaties, signed on November 28, 1840, forfeited the remainder
of the Miami's traditional territories to white settlers and required the
forced removal of the Miami tribe to the west (Anson 1970:205). After a
delay of several years, more than three hundred Miami boarded canal
boats on October 6, 1846, for transportation to an unwanted reservation in
Kansas. Significantly, a few prominent Miami families were able to purchase exemptions and keep what had been titled as family property in Indiana, effectively avoiding removal.

The Miami who were relocated to Kansas did not stay there very long.
Almost from their first settlement in Kansas (near what is today Kansas
City), they had to deal with regular encroachment of whites onto their
lands. In 1854 the Miami (and other Indian groups) were compelled to

sign another treaty that reduced their Kansas lands from approximately 325,000 acres to approximately 71,000 acres. These lands taken from the Miami were then opened up to white settlement, while the remaining lands were divided up into two-hundred-acre allotments to be held by individuals (Anson 1970:239–40). Conflicts between whites and Indians continued, however, and in 1867 the Bureau of Indian Affairs (BIA) initiated another relocation effort. Under terms of an 1867 proposal by the government, the Miami and several other Indian nations residing in what was now the state of Kansas were presented with a choice. One option was to stay where they were, receive title to the land they currently resided on, and become American citizens—while at the same time renouncing their Indian heritage, removing themselves from tribal rolls, and giving up access to further support from the BIA. The other option was to move to new lands in what is today the northeastern corner of Oklahoma but at the time was simply "Indian Territory." The move would have put the Miami in close association with seven other Indian Nations from all over the United States (the Modoc, Ottawa, Peoria, Quapah, Seneca-Cayuga, Shawnee, and Wyandotte) and was an attempt by the government to consolidate many smaller groups for the sake of administrative efficiency (Anson 1970: 243–44).

Ultimately, fewer than eighty Miami emigrated in 1873 to Indian Territory, where the U.S. government continued its efforts to assimilate them into white America. The most notable effort was the Dawes Act of 1887, which attempted to facilitate assimilation of the Indians by eliminating the reservation system of collective land ownership and mandating the division of land into individually owned parcels. This is what happened to Miami lands, and it became a selling point for continued white expansion in the region. Illustrating this was a 1902 publicity booklet for the region which states in the introduction that "this is the only place in the Indian Territory where . . . a purchase of an Indian's title to land is possible" (Odell 1902:2).

Overall, the history of the Miami during the last two hundred years is one of persistent efforts by the U.S. government to take lands and destroy tribal culture. To some extent the government has been successful; today, for instance, there are no remaining native speakers of *Myaamia Iilaataweenki*, the language of the Miami. Despite early federal efforts at assimilation, however, the tribe has persisted. Today there are two communities of Miami, one in Indiana (which is not federally recognized) and one federally recognized community in Miami, Oklahoma. There are approximately 7,700 members on the tribal rolls of the two branches; 2,400 members are associated with the Western Miami, while the Eastern Miami claim 5,000.[3] Beyond numerical growth, the Miami have been extremely active in a number of areas. A particular emphasis has been aimed at the revitalization of Miami culture. In the past decade the Miami have initiated a project that teaches the Miami language, *Iilaataweenki*, to interested members through regular language camps and a CD-ROM. In addition they are producing a tribal newspaper, have established a regular pow-wow and stomp dance, and have created an oral history project in conjunction with Miami University (see the tribal webpage at: http://www.miamination.com/). It is the oral history project that was the catalyst for the archaeological work with the Miami Nation.

Tribal Infrastructure Today: Baldwin

The Miami tribe of Oklahoma consists of a population often referred to as the "general council" and then a five-person business committee, which oversees the day-to-day operations of the tribe. The tribe also has an elected chief and vice-chief, who serve executive duties on behalf of the nation. Several government-funded programs exist, including a library, day-care, elders' food program, environmental department, and so on. Committees handle most other tribal matters; these include a language and cultural committee, cemetery committee, traditions committee, finance committee, and tourism committee. Tribal infrastructure has grown considerably in the last twenty years, primarily due to the growth of the nation, stable leadership, and successful business ventures. All of this has allowed for an increased ability to channel tribal support toward the management of cultural resources.

Taking on the responsibility of cultural resource management is still relatively new for the Miami. As the tribe begins to play a more active role in managing these resources, a certain amount of tribal infrastructure, including key positions and appropriate protective measures, will be needed. Along with infrastructure development comes the ability to strategically place knowledgeable and trained individuals into key positions within the tribe. Recently, the Miami tribe has provided enough resources to fully fund a cultural preservation office, which currently has one full-time employee. This is a good first step in assuring Miami participation in ongoing culture-related activities, including overseeing any research that might directly affect the tribe or tribal lands.

Today, we have tribal members earning degrees in history, linguistics, anthropology, and other related fields in order to assist the tribe with our current need. Most of these tribal members have provided support for the community in some form or another. Our own members who become actively involved in research bring with them a sentiment that is typically only shared among Miami people. After all, many of the material objects used in any given research project have direct ties to personal ancestors. The downside to this is the issue of personally biased research, but the upside is the internal motivation to know one's own past and to learn from that past. An important skill for many to develop in any given research project is the ability to distinguish between emotional, spiritual, and critical or objective thinking. Much of this is not taught in an academic setting but is essential to working in a tribal environment.

Another recent development worthy of noting is the Myaamia Project at Miami University (Myaamia being the Miamis' name for themselves). Both the Miami tribe and Miami University support this project, and its purpose is aimed at preserving, promoting, and researching Miami tribe history, culture, and language. This is an interesting development that brings university students and resources and matches them with the needs of the tribal community. Projects are identified and managed by the project director Daryl Baldwin to ensure that they directly serve the tribal community. In turn, Miami University gains experience in hands-on community development, and students get cross-cultural experience in tribal language and cultural development. The Miami have learned the value of good, long-term allies and how they are able to mesh with communal needs.

All of these new internal and external developments have allowed the Miami tribe to regroup and begin looking at the issues around cultural resource management. This is an important sovereign step for the nation and one we will ultimately be glad we took.

Needed Research: Baldwin

The Miami tribe has many political, social, economic, historical, and cultural needs as a result of their recent history. Removals, boarding schools, allotments, and community fragmentation have negatively impacted our ability to maintain the social and cultural infrastructure needed for a healthy contiguous community. Since the 1930s the Miami tribe has been in a constant state of rebuilding. The needs are tremendous, and with threats of federal budget cuts and other issues, the urgency is even greater. In order to rebuild, identify needs, develop social understanding, and ultimately create a healthy community again, a certain amount of research is necessary. The Miami must play a lead role in this process in order to ensure that appropriate research is conducted.

There is a certain amount of physical knowledge derived from good research that is of interest to the Miami. For example, in order to better understand the effects of removal and allotments, during which period the Miami population fell to its lowest, knowledge of the physical lives of

Miami ancestors is important. The least-known period in Miami history is the removal period. It was a very dark time for the Miami, and it stands to reason that not much was passed down orally. Only recently have tribal members been more willing and open to discussing this part of our past. But even today a wide range of emotions is often stirred up when the topic of removal comes up. Due to the sensitivity of this issue, any research that involves the issue of removal must be conducted in a way that does not further inhibit much-needed healing from that period.

It was also during this era that much of the language and culture began to fall dormant. For modern reclamation and historical purposes, it will be important for us to know all that contributed to the decline in hopes of understanding how this history has shaped the modern community and, more importantly, to ensure these sorts of atrocities our ancestors lived through do not happen again. Traditionally our people were very knowledgeable about our history, but with so much pain associated with the last two hundred years, it is difficult to justify remembering.

The removal period has been opened slightly on many fronts. In the summer of 2002, the Miami tribe sponsored a tribal member to visit the old reservation area in Kansas and begin looking over available records. In 1996 the Miami tribe opened its enrollment to allow those Miami who remained in Kansas during the final removal to Indian Territory (Oklahoma) to reenter the rolls. This has allowed families in Kansas to reestablish communal and kinship ties to the Miami tribe, which opens up avenues for knowledge sharing, especially relative to the removal period. There is also discussion about the need for an archaeological survey of properties in Kansas and Oklahoma, either owned today by Miami families or on other tribal properties. Either way, a better understanding of the removal period must be handled from several different perspectives and with help from inside and outside the community. Archaeology will play a pivotal role in understanding the material lives of our ancestors during the removal period.

The Development of Miami Collaboration with Archaeology

The origin of archaeological involvement with the Miami nation was an informal conversation between Jim Hamill and Mark Warner in early 1997. Hamill is a cultural anthropologist who teaches at Miami University. In 1994 members of the Miami nation approached Miami University about developing strategies for recovering tribal histories and building closer ties between the tribe and the university. The first sustained outcome of this contact was the development of an ethnohistory summer field program run by Hamill (see Hamill 2000:291–92). After outlining his pro-

ject Hamill basically asked, "What sort of things could a historical archaeologist do in Miami?" That conversation led to a week-long visit to Miami,
Oklahoma, in the summer of 1997, when Warner conducted a "windshield"
survey of the region, met with several tribal members, and shovel-tested
two properties to determine their archaeological integrity. The original intent was to locate and excavate Pumpkin Center, which had been the tribal
general store and was a prominent landmark in tribal memories. It was ultimately not practical to locate the store due to a lack of access to the property, but an alternative location was identified. The property that became
the focus of the excavations is one of the few properties that have been
continuously occupied by tribal members since their relocation to northeastern Oklahoma in the 1870s. The site is a farmstead with a standing
house dating to the 1890s, which is coincidentally owned and occupied by
the Miami tribal cultural preservation officer and her husband.

Two summers of excavations have been conducted on the property (in
1998 and 2000), which has resulted in the recovery of approximately
28,000 artifacts. (A third field season will be conducted on the site when
funding is secured—most likely during the summer of 2004.) The analysis
of the materials is ongoing; so far, based on this work, two masters theses
are in progress, and several conference papers have been presented that uti-
lized data from the excavations (Ruedrich in prep; Warner 2001a, b; Yoder
in prep).

Archaeological Motivations for the Project: Warner

My motivations for undertaking this work with the Miami are based on a
combination of personal and professional issues. On a personal level the
nagging question that existed for me as an undergraduate was, What is the
social utility of archaeology? Does archaeology have a viable utility for
people beyond other archaeologists? Fortunately, my time in graduate
school provided me with some tentative answers to this issue. For this I
owe a debt to Mark Leone and my cohorts in the Archaeology in Annapolis
project. For more than twenty years the project has operated with the intent of making archaeology meaningful and relevant to an audience beyond merely other archaeologists (Potter 1994, Potter and Leone 1987,
Shackel et al. 1998:xvi–xvii). While this is a noble model in theory, the reality left something to be desired. In the case of Annapolis, the question remains open on the extent to which the public archaeology program has
elicited change in how the city is viewed and marketed to tourists, especially to the city's African-American community.

In turning to the Miami project, my establishment of a relationship
with members of the tribe has provided me with a clear illustration of the

potential significance of archaeology to nonarchaeologists. The splitting of the tribe and the two forced relocations by the U.S. government during the nineteenth century ultimately did lead to a profound loss of tribal memory. Since 1990 the Miami have been aggressively taking steps to address this loss through a variety of initiatives that were mentioned above. The expectation is that archaeology will ultimately be able to contribute to this initiative in a somewhat more sustained manner than with the Annapolis work. The reason is simply that in Annapolis we were essentially attempting to insert ourselves into the community, while in Miami it is the community that is inviting anthropologists in, on their terms and under their initiative.

Project Expectations: Warner

In the academic realm there are three factors that shape this project. First, this work is clearly a product of the Indian-driven critique of anthropology and archaeology that was initiated more than thirty years ago by Vine Deloria, Jr. (1969), which has forced a fundamental reevaluation of the nature of archaeology's relations with American Indians. Much of this reassessment initially focused on the issue of repatriations of excavated Indian burials and associated funerary remains ("Special Edition" 1992; *Arizona State Law Journal* 1992). Out of the repatriation issue, however, has come a related body of literature written by both Indians and whites that strives to rearticulate the relationship between Indians and archaeologists (Adams 1984; Ferguson 1984; Anawak 1989; Handsman and Richmond 1995; McGuire 1997; Swidler et al. 1997; Mason 2000; Echo-Hawk 1990; and Watkins 2000 among many others that could be cited). It is clear that the relationship between Indians and archaeology is still being renegotiated, but as a result of the dialogue of the past fifteen years or so, an increasing number of archaeologists have been striving to build relationships with Indians that are sensitive to Indian values rather than simply the pursuit of scientific knowledge. From an archaeological standpoint it is my hope that this work is part of that renegotiated relationship between Indians and archaeology.

The second issue is, What are the research objectives for this project? In brief, this work represents an expansion of one of my primary research focuses, namely the issue of minority group identity. My earlier work explored the issue of African-American identity vis-á-vis white society (Warner 1998). The Miami project represents an expansion of this research. I am asking the same questions about how minority groups have redefined and maintained identities that are at least partially separate from white America. Yet I am exploring these questions with a different group in a different geographical location.

Finally, there is a long-term research framework, which can link to tribal interests as well as make a unique contribution to archaeology. As mentioned earlier, the Miami have been relocated twice, with portions of the tribe moving from Indiana in 1846 and from Kansas in 1877. One of the questions to be explored in the future is the question of change over time; namely, what happened to the Miami materially from the 1800s to the present? In what ways did assimilation take place, and in what ways was it resisted? Surprisingly, this is a fairly accessible question to explore. The current excavations in Miami present an initial understanding of life in the early twentieth century, while a variety of technical reports on salvage excavations on preremoval Miami-occupied sites in Indiana provide an image of Miami life in the early 1800s (see Cochran 1990; Mann 1996, 1999; Rose 1979; Stillwell 1990; Wepler 1984). The missing piece of this puzzle would be Kansas, where several tribal members continue to own lands. This large-scale view has been previously mentioned to the tribe, and the assessment is that it does fit in with overall tribal efforts to understand tribal life over the past one hundred years or so.

What is interesting about such a model of looking at change over time is that change in lifeways is a core question for precontact explorations of Indians, yet in historical settings it is a question that has generally not been explored. Indeed, when compared to other minority groups, postcontact Indian lifeways have received comparatively little attention from archaeology.

Outcomes and Future Directions

At this early stage there are a few themes that can be noted—though it is also fair to say that the primary benefit has been to archaeologists. The property that has been partially excavated has produced an extremely large volume of material culture artifacts; nearly 28,000 have been recovered, and those artifacts have led to several conference papers and masters theses. So far there are at least three avenues that will be of significance to the Miami. First, mechanisms need to be developed to increase the involvement of tribal members in the archaeological process. Thus far a combination of factors (for example, dig logistics, funding, and property owner privacy concerns) have profoundly limited community involvement in the project. Yet this is a project where tribal involvement could be considerable. Well-funded archaeological projects that are exploring the history of any descendant community have the potential to incorporate people at every step of the process, from the fieldwork to the lab processing and analysis to ultimately the intellectual production stemming from the excavations. In the best of all situations, this project could foster tribal interest in archaeology to the degree where eventually tribal members will be fully trained as archaeologists and will take the lead in managing archaeological resources on tribal lands as well as any other research on Miami-related themes.

Second, the archaeological data from multiple sites will have to be woven together to produce a *meaningful* history. Certainly, such a project can produce multiple stories that will be presented in varying forums (for example, academic conference papers), but what I ultimately will owe the tribe is the production of a history, which is based on archaeology that is useful to the tribe. How exactly this will be accomplished remains to be seen but the point is the work should be as relevant to the tribe as it is to other academics.

Finally, a mechanism needs to be developed wherein archaeology can be integrated in tribal management plans. The Miami have been reacquiring lands in northeast Oklahoma that were part of their original reserve. In the last three years or so they have acquired roughly one thousand acres of land. A good deal of the land has been farmed in the past, but other than that there has been almost no development on it. As part of the land acquisitions, the tribe is developing management plans for these properties, including environmental impact surveys. They are not planning on developing these lands at this point, but they are very interested in identifying what the cultural remains are on these lands. From an archaeological standpoint this would likely entail a detailed survey of their lands to identify the presence of archaeological sites. For the Miami what is important is knowing what cultural resources are present on their lands. The clear goal for the tribe is not development but rather stewardship. The tribe desires knowledge of what is on their lands as a way to avoid the pitfall of accidentally destroying precontact resources.

Conclusion

Seeking knowledge is a concept that is embedded in traditional Miami culture and language. *Nipwaahkaalo* is a term with several meanings, but it basically embodies the concept of knowledge, wisdom, as well as consciousness. This term is closely related to *nipwaaminki* "teaching/learning." The Miami have always been a people interested in seeking knowledge. It is one of their fundamental purposes for living, but their traditions tell them that knowledge must be sought in a healthy way—their health being guided by their traditional culture and a way of living that has evolved over many thousands of years. It stands to reason that modern European-based approaches to seeking knowledge may conflict with traditional Miami ways of knowing. In other words they see the value that fields like archaeology contribute to human knowledge, but when the display and mishandling of human remains occurs, it has devastating effects on their people and cultures. It is not that the field of archaeology is bad, but the manner in which it has been practiced in the past violates traditional beliefs and values. The Miami will eventually try the modern tools offered by archaeology, but they will use them in ways that do not violate traditional beliefs and values. This is a form of cultural boundary maintenance where the Miami maintain control of that boundary between themselves and mainstream society. Objects and knowledge can cross that boundary, but their use is best defined by the culture. This is a delicate balance the Miami are still figuring out, and the process will likely continue for many generations.

The collaboration between archaeology and the Miami tribe is still recent, and so an assessment of the project at this point in time is far too preliminary. Our respective motivations are clear, as are the expectations, yet the success in this work will only be determined years from now when there is an extensive history of the postrelocation Miami, when archaeologists are interested in the everyday lives of native people, and when excavations on Miami lands are directed by archaeologists who are tribal members. In short, we are off to a positive start, but the long-term goal of substantive integration of archaeological and tribal interests is still being negotiated.

Both parties are crossing a cultural boundary. We both believe there are profound benefits to come from this kind of collaboration, but more fundamentally, we both believe this sort of collaboration is necessary to create the understanding needed to advance our collective knowledge of Miami archaeological history. Without question there is a history of unequal relations between races, and we should never forget that history. It is likely that this type of work will continually force us to remember that history, and as that shared history begins to emerge from the soil, we hope it creates an understanding of the past that allows us to move on in a respectful way. The Miami are in the midst of a period of dramatic cultural rediscovery, and certainly, the tools of anthropology and archaeology can contribute to that. What is key from our perspective is to remember archaeology's role, which is to *contribute* to the stories being told and not to *create* those stories on our own.

Notes

The authors would like to thank several people for reading earlier versions of this article and supporting this work. We particularly would like to thank Julie Olds, whose efforts on behalf of the tribe are tireless, and Dr. Beverly Rodgers, for her insight and comments. We also wish to thank Chief Floyd Leonard and the other members of the business committee for their leadership on behalf of the tribe. A portion of the archaeological work with the Miami was supported through a seed grant awarded by the University of Idaho Research Office. Finally, we would like to thank our spouses, Amy Grey and Karen Baldwin, for helping us maintain a small sense of balance in our lives.

1. The term *cultural resource management* as used in this work should be understood to have a broader meaning than is typically used in archaeological writings, where the term tends to refer to compliance-driven work. In this instance it should be read as a more inclusive phrase that incorporates any actions relating to cultural heritage, regardless of whether they were mandated by legislation or by other concerns.
2. While this paper is jointly authored, there are segments of this work that are, of necessity, single-authored. Simply put, we feel it would be inappropriate to imply that Warner is speaking as a tribal member or Baldwin is speaking as an archaeologist. Our solution to the issue of a shifting voice in this work is to make explicit which segments are effectively single-authored; in those segments we chose to write in the first person to further clarify our respective contributions.
3. Two points of clarification should be made on these figures. First, the large growth in numbers of enrolled Western Miami is attributable in large part to the later reenrollment of many of the Miami families that had stayed in Kansas. Second, the totals for the Eastern Miami are at this point not verifiable.

References Cited

Adams, E. Charles. (1984). "Archaeology and the Native American: A Case at Hopi." In *Ethics and Values in Archaeology*, ed. Ernestene L. Green, pp. 236–63. New York: Free Press.

Anawak, Jack. (1989). "Inuit Perceptions of the Past." In *Who Needs the Past?: Indigenous Values and Archaeology*, ed. R. Layton, pp. 45–50. London: Unwin Hyman.

Anson, Bert. (1970). *The Miami Indians*. Norman: University of Oklahoma Press.

Arizona State Law Journal. (1992). "Symposium: The Native American Graves Protection and Repatriation Act of 1990 and State Repatriation-Related Legislation." *Arizona State Law Journal* 24.

Callender, Charles. (1978). "Miami." In *Handbook of North American Indians, vol. 15: Northeast*, ed. Bruce Trigger, pp. 681–89. Washington, D.C.: Smithsonian Institution Press.

Cochran, Donald. (1990). *Excavations at the Richardville/LaFontaine House*. Report #26. Muncie: Archaeological Resource Management Service, Ball State University.

Deloria, Vine Jr. (1969). *Custer Died for Your Sins*. New York: Macmillan.

Echo-Hawk, Roger C. (1990). "Ancient History in the New World: Integrating Oral Traditions and the Archaeological Record." *American Antiquity* 65:267–90.

Ferguson, T. J. (1984). "Archaeological Ethics and Values in a Tribal Cultural Resource Management Program at the Pueblo of Zuni." In *Ethics and Values in Archaeology*, ed. Ernestene L. Green, pp. 224–35. New York: Free Press.

Hamill, James. (2000). "Being Indian in Northeast Oklahoma." *Plains Anthropologist* 45:291–303.

Handsman, Russell G., and Trudie Lamb Richmond. (1995). "Confronting Colonialism: The Mahican and Schaghticoke Peoples and Us." In *Making Alternative Histories: The Practice of Archaeology and History in Non-Western Settings*, ed. Peter R. Schmidt and Thomas C. Patterson, pp. 87–117. Santa Fe: School of American Research Press.

Mann, Rob. (1996). *Archaeological Excavations at the Ehler Site (12Hu1022): An Early 19th Century Miami Indian Habitation Site Near the Forks of the Wabash, Huntington County, Indiana*. Report of Investigation 95IN0062-P3r01. Sheridan, Ind: Landmark Archaeological and Environmental Services.

———. (1999). "The Silenced Miami: Archaeological and Ethnohistorical Evidence for Miami-British Relations, 1795–1812." *Ethnohistory* 46:399–427.

Mason, Ronald J. (2000). "Archaeology and Native American Oral Traditions." *American Antiquity* 65:239–66.

McGuire, Randall H. (1997). "Why Have Archaeologists Thought the Real Indians Were Dead and What Can We Do about It?" In *Indians and Anthropologists: Vine Deloria Jr., and the Critique of Anthropology*, ed. Thomas Biolsi and Larry J. Zimmerman, pp. 63–91. Tucson: The University of Arizona Press.

Odell, Risdon Moore. (1902). *A Pen Picture of Miami, Indian Territory and Tributary Lands*. Miami, Okla.: Press of the Miami Republican.

Potter, Parker B., Jr. (1994). *Public Archaeology in Annapolis: A Critical Approach to History in Maryland's Ancient City*. Washington, D.C.: Smithsonian Institution Press.

Potter, Parker B., Jr., and Mark P. Leone. (1987). "Archaeology in Public in Annapolis: Four Seasons, Six Sites, Seven Tours and 32,000 Visitors." *American Archaeology* 6:51–61.

Rafert, Stewart. (1996). *The Miami Indians of Indiana: A Persistent People*. Bloomington Indiana Historical Society.

Rose, Mark. (1979). *A Nineteenth Century Miami House on the Mississinewa*. Undergraduate honors thesis, Ball State University.

Ruedrich Kathryn. (In prep). *Miami Identity as Seen through the Ceramic Assemblage Recovered from a Historic Miami Farmstead Site*. Masters thesis, University of Idaho.

Shackel, Paul A, Paul Mullins, and Mark Warner. (1998). "Introduction: The Archaeology in Annapolis Project." In *Annapolis Pasts: Historical Archaeology in Annapolis, Maryland*, ed. Paul A. Shackel, Paul R. Mullins, and Mark S. Warner, pp. xv–xxxiii. Knoxville: University of Tennessee Press.

"Special Edition: Repatriation of American Indian Remains." (1992). *American Indian Culture and Research Journal* 16.

Stillwell, Larry N. (1990). *The Richardville/LaFontaine House and the Troyer Site: A Material Culture Comparison*. Masters thesis, Ball State University.

Swidler, Nina, Kurt Dongoske, Roger Anyon, and Alan Downer, eds. (1997). *Native Americans and Archaeologists: Stepping Stones to Common Ground*. Walnut Creek, Calif.: Altamira Press.

Warner, Mark S. (1998). *Food and the Negotiation of African-American Identities in Annapolis, Maryland and the Chesapeake*. Ph.D. dissertation, University of Virginia.

———. (2001a). "Collective Otherness:? African American and Indian Responses to White America." Paper presented: at the 66th annual meeting of the Society for American Archaeology, New Orleans.

———. (2001b). "Experiencing Ethnicity: The Interplay of Minority Identity and Material Culture." Paper presented at the 100th annual meeting of the American Anthropological Association, Washington, D.C.

Watkins, Joe. (2000). *Indigenous Archaeology: American Indian Values and Scientific Practice*. Walnut Creek, Calif.: Altamira Press.

Wepler, William. (1984). *Miami Occupation of the Upper Wabash Drainage: A Preliminary Study Unit*. Report #16. Muncie: Archaeological Resource Management Service, Ball State University.

Yoder, Stephen. (In prep). "Consumer Behavior among the Miami Tribe of Oklahoma." Masters thesis, University of Idaho.

CHAPTER 9

"The Burra"
Archaeology in a Small Community in South Australia

PETER J. BIRT

While we often tend to see the public virtues of archaeological work in rather abstract and idealistic (but nonetheless important) terms, in this chapter Peter Birt reminds us that archaeology can also have some very practical and worldly values. He describes the partnership that has developed between archaeology and a small Australian community, based primarily on the promotion of heritage tourism. The Burra community archaeology project depends on community support to achieve its scholarly aims. In turn, the town of Burra relies on archaeology to provide recognition and legitimization of its past as well as to provide significant economic gain.

Introduction

One thing that most archaeologists will likely agree on is that archaeology is important, and each will undoubtedly give a variety of reasons as to why, ranging from its academic value to its social and political relevance (see Renfrew and Bahn 1994:483–84; Johnson 1999:1; Hodder 1999:208). Unfortunately, it is probably difficult for the average person—whose tax dollars often support our research—to see archaeology in the same light. Essentially, archaeology's importance stems from one fact: the past is powerful (Johnson 1999:1). The power that the past has in modern politics and in people's minds is easily seen in nightly news services. Legislation to protect and conserve heritage, and the popularity of the past as seen through screen and television, demonstrate public interest in the past; but the past is not necessarily archaeology. Certainly, archaeology has an importance to indigenous issues in many parts of the world, playing a role in social issues like land claims and the repatriation of cultural material, but how much of this is seen by the general public as relevant to them? Much of the research undertaken by archaeologists, while having academic value, generates only passing interest within the discipline and totally escapes the attention of a wider audience. Public and community-based archaeological projects can help to redress this, and there does seem to be a greater awareness among archaeologists of working with and not just in communities. All archaeological projects can only benefit from this sort of inclusiveness, and it can also allow archaeology to achieve a real, if localized, importance.

This chapter is about academic archaeology working with interested community groups in the small rural South Australian town of Burra (fig. 9.1). Burra is a place where people think archaeology has importance, and

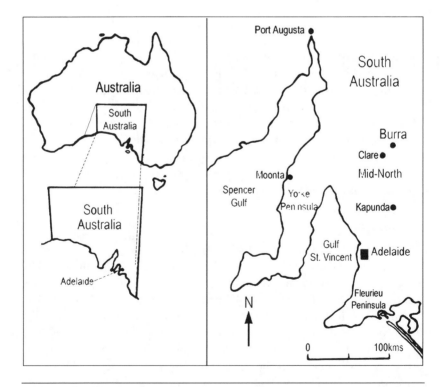

Fig. 9.1 The location of Burra in South Australia

they have put up the money to back this. It is not a big project in any sense, but it has been undertaken with the aim of generating both archaeological and community results. This paper is about an attitude toward research, rather than a community archaeology model for others to follow. The variety of individual community circumstances in different parts of the world would make such a model of little value, but we can bring an awareness of and consideration for local community interests to our research. The archaeological methods used in this research present nothing new or unusual, other than perhaps the sense of partnership in which the project operates. This project's academic and community partners share a commitment to the research; this in turn can generate tangible benefits to the community. It is often the small things that count when working with communities, like ensuring that information is given back, or even simply seeing to it that professionals like archaeologists are present; these can make a difference.

Burra lies nestled in a small valley, on the edge of the outback, 156 kilometers north of Adelaide in South Australia's mid-north region. The town is now reliant on rural industries and heritage tourism, but its early history was very different.

"The Burra": History and Heritage Tourism

Six years before the 1851 Victorian gold rush ignited the imaginations of so many around the world, the fledgling colony of South Australia was already in the grip of its own rush, but it was copper not gold that was responsible. The centerpiece of South Australia's first mineral boom was the South Australian Mining Association's (SAMA) Burra Burra mine, which opened in 1845 and was touted in the press as "the Monster Mine" and "the Eighth Wonder of the World" (Auhl 1986:73). "The Burra" encouraged immigration, brought valuable export earnings to the colony, and enriched its shareholders (Blainey 1981:112). In 1850 the mine had paid dividends to its shareholders of 800 percent (Auhl 1986:139), and by 1851 it directly employed 1,000 of the 35,302 males in South Australia ("Visit" 1851: May 3:2 and May 10:2; Colonial Secretary's Office 1851:189). Burra was a remarkable place, both in the public mind and in reality.

The mine was operated under the Cornish system: run by Cornish captains for most of its life and worked predominantly by Cornish miners. It is impossible to quantify, but the early accounts of the area strongly suggest a Cornish social and cultural dominance (Payton 1984:71; see Auhl 1983). Certainly, within the townships were to be found significant numbers of English, Scots, and Irish; Welsh smelters; and German smelters and miners, among others (Auhl 1986:86). The nearly invisible group in Burra's

European history, other than a handful of mentions in early accounts, are the Ngadjuri traditional owners (see Auhl 1983:20, 81–81).

The original company township of Kooringa, immediately south of the mine, was surveyed in early 1846 but was later joined by several government and private townships built to the north (fig. 9.2). These other townships, including Redruth and Aberdeen, both surveyed in 1849, lay on the boundaries of SAMA's property and were collectively known as "the Burra." This gave Burra its distinctive divided layout, but there was one other unofficial township. The Burra Creek dissected all these townships and in—not on—its banks were hundreds of dugout homes (Auhl 1986:124). In 1851, 1,800 of the 4,172 people living in the Burra had made their homes in the creek;

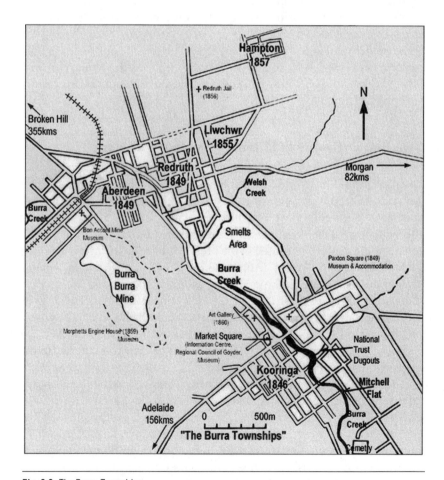

Fig. 9.2 The Burra Townships

most of them were miners and their families (Colonial Secretary's Office 1851:189). Largely ignored by officialdom and by SAMA, the creek provided rent-free homes for a large proportion of the workforce until 1851. By 1860 the creek was abandoned, mainly due to periodic flooding and the exodus to the Victorian gold rush between late 1851 and 1854, which had lessened the demand for housing in the town. The mine closed in 1877, but the town survived as a rural center, albeit in a much-reduced state.

Burra has been described as an "open air museum" (Linn et al. 1990:522), with many of its early domestic and mine buildings extant and often still in use, while areas of significant archaeological potential have remained relatively untouched (Auhl and Gilbert 1978:74; Lester et al. 1978:79–80). The importance of Burra's heritage was recognized officially from the early 1970s, with numerous individual listings on the Register of the National Estate and the South Australian Heritage Register, including a blanket listing of the whole town (Australian Heritage Commission 2002). The town has been innovative in dealing with its heritage, for example, producing the "first heritage study to be prepared in SA [South Australia]" in 1978 (King 1999:4; see Auhl and Gilbert 1978; Lester et al. 1978) and the development of the Burra Heritage Trail and the Burra Passport system for tourists in the 1980s (Drew 1988). The Australian Heritage Commission (2001:40–41) has used the town as a case study for its "effective commercial management systems" and "local government, tourism and community partnerships." The Burra Burra branch of the National Trust, a community-based volunteer organization, has been described as "the jewel in the crown" of the National Trust branches in South Australia (Jozeps, pers. comm. 2002; Wright 2001). The National Trust manages the town's heritage sites, as well as operating and maintaining the eleven-kilometers-long Burra Heritage Trail, which includes several locked sites and four small museums. The heritage trail is a self-drive and walking tour that includes the town's business precinct, the mine precinct, the Smelts, Hampton (an abandoned township), Redruth Gaol, Police Lockup, reconstructed miner's dugouts, and museums (fig. 9.3). Visitors access the heritage trail by purchasing a Burra Passport, a unique self-guided tour that includes a guidebook, museum entries, and a key to the locked sites.

Heritage is important to Burra and has been described as "the key to the area's ever-increasing tourist industry" (Linn et al. 1990:25). Just how important is hard to quantify as no comprehensive data has been collected, but one recent study estimated that 40,900 visitors spent just under $4.5 million annually in the town (Cegielski et al. 2001:40). Burra is now a town of around one thousand people reliant on rural industries, but with an important tourism component. Recent years have been tough in many Australian rural areas; a poor economy can threaten the survival of heritage places through neglect (King 1999:1). Burra is not immune to this, but tourism is probably

Fig. 9.3 A reconstructed miner's dugout on the heritage trail

the difference between Burra and similar rural towns that struggle to survive. It also means that many people in the community recognize the value of Burra's extant heritage and actively work to protect, conserve, and use it.

Burra's historic importance, extant heritage, and undoubted archaeological potential make it an attractive place to the researcher, but little archaeology had been undertaken prior to 1998 (see Bannear 1987, 1988, 1990; Bell 1990; Kostoglou 1988). Fortunately, one of the National Trust's objectives is the formation of "alliances with recognized authorities in archaeology, history and tourism" (Australian Heritage Commission 2001:40–41), which has directly led to the current project.

The Burra Community Archaeology Project

The Burra community archaeology project was instigated in 1998, when the National Trust approached Flinders University about having archaeological work undertaken at suspected dugout home sites in the Burra Creek. The result of this was a preliminary survey of dugout sites (Anson 1998), which in turn formed the basis for a more in-depth conservation study (McCarthy and Parkinson 1999). From the outset, Flinders University recognized the potential Burra held as a site for long-term research, and negotiations with the local community began. Groups within the community were canvassed, and the necessary money and in-kind support for an industry-based doctoral scholarship application was gained, largely through the efforts of Dr. Claire Smith. The commitment of this small community to what was, in essence, an academic project is remarkable and illustrates the recognition and importance of heritage to the town of Burra.

The progression of the project hinged on gaining the doctoral scholarship, which would ensure funding and bring a continuity that occasional research activity could not. The success of this application in 1999 has led to what is now the fifth year of a successful partnership between the National Trust of South Australia Burra Burra Branch, the Regional Council of Goyder, the Mid-North Regional Development Board, and Flinders University. Each of the partners has specific objectives, but there are a number of common community aims that archaeology can further, namely:

- promotion and marketing of heritage tourism;
- raising public awareness and appreciation of Burra's heritage;
- increasing public awareness in Burra of the role these community groups play;
- raising visitor numbers to Burra, consequently benefitting business and creating more jobs;
- and, not least, gaining specialist and "authentic" information on Burra's heritage.

Flinders University's aims are primarily academic, but they are not incompatible with those of the community. For the university Burra offers a research platform for postgraduate and honors level study and fieldwork training opportunities for undergraduates in one of South Australia's most historic towns. The community partners' commitment to having quality information about their heritage has meant that there have been no unrealistic expectations about the archaeological results, only interest in what has been found. The other outcomes have been more of a learning experience for all parties, as the project has explored the ways in which academic archaeology can affect these outcomes. This has not been a large-scale project to date, with only enough funding available to support one full-time student, although there has been invaluable research support from the community, including money and in-kind support like accommodation. Significant results have been achieved, but the project can be described as being near the end of the beginning and as ready to take the next steps forward.

Project Outcomes

The heart of this project is an academic one, but its soul resides in the local community, and it has returned results to all parties. The academic outcomes are easiest to evaluate, but many of the community's aims have at least been met in part. This is important, as the Burra project is not only a community archaeology program (see Start 1999 for an example), but it must also produce academic results for the project to work. Regular archaeological fieldwork has been undertaken in the town since 1998, producing theses, reports, interpretive material, conference presentations, an exhibition, field experience for undergraduates, media exposure, and public archaeology. There is nothing unusual in any of this, other than the equal weight given to both academic and community results.

Academic Outcomes

From the project's inception the main research focus has been on the collapsed miners' dugouts in the banks of the Burra Creek, but other aspects of Burra's social and industrial past have also been included. The dugouts have provided a good opportunity for archaeology to add to both the story of European settlement in South Australia and to the tourist experience in Burra. Three twentieth-century reconstructed dugouts form one stop on the heritage trail (see fig. 9.3), but only one of these has recently provided evidence that it was probably based on an original feature (Birt 2002:7). Other than a few early accounts, paintings, and reminiscences (see Auhl 1986: chapter 12), the only other evidence for dugouts is subsurface. The original dugouts were collapsed by flood and time, and all that remains are multiple depressions in the creek banks at a few locations relatively untouched by subsequent development.

One of these locations is Mitchell Flat, about five hundred meters southeast of the town's center, which has been the main focus for fieldwork (see fig. 9.2). Originally surveyed in 1998 (Anson 1998), the area has now been the subject of four excavation seasons, as part of this author's doctoral research, and has provided the community with two interim reports (Birt 2001, 2002). There are at least fourteen large depressions, in a 250-meter section of the Burra Creek's eastern bank at Mitchell Flat, three of which have now been investigated. Each has contained evidence of mid-nineteenth century European occupation, and each has ample evidence of the floods that effectively destroyed the creek settlement. The dugouts were clay houses in a clay creek bank, which were destroyed by flooding. Remaining evidence is dependent on a dugout's position within the creek, the severity of the flood event that collapsed it, and whether or not it was occupied at the time of the collapse (Birt 2001:46). Of the three excavated depressions, one had literally been gutted, with little occupational evidence remaining; one contained considerable structural remains, but inconclusive amounts of material culture; while the third has ample evidence of both (fig. 9.4; Birt 2001:46–57).

Burra's collapsed dugouts are an ideal archaeological project, being an unusual and significant feature of colonial South Australian settlement, the

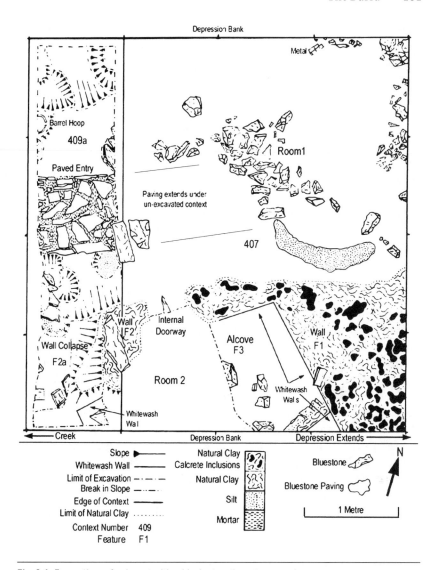

Fig. 9.4 Excavations of a dugout with mid-nineteenth century remains

remains of which are subsurface. Spatially, the location of the Burra's dugouts, dissecting both the company and other townships, says much about expediency and something about the power relationships in the settlement. Burra's dugouts were improvised working-class housing, but the archaeological and documentary evidence suggests that they were homes, not hovels: used for years and made as comfortable as possible (Birt

2001:46–57). Dugouts were not unusual features of nineteenth-century European settlement, being used in many places where there was a need for "quick fix" housing and where the environment was suitable. Burra was possibly unique, simply for the scale and longevity of dugout use. They are also features on which little archaeological work seems to have been undertaken (see Hardesty 1988:84–86; Ziegler 2001:98–132 for exceptions). Burra's dugouts are an appropriate focus for historical archaeology, speaking to issues ranging from class, the growth of a labor movement and the relationships to the dominant capitalist ethos, to simple adaptation and expediency (Leone and Potter 1988; Karskens and Thorp 1992; Little 1994; Orser 1996; Delle et al. 2000). The archaeological results will also affect the future interpretation and presentation of the National Trust's dugouts, while Mitchell Flat could be added to the heritage trail using the archaeological results to interpret an otherwise bare creek bank.

The dugouts remain the primary project focus, but other research has been conducted in the town and has produced three honors theses to date. The first of these dealt with the commercial use of archaeology, using Burra as the case study (Saeki 1998). The second thesis was a direct result of the 1998 survey, with one member of the undergraduate field team taking on one of the town's other projects. This was a study of the small 1857 abandoned township of Hampton on Burra's northern edge, focusing on the built environment and the role of ideology in the creation of a colonial social order (Birt 1999). The third was an industrial study of the remains of the smelting works (Wood 2001), which extended research on this site from an original survey undertaken in 1988 (Bannear 1988). Both the Hampton and smeltery sites are on the heritage trail and are areas where additional information can improve future interpretation (see fig. 9.2).

One of the university's aims was to use Burra for student training, and this has been a feature of the fieldwork; the site has been used for field schools in 1998 and 2000, providing volunteer fieldwork opportunities for students. Apart from the obvious training advantages that fieldwork offers, the influx of twenty or more university personnel and students for periods of up to two weeks has in itself had an effect on a town of Burra's size, especially the hospitality sector. This is also the closest archaeology has come to fulfilling the partners' aim of increased visitor numbers. The field schools have also directly benefited the project by focusing student interest on Burra, which has resulted in two of the three completed honors theses.

Community Outcomes

The community aims have equal weight with the academic aims, and the archaeologists have sought to return something to the town and to include visitors whenever possible. This is important in any project that is partly funded by communities, who wish to see some return for their investment. Burra's support of archaeological research is a direct investment in their heritage. The archaeology has produced valuable information for the community, which helps legitimate the tourism product in Burra and has in itself provided an authentic experience for visitors. What constitutes *authenticity* is problematic, but tourist surveys show that at least the perception of authenticity is important to visitors (Cegielski et al. 2001:43), and this is reinforced by the project's public outcomes. Results have included public archaeology and schools programs, an archaeology exhibition, a website, and other published material.

Public Archaeology

All of the archaeological fieldwork undertaken in Burra has welcomed public visitation, with dedicated guides or members of the field crew available to interpret the site. In an urban area this second approach would be a major distraction, but here visitor numbers at any given time are low and consist mostly of couples and small groups touring in their own vehicles. Promotion of the archaeology has mainly been undertaken by the Burra Visitors Center, which opens seven days a week and informs visitors of our presence when they pick up their Burra Passport key. Sites like Mitchell Flat can be discouraging, with most of the archaeological excavations happening in the banks of the creek below eye level, with long grass, no paths, and the odd brown snake during the warmer months. It is only the very interested who generally take this on, but some people have stayed for hours, becoming involved in the excavation. At the very least people get a one-on-one conversation with one of the team, which makes for an intimate introduction to archaeology. Visitors to the site have included both tourists and locals, but as a community-based project, it was felt that something more proactive in attracting local visitation was needed.

One of the easiest ways for archaeologists to include a community in a project is through local schools, enabling us to reach a significant proportion of the community at a more personal level than most other forms of communication allow. The involvement of schools in archaeological projects is not new (see Start 1999:56–58; Kostoglou 1988), but in South Australia there seems to be a more systematic approach to how we involve schools and other community groups. This has certainly been the case at Flinders University, with many of the projects conducted in recent years incorporating a public and community component. Arising out of this background has been the development of a schools education program, written by two postgraduate students, Jody Steele and Tim Owen. The program is aimed at children aged from five to fourteen and is based on worksheets and activities (Owen and Steele 2001). The program is flexible, but it has worked best when children have an introductory session in class, followed by a session on the archaeological site. Not everything in the book will work for all ages, and teaching must be tailored to each class. This can be an interesting exercise in itself, talking to twelve-year-olds in the morning and then having to keep six-year-olds engaged in the afternoon.

In April 2001 Burra was fortunate to have been one of the trial projects for the schools program, teaching all of the Burra Community School's primary classes (more than 140 K–7 children) and an impromptu on-site session with a busload of children from Peterborough, north of Burra. Each group had a classroom introductory session, followed by one to two hours at Mitchell Flat. This was very much a hands-on experience for the children, one that allowed them to participate in the archaeology to varying degrees—depending on age—as well as teaching them about their local heritage and archaeology generally (fig. 9.5). The involvement of local schools is also an effective and enjoyable way of including a large proportion of the community within the project, since for every child we teach, we also reach parents and friends and provide a focus for the local media. Inclusion is an important aspect of community archaeology, and it is im-

Fig. 9.5 A school group visits the heritage area

portant that local people retain a sense of ownership and of participation in what happens in their "place" (Nethery 1993:101).

One of the key elements of this project is the sense of collaboration in which it has occurred, with all parties working well together and helping to shape the direction in which it moves. This was obvious when putting together an exhibition called "Fragments of the Past" (Smith et al. 2000b), based on the 1998 survey, the Hampton research, the first season's excavation, and the National Trust's archival collection. The exhibition was shown in Burra in May and June 2000 and later at the Flinders Art Museum in Adelaide. This exhibition was a National Trust idea, funded mostly by the Mid-North Regional Development Board and put together by university personnel. Other returns to the community have included a public lecture in March 2000, the presentation of the interim excavation report to the National Trust in July 2001 (Birt 2001), a website of the archaeology (Smith et al. 2000a), interpretive brochures on Hampton and the dugouts, and media coverage of the exhibition and the fieldwork. Media exposure is important, but it has proved difficult convincing Adelaide's media to make the two-hour trip. Nevertheless, Burra's archaeology has proven popular with the local regional media, and it has received air time on Adelaide radio and has been a featured story on *Postcards*, a popular television tourism program in South Australia. The local media attention has been important in fulfilling one of the partners' aims by informing the region's residents of the active role played by the project's community partners. All of these things help build community awareness of their heritage, but there are other valuable if less tangible contributions that we as archaeologists make in helping create a credible past.

Only a minority within the community ever sees many of the outcomes mentioned above, but one thing that archaeologists unwittingly do is raise community awareness of local heritage simply by our presence. It is manifested in the recognition and the "g'day" that you get on entering a local hotel, quickly followed by "What are you doing this time?" and "Found anything interesting yet?" Local history is something that is often taken for granted, something that may surround people without them ever really realizing its significance. In Burra this has been the case, with a core of dedicated people being fully aware of the town's past, but with others not really caring. In a small town like Burra, having archaeologists actively and regularly at work helps to put heritage into people's minds. It is something that also probably affects tourist perceptions, helping to build that sense of authenticity. The presence of archaeologists implies that there is something important here, something that is yet to be revealed, and something that is real. It does not matter that the reality of archaeological fieldwork is not usually quite this mysterious; it positively influences peoples' attitudes to their visit or makes local residents think about their area. One problem that small communities like Burra face is that of gaining both the financial support and also the people willing to give their time to protect, maintain, and use their past. Archaeology in Burra has not brought a rush of volunteers to the National Trust, but it has made the local community more aware and has fulfilled one of the partners' aims in having their roles within the community highlighted.

Project Limitations and Future Directions

A range of both academic and community results have been achieved, but the full potential of this project is yet to be realized. Funding has been available to undertake the archaeology, but not to help the community fully exploit the archaeological results. This is the next step, with the potential to rethink the interpretation and presentation of the National Trust's reconstructed dugouts, of Hampton, of the smelteries, and of adding at least the Mitchell Flat site to the heritage trail. This raises a new set of issues, including how to interpret a site where the visual component is fragile and entirely subsurface, and how to make it engaging.

Many potential research projects remain, including sites central to early Burra. Some, like the mine, have yet to be investigated archaeologically, while the area's indigenous past is all but invisible. There is scope to keep research students busy for years and allow the field schools and public archaeology to be developed further. The most obvious academic outcomes are the theses and the information generated, but a range of public literature will also be produced. Monographs on the township of Hampton, the Burra dugouts, and the smelteries are planned and will be written for the public in a low-cost format. Additional brochures and improved versions of the ones already produced are another relatively easy way to provide public interpretation that only requires a photocopier to produce.

Discussion

The Burra community archaeology project is not a model for long-term relationships between academic archaeology and small communities, but the positive experience of the last four years does provide some useful guides. Information is the single most important thing that archaeology produces, and it should be disseminated by publication, at conferences, and through public archaeology programs. More importantly, this information must also be returned to the communities if it is to be of any real use. In essence it is a matter of thinking through the research issues and beyond to the community implications. What does a place or site mean to a community? Talk to the interested community bodies in an area, not only to see how they can help the project, but also what results they would like to achieve. Be realistic when discussing what can and cannot be done, because most people will not expect archaeology to change their world. It takes time to build effective community networks and effort to maintain them, and they should not be taken lightly. Undoubtedly, there are many other archaeological projects around the world working in similar ways; these will be able to identify with our experience in Burra and add new insights themselves. Projects like the one occurring in Burra are important academically, but they can also have a significant contemporary importance to the communities in which they occur. This importance stems from consideration for and inclusion of the communities that host us.

Burra acknowledges its past and uses it to bring a significant economic input into the town. In Burra we have been able to meet some of the community's aims, including helping to promote the town, raising public awareness of the town's heritage locally and beyond, generating information about Burra's past, and disseminating this in various ways. From greater community awareness will hopefully flow greater support that will translate into more resources and volunteers to help maintain, operate, and improve the product that Burra has. The academic aims of this project are being met, with Burra's heritage providing a firm foundation upon which archaeological research builds. For the community this is an additive role in an already recognized past. The outcomes we have achieved in Burra sometimes seem small, but they are nevertheless important and appreciated by the local community. These outcomes translate into a past that this community can further use, while meeting the demands of academic research.

Acknowledgments

As always thanks must go to the National Trust of South Australia Burra Burra Branch, the Regional Council of Goyder, and the Mid-North Regional Development Board for their continued support. Special thanks to Maureen and Barry Wright of the trust, John Brak of the council, and Craig Wilson of the development board; to my supervisors at Flinders University, Dr. Claire Smith, Dr. Mark Staniforth, and Dr. Heather Burke; to my fellow students Jody Steele and Tim Owen, without whom we would have achieved half as much and had half the fun; to Catherine Hunt, Katrina Stankowski, Sally May, Julie Ford, Chris Langeluddecke, Donna Flood, Cass Philoppou, Matt Shlitz, Gary Jackson, and all the other volunteers who have helped; and finally, thanks to Paul Shackel and Erve Chambers for the opportunity to present this project to a wider audience.

References

Anson, Timothy. (1998). *Burra Dugouts Heritage Site: Survey and Assessment.* The Flinders University of South Australia, Adelaide. Submitted to the National Trust of South Australia, Burra, Burra Branch and the Regional Council of Goyder.

Auhl, Ian. (1986). *The Story of the Monster Mine: The Burra Burra Mine and Its Townships 1845–1877.* Hawthorndene, South Australia: Investigator Press.

Auhl, Ian, ed. (1983). *Burra-Burra Reminiscences of the Burra Mine and Its Townships.* Hawthorndene, South Australia: Investigator Press.

Auhl, Ian, and S. Gilbert. (1978). *Burra Conservation Study: Historic Buildings and Areas Survey.* Submitted to District Council of Burra, Burra; the Department of Housing, Urban and Regional Affairs; the Department for the Environment and the National Trust. Burra: National Trust Burra.

Australian Heritage Commission and the Department of Industry, Science and Resources. (2001). *Successful Tourism at Heritage Places: A Guide for Tourism Operators, Heritage Managers and Communities.* Canberra: Pirie Printers.

————. (2002). Website, Register of the National Estate and SA Heritage Register. http://www. heritage.gov.au/aphi/search.html. Accessed 10 August, 2003.

Bannear, David. (1987). *Burra Waterworks.* Submitted to the History Trust of South Australia.

————. (1988). *Report of a Preliminary Survey of the Bushmen's Rest Hotel, Burra.* Submitted to the SA State Heritage Branch.

————. (1990). *The Burra Smelting Works, A Study of Its History and Archaeology.* Submitted to the District Council of Burra, Burra.

Bell, Peter. (1990). "Continuity in Australian Timber Domestic Building: An Early Cottage at Burra." *Australian Historical Archaeology* 8:3–12.

Birt, Peter. (1999). *A 'Less Favoured' Place: Ideology and Social Order in the Built Environment of the Township of Hampton, Burra, South Australia.* Unpublished honors dissertation. Adelaide, Australia: Department of Archaeology, Flinders University.

————. (2001). *Whitewash and Red Clay: The Archaeology of the Burra Creek Miner's Dugouts.* Flinders University, Adelaide, Australia. Submitted to Heritage South Australia, the National Trust of South Australia Burra, Burra Branch, the Regional Council of Goyder, and the Mid-North Regional Development Board. Burra: National Trust.

————. (2002). *Burra Creek Dugout Survey: A Walking Survey of Miner's Dugout Sites on the Burra Creek, Burra, South Australia.* Submitted to the National Trust of South Australia Burra Burra Branch, the Regional Council of Goyder, and the Mid-North Regional Development Board. Burra: National Trust.

Blainey, Geoffery. (1981). *The Rush That Never Ended: A History of Australian Mining.* Carlton, Victoria: Melbourne University Press.

Cegielski, Michele, Ben Janeczko, Trevor Mules, and Josette Wells. (2001). *Economic Value of Tourism to Places of Cultural Heritage Significance: A Case Study of Three Towns with Mining Heritage.* University of Canberra, Australia. Submitted to the Cooperative Research Center for Sustainable Tourism and the Australian Heritage Commission, University of Canberra Tourism Program.

Colonial Secretary's Office. (1851). Census Abstract. *South Australian Government Gazette No. 13.* Adelaide, South Australia (March 20) 189.

Delle, James, Stephen Mrowzowski, and Robert Paynter. (2000). "Introduction." In *Lines That Divide: Historical Archaeologies of Race, Class, and Gender,* ed. J. Delle, S. Mrowzowski, and R. Paynter, pp. xi–xxxi. Knoxville, Tenn.: The University of Tennessee Press.

Drew, G. J. (1988). *Discovering Historic Burra: South Australia.* Adelaide, South Australia: National Trust, Burra Mine Museum and Department of Mines and Energy.

Hardesty, Donald L. (1988). *The Archaeology of Mining and Miners: A View from the Silver State.* Special Publication Series No. 6. The Society for Historical Archaeology.

Hodder, Ian. (1999). *The Archaeological Process: An Introduction.* Oxford: Blackwell.

Johnson, Mathew. (1999). *Archaeological Theory: An Introduction.* Oxford: Blackwell.

Jozeps, Rainer. (2002). Personal communication with Rainer Jozeps, Director, National Trust of South Australia, e-mail, April 29.

Karskens, Grace, and Wendy Thorp. (1992). "History and Archaeology in Sydney: Towards Integration and Interpretation." *Journal of the Royal Australian Historical Society* 78:52–75.

King, Peter. (1999). Revitalising Rural Regions: New Opportunities through Heritage, Disappearing Rural Heritage—A Case for Concern. *Regional Australia Summit.* www.holg.gov.au/regional/summit/index.htm. Accessed 10 August 2003.

Kostoglou, Parry. (1988). *The Ludgvan Street Bypass Archaeological Survey.* Submitted to the Burra Branch of the National Trust and the State Heritage Branch.

Leone, Mark, and Parker Potter, Jr. (1988). "Introduction: Issues in Historical Archaeology." In *The Recovery of Meaning: Historical Archaeology in the Eastern United States,* ed. M. Leone, and P. Potter, Jr., pp. 1–22. Washington, D.C.: Smithsonian Institution Press.

Lester, Alf, Howard Murton, and Stephen Anders. (1978). *Burra Conservation Study.* Adelaid: Lester Firth and Murton. Submitted to District Council of Burra, Burra; the Department of

Housing, Urban and Regional Affairs; the Department for the Environment; and the National Trust. Burra: National Trust Burra Branch.

Linn, R., J. Linn, C. Lane, J. Gratton, and A. Tuttle. (1990). *Heritage of Eight Lower North Towns.* Adelaide: South Australian Department of Environment and Planning.

Little, Barbara. (1994). "People with History: An Update on Historical Archaeology in the United States." *Journal of Archaeological Method and Theory* 1, no. 1:5–40.

McCarthy, Justin, and Charles Parkinson. (1999). *Burra Creek Dwellers Dugout Conservation Study.* Adelaide: Austral Archaeology. Submitted to the Regional Council of Goyder and the Burra Branch of the National Trust of Australia (SA). Burra: National Trust Burra Branch.

Nethery, B. (1993). "Built Heritage, Tourism and the Management Expectations." *Embracing Interpretation in the Year of Indigenous Peoples.* Proceedings of the 1993 National Conference of the Interpretation Australia Association, pp. 97–107.

Orser, Charles. Jr. (1996). *A Historical Archaeology of the Modern World.* New York: Plenum Press.

Owen, Timothy, and Jody Steele. (2001). *Digging Up the Past: Archaeology for Kids.* Adelaide: Southern Archaeology.

Payton, Phillip. (1984). *The Cornish Miner in Australia.* Kernow, U.K.: Dyllansow Truran.

Renfrew, Colin, and Paul Bahn. (1994). *Archaeology: Theories, Methods, and Practice.* London: Thames and Hudson.

Saeki, Paul. (1998). *The Business of Archaeology: A Production and Value Added Approach.* Unpublished honors dissertation. Adelaide: Department of Archaeology, Flinders University.

Smith, Claire, Peter Birt, Jody Steele, and Timothy Owen. (2000a). *Burra Web Site.* http://wwwehlt.flinders.edu.au/archaeology/*Smith/burraweb/projectfront.htm. Accessed 10 August 2003.

Smith, Claire, Peter Birt, Paul Saeki, and Cherrie De Leiuen. (2000b). *Fragments of the Past: An Exhibition of Historical Archaeology from Burra 1845–1877.* Exhibition Catalogue, Burra Community Archaeology Project, Bedford Park: Flinders Press.

Start, David. (1999). "Community Archaeology: Bringing It Back to Local Communities." In *Managing Historic Sites and Buildings: Reconciling Presentation and Preservation*, ed. G. Chitty and D. Barker, pp. 49–59. London: Routledge.

"Visit to the Burra Burra Mines and the Great Smelting Works in South Australia." (1851). *Sydney Morning Herald*, May 3:2;`May 10:2; May 17:2.

Wood, Ian. (2001). *The Burra Smelting Works, South Australia.* Unpublished honors dissertation. Adelaide: Department of Archaeology, Flinders University.

Wright, Maureen. (2001). Chairman's Report. Annual General Meeting and Reports. Burra: National Trust of South Australia, Burra Branch.

Ziegler, Robert J. (2001). "Archaeological Investigations." In *Historical Archaeology at Locality 6 of the Fort Ellsworth Site (14EW26) Kanopolis Lake, Ellsworth County, Kansas*, ed. R. J. Ziegler, pp. 75–132. Kansas City: U.S. Army Corps of Engineers, Kansas City District.

CHAPTER 10

Archaeological Interpretation and the Irish Diasporic Community

CHARLES E. ORSER, JR.

In this discussion of his long-term involvement with public archaeology in Ireland, Charles Orser, Jr., challenges us to reconsider the way we think about descendant communities. While such communities are often identified in relation to their contemporary proximity to an archaeological site, Orser describes a case in which strikingly different reactions to the interpretation of local history are apparent between long-term residents and visitors of Irish descent. Understanding the contemporary cultural situations of both the local and the diasporic Irish communities has helped Orser to appreciate the rationale beneath these different views of regional history, as well as to negotiate his own place in the interpretation of Irish history.

Introduction

Within recent years, archaeologists have come to understand, often in vivid detail, that their field of study is not simply about the past. Often motivated by the wishes of descendant communities, archaeologists have been forced to confront the often-complex social realities of today's world and have had to admit, sometimes quite reluctantly, that archaeologists do not own history. Archaeologists now acknowledge that men and women who are not trained in the discipline may be intensely interested both in the archaeologists' findings and in the nature and tenor of their interpretations, even though these same individuals may lack any precise knowledge of archaeological practice.

Archaeologists conducting research in prehistoric North America were some of the first scholars to confront the realities of the present, as Native American spokespersons stressed their right to have a voice in the telling of their histories and traditions. The many encounters between non-Native American archaeologists and nonarchaeologist Native Americans have run the gamut from mutual respect and cooperation (e.g., McDonald et al. 1991) to fierce conflict, perhaps best exemplified in the late 1990s by the discovery of the controversial "Kennewick Man" (e.g., Thomas 2000). Though some archaeologists continue to express racist opinions against Native Americans (Custer 2001:21), most American archaeologists have come to accept that they have much to learn by working in concert with descendant communities. The many archaeologists who have become convinced of this reality are experimenting with innovative methods to promote cooperation and mutual learning (e.g., Biolsi and Zimmerman 1997; Klesert and Downer 1990; Swidler et al. 1997; Watkins 2000).

Nowhere is the interplay between the archaeological past and the present greater than in the archaeology of recent history. Historical archaeologists, because they examine the cultural and historical experiences of the most recent centuries, usually find it impossible to hide behind the veil of antiquity, because the sites and people they study are often direct ancestors of men and women who are identifiable today. In the United States, for example, many African Americans have been justifiably vocal about acquiring the right to tell their own histories in their own ways, and many have sought to interact with archaeologists who are attempting to interpret their past. The excavation of the African Burial Ground in New York City provides an especially enlightening example of this desire and the realities that archaeologists must now confront (Harrington 1993; LaRoche and Blakey 1997).

Historical archaeologists often find themselves attempting to juggle the perceived needs of the archaeological discipline and the stated wishes of communities who may have little or no interest in the stories archaeologists wish to tell one another. Some members of the community may believe that the jargon of archaeological science and the often narrow confines of scholarship have little or no real use in their daily lives. Others who are more interested in the past may wish to see scholarship reflect history on their terms. When forced to emerge from behind the shadow of "objective science," historical archaeologists often find themselves confronting the complex realities of modern life in many of the same ways as cultural anthropologists. My research in the Republic of Ireland provides a useful case study of the realities of contemporary archaeological interpretation, in this instance made even more difficult than usual by the presence of a diasporic community of men and women who reside at great distances from one another.

A Reflexive Background

My introduction to the rigors of diasporic research was anticipated by twelve years of research on African-American slavery and freedom, aided by three additional years investigating Palmares, the infamous, seventeenth-century maroon kingdom in northeast Brazil. This program of research convinced me that historical archaeologists, where possible, must collaborate with interested members of descendant communities.

Palmares was one of the most important maroon communities in the New World, and today it holds a central place in the ideology of the Black power movement in Brazil. Many Brazilians view its final leader, Zumbi, as a national culture hero (Anderson 1996; Funari 1999; Orser 1996a:41–55; Orser and Funari 2001; Schwartz 1992). When conducting research on this significant place—and especially when excavating what many perceive as its sacred soil—archaeologists find it virtually impossible to ignore the reverence most African Brazilians feel for Zumbi. Their idealized image of Zumbi, as steadfast rebel leader, constitutes an integral component of their conceptualization of Palmares as a resilient symbol of resistant power. Many men and women in today's Brazil quite simply do not accept that Palmares died when the Portuguese destroyed its buildings and stockades in 1694. They believe, on the contrary, that Palmares lives, and that its very existence provides a significant vector of self-identification.

My experiences in Brazil led me to understand with clarity that historical archaeology can never be truly disengaged from the present. If historical archaeology is practiced with conviction, it should illuminate the historical circumstances of the modern world (however defined) and should seek to link past and present. It should in fact become a "modern-world archaeology."

My commitment to the construction of an overtly modern-world archaeology that exists within yet apart from the often-detached world of historical archaeology stems from my firm belief in the power of archaeology to inform contemporary history. Modern-world archaeologists do not simply examine the past; they attempt to explain the condition of the world on both global and local scales. They seek to use archaeology to interpret the historical roots of inequality in all its myriad forms. Such an analysis can be pursued anywhere in the world, including nineteenth-century rural Ireland.

I have been reading about Ireland since the late 1960s, but since beginning a long-term research program there in 1993, I have replaced my superficial understanding with a more nuanced conceptualization of the many complexities Ireland presents to the modern-world archaeologist. One of my most valuable discoveries has been the realization that to provide truly meaningful interpretations of early-nineteenth-century rural life—my temporal focus—one must fully acknowledge the diasporic history of modern Ireland. The historical reality of the diaspora means that the archaeology of early-nineteenth-century Ireland presents challenges that extend beyond making connections with a single resident community. At a minimum, it involves the linking of two disparate communities, composed of at least two cohorts of individuals: those who were born in and still live in Ireland, and those who were born and still live outside Ireland, but who still self-identify in some fashion as Irish. Members of both communities believe intensely that they have a personal stake in the telling of Irish history.

Diasporic Ireland

According to at least one writer, "Ireland" is synonymous with "diaspora": "Ireland is a diaspora, and as such is both a real place and a remembered place" (O'Toole 1999:12). History confirms that the island has experienced numerous waves of in- and out-migration. Within the most recent centuries, its people have sought to flee religious persecution, to escape military assault, and to avoid the oppression of unfair, impoverishing agricultural arrangements. Others simply wished to find a better life in another place (see Akenson 2000; Allen 1994; Collins 1990; Ellis 1988; O'Callaghan 2000). At the end of the Great Starvation (variously also called the Great Hunger, the Great Famine, or the Irish Potato Famine), Ireland's population was reduced from about 8 million to about 6.5 million (Kinealy 1995:295). Some scholars have considered the steady population drain from 1850 until about 1999 as "the Famine's most important legacy" (Ó Gráda 1989:69). So important is the idea of "leaving" that the Irish have practically developed a "culture of exile" (Miller 1985:102).

Scholars who have studied traveling in relation to identity formation acknowledge that self- and group-sustaining identities can be created during the journey itself, as individuals renegotiate their conceptualization of their homeland and their place within it (Leed 1991). An aspect of ritual death accompanies the leaving of one's ancestral home, particularly for those who have been forcibly removed or who are fleeing racial and ethnic persecution. Even so, travelers also experience the effects of entering a new place, composed of unfamiliar albeit intriguing natural and social landscapes. The act of belonging to a diaspora is an identity-forming process, one that serves to link the homeland with the home (Cornwell and Stoddard 2001:7). In many cases the diaspora is composed of many journeys throughout various parts of the world, and a confluence of narratives creates both an individual and a collective diasporic memory (Brah 1996:183).

Ireland has a prominent place in the history of the world's great diasporas because of its long association with emigration (Bielenberg 2000), and studies show that emigrant Irish men and women settled in every continent in the world. Thousands went to the United States, where today the label Irish American is an accepted identity (Walter 2001:9). Contemporary Americans who self-identify themselves as having Irish ancestry number around 44 million people.

Negotiating the Irish Diaspora

Historical archaeologists who wish to conduct research in the Republic of Ireland must understand that many members of the Irish diasporic community are deeply interested in their research. Any modern-world archaeology conducted in Ireland is thus inherently diasporic in character, if perhaps not in explicit design, because it is impossible to delink the Irish in Ireland from those individuals of Irish ancestry who live throughout the world. Whereas descendants of the African diaspora may find it difficult or even impossible to trace their direct line of descent because of the disruptive horrors of capture and transshipment, many diasporic Irish can not only identify their direct ancestors, in many cases they can travel to the precise location from which their family was dispossessed.[1]

American historical archaeologists concentrating on the Irish nineteenth century face potential pitfalls that may not be readily apparent. For example, even the focus of my research contains potential controversy because I am investigating the early nineteenth century, a period of history that I have studied throughout my professional career. I have concentrated on rural townlands in north County Roscommon that were occupied in the years immediately preceding the Great Famine of the 1840s. Even this apparently innocuous statement may be contentious because the term *Great Famine* is fraught with political meaning and implication. The famine still matters today in profound and important ways to many men and women in Ireland, the United States, Canada, and elsewhere, just as Palmares remains vitally significant to many Brazilians. Whereas many people commonly refer to the horrors of the late 1840s as the "Great Potato Famine" or the "Irish Potato Famine," others note that many of the people directly affected by it referred to it as "the Great Hunger" (*An Gorta Mór*, in Irish). Other men and women refer to it as "the Great Starvation," while some interpreters term it "the Irish Holocaust" (see Daly 1996; Davis 1997; Metress and Rajner 1996). Attempts to mandate the teaching of the Irish famine in the public schools of California, Illinois, and New York—alongside the mid-twentieth-century Holocaust in Europe—have often devolved into hotly contested political and ideological battles. Those opposed to teaching the Irish famine as genocide argue that the Nazis consciously set out to murder millions of people in Europe, whereas a naturally occurring crop fungus initially caused the famine. Those individuals in favor of teaching the Irish famine as genocide counter that the British did little or nothing to prevent the human tragedy. A more poetic way of framing this last argument is: "The Almighty, indeed, sent the potato blight, but the English created the famine" (Mitchel 1868:596).

One's interpretation of the 1840s—and even the words one employs to describe the period—thus depends upon whether one chooses to perceive the starvation of the Irish people as having been ultimately caused by one of three oft-cited reasons: (1) the biology of the potato blight and the devastating loss of the crop, on which millions of families depended; (2) God's punishment for the imprudence and ignorance of the rural Irish for relying largely on one food crop and for the overpopulation that accompanied their Roman Catholic beliefs; or (3) the conscious, hard-hearted actions of the British government to starve and deplete a population they viewed as racially and culturally inferior (see, e.g., Bourke 1993; Mokyr 1985). Even the numbers of famine dead range wildly from 500,000 to 1.5 million. The lower number suggests that the devastation was bad but not total, whereas the second number proposes that the famine was truly horrendous in its proportions. As a corollary, historians variously argue that the famine was a turning point in Irish history (because it affected the nation so profoundly), a turning point in world history (because of the worldwide Irish diaspora), or that it was terrible but not entirely devastating (because the nation's people were able to rebuild and eventually even to prosper) (see, e.g., Davis 1997; Morash and Hayes 1996; Cullen 2001).

Much of the continuing controversy over the Irish famine undoubtedly results from the ongoing conflict in Northern Ireland. It is thus not difficult, when viewed from this perspective, to perceive the Great Hunger as a prelude to the early-twentieth-century partition of the island and the lasting British presence in the north. The British colonization of Ireland began in the twelfth century, and the events of today—like those of the 1840s—can be construed as the historical consequences of colonialism (Allen 1994; Collins 1990; Howe 2000; Ó Ceallaigh 1998). As a result of this still-unfolding legacy, the archaeological interpreter of the early nineteenth century must be mindful of the reality that many political parties today are jostling for partial or total control of the island, in a contest that is undeniably real. Not only are Republicans and Unionists in conflict, so are various offshoots of each, ranging from individuals who believe in the continuation of the armed struggle to those who argue for a constitutional solution

(O'Brien 1999). The research locale reported upon here—though situated about thirty-two kilometers from the northern border—was part of the British Empire in the early nineteenth century.

Adding the diasporic Irish to the contemporary equation increases the complexities of community-sensitive archaeological interpretation. The descendant community encompasses a global cohort of thousands of people who were forcibly evicted from their homes as a direct result of landlord power. Many of these men and women find themselves living in North America and elsewhere simply because their ancestors were dispossessed in Ireland. Many diasporic Irish thus on some level may empathize with exiled deportees. Many Irish Americans, for example, can be described as "inhabitants not just of a geographical country but of a country of the mind" (Heaney 1980:132). Personal experience indicates that even men and women who may consider themselves to be political conservatives at home can hold radical, anti-imperialist views when considering Ireland.

The Context and Constituents of Ballykilcline

In 1998, after four years of fieldwork at two nearby townlands, I instituted a five-year study of Ballykilcline, a townland[2] in north County Roscommon (fig. 10.1). Roscommon is one of five counties in the province of Connacht, the westernmost and traditionally the poorest part of Ireland. In the early 1840s, 935,448 people lived in the Irish countryside, most of them as rural tenant farmers. Of this number, 54 percent rented fewer than ten acres (4.05 ha) of farmland, and 34 percent rented less than five acres (2.02 ha) (Bourke 1993:79). Another 650,552 individuals were landless laborers. Folklorists have shown that for generations the residents of the island's more than 62,000 nineteenth-century townlands faithfully observed their seasonal cycle of festivals and agricultural observances (Danaher 1972; Ó hAllmhuráin 1999: 24). Many of these celebrations—along with many of their agricultural practices—promoted townland cohesion and cooperation (O'Dowd 1981). At the same time, however, many tenant farmers were also engaged in an ongoing struggle over control of the land.

As with most tenant farming areas, access to land in Ireland was rooted in a social hierarchy. The ranked system that was created has been termed the *agricultural ladder* in the United States (Spillman 1919), but the term applies to any setting that includes tenant farmers. The utility of the concept holds even in those sociohistorical situations in which climbing the ladder was not a realistic option for those at or near the bottom. In a familiar pattern, landlords always occupied the top of the ladder, and in Ireland, farmers and cottiers held lower positions. *Cottiers* were families who rented less than five acres (2.02 ha) for a single growing season (and were merely

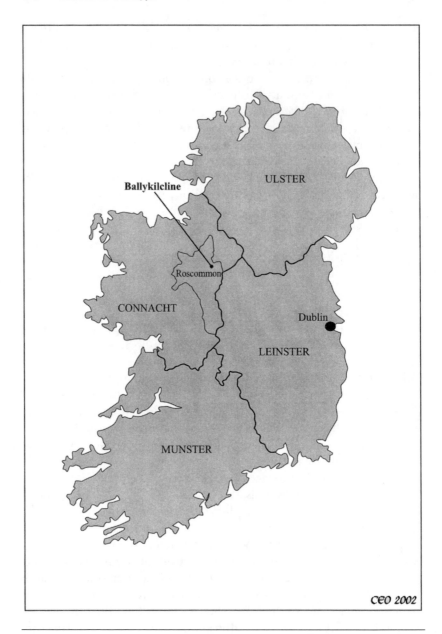

Fig. 10.1 Map of Ireland, with the location of the four provinces, County Roscommon, and Ballykilcline Townland.

tenants-at-will), while *farmers* were families who rented the same piece of land year after year. Scholars often incorrectly conflate the two groups as *peasants*, but farmers are thought to have been generally better off materially than cottiers (Pomfret 1969:7). Residents of townlands regularly cooperated, but class divisions created by the agricultural ladder meant that internal conflicts did occur (Sigerson 1871:137–68; Whelan 1993:211). Even so, farmers were only "one degree less miserable" than cottiers, and one of the farmers' great fears was that they would sink to the level of cottiers (O'Brien 1972:24; Pomfret 1969:7). By the same token, the landlords—often with overextended expense accounts and high debts—also worried about a drop in their social rank (MacDonagh 1989:220). Some landlords created unnecessary tension when they sought to maintain their superior social positions through *rack renting*, or charging exorbitant and often unrealistic rents.

Existing alongside the agricultural ladder was a classification based on dwelling quality. When the Crown's census takers assessed the value of Ireland's houses in 1841, they organized their statistics into a four-tiered system. Fourth-class houses were "all mud cabins having only one room," while third-class houses were of "a better description of cottage, still built of mud, but varying from two to four rooms and windows." Census enumerators described a "good farmhouse"—that is, a second-class house—as "having from five to nine rooms and windows," and a first-class house as being of "a better description than the preceding classes" (Pim 1848:298). In 1841, 36.3 percent of the Irish lived in fourth-class housing, and 40.4 percent lived in third-class dwellings. Only 3.3 percent lived in first-class houses (Keating 1996:12).

Thousands of rural families in early-nineteenth-century Ireland subsisted on potatoes (Salaman 1949:286), and when the potato blight reached Ireland in 1845, these men and women were soon devastated, as seven million tons of potatoes were needed annually to feed them (Gray 1995:32). As noted above, scholars from many disciplines still hotly debate the cause and implications of the blight and the subsequent famine and disease that followed. Nonetheless, historical records indicate that significant exports of food flowed out of Ireland during the period of intense starvation (Kinealy 1997; also see Grant 1991:268).

In the decades preceding the appearance of the potato blight, "serious economic conflict arose between the Irish tenant farmers and their landlords" (Mokyr 1985:124). Landlords, seeking to convert their mode of production from agriculture to grazing, attempted to clear their land of their often bothersome and financially burdensome tenants. Historical accounts repeatedly mention the tenants' theft of their landlords' timber, wool, and personal possessions in the early nineteenth century (Grant 1991:82, 117, 224; see also Orser 1996b:89). The tenants, whose families may have occupied the land since before the landlords' families arrived in the region, often overtly fought all efforts at dispossession. In this tense environment it is perhaps easy to understand why "Irish society was shaken repeatedly by outbreaks of agrarian and sectarian violence in the countryside" during the one hundred years before 1845 (Garvin 1982:133). To avert a full-scale, island-wide peasant revolution and to keep the tenant farmers from becoming a vast army of expensive paupers, the British government in 1838 passed the Irish Poor Law and created the workhouse system (Kinealy 1995:23–26). Dispossessed tenants could be shunted off to these dismal institutions to work for their sustenance.

At the height of its occupation in the 1840s, Ballykilcline consisted of about 243 ha, and was inhabited by about five hundred people. The earliest extant historical records indicate that people lived there in the seventeenth century, and the nearby remains of ring forts and crannogs show that the human settlement of the area occurred long before the creation of Ballykilcline (O'Conor 2001:337).

Ballykilcline was one of several parcels of land given or leased to Nicholas Mahon in the 1650s as part of the Cromwellian colonization of the west of Ireland (Campbell 1994:10; Hanley 1961:228). Arthur Young (1780:184), writing in the late eighteenth century, described the tenants of the Mahon estate as "upon the increase, but not much; they are better fed than 20 years ago, and better cloathed [sic], but not more industrious, or better housed. They live on potatoes, milk, and butter." Visiting the same area a few years later, Edward Wakefield (1812:274) noted that he "found every where, cabins of the most wretched aspect, infamous stone roads, very minute divisions of land, and what usually follows it, a superabundant but miserable population." Isaac Weld (1832:317), who surveyed County Roscommon for the Royal Dublin Society in 1830, reported that among Mahon tenants, even though "want and wretchedness . . . are by no means obliterated entirely," conditions were certainly better than they had been during Wakefield's tour. According to Weld (1832:317), the new cottages built on the Mahon estate were among the very best he had observed anywhere in Ireland.

The Mahon family's lease to Ballykilcline expired on May 1, 1834—four years after Weld's visit—and the family immediately opened negotiations with the Crown for its continuation. The two sides could not agree on the terms, and later that year, the lands and people of Ballykilcline came under the direct control of the British Crown, administered by His (and later Her) Majesty's Commissioners of Woods, Forests, Land Revenues, Works, and Buildings.[3]

Upon taking control of Ballykilcline, the commissioners discovered that the townland was divided into seventy-four distinct tenancies. The people were tenants-at-will, meaning they lived on the land and tilled the fields at the pleasure of the landlord. Even so, the Crown's agents learned that they would have significant difficulty collecting the rents. A general perception was that the region around Ballykilcline was "proverbial in this part of the county for its wickedness" (O'Donovan 1927:57). So-called agrarian unrest was nothing new to County Roscommon, and underground protective associations—calling themselves Threshers, Carders, Rockites, Ribbonmen, and White Boys—were all present in one form or another within the county (Coleman 1999).

To solve the rent strike as quickly as possible, the commissioners issued notices to the tenants requiring them to surrender possession of their holdings. Fifty-two of them complied and were reinstated as caretakers with a small monthly allowance. One condition of this arrangement was that the tenants, now simply occupiers of the land, were required to surrender possession immediately upon the Crown's demand. Other tenants, however, "absolutely refused to give up the Possession or to account with the Crown's Receivers for the Value of the Holdings in their Occupation" (House of Lords 1847:4), and they began a full-blown rent strike. When visited by the Crown's receivers, several of the tenants, including many who had originally agreed to the Crown's arrangement, refused to surrender. Faced with this volatile situation, the under secretary asked the police to protect the rent collectors. The police feared for their own safety and declined to intervene, stating that any effort to collect the rents would cause "a certain Breach of the Peace and probable personal Injury to those employed" (House of Lords 1847:5).

The British government decided to institute legal proceedings against eight ringleaders of the rent strike and ordered their arrest. On April 6, 1842, a process server attempted to give notice to four of the tenants, but a mob soon assembled and he was "driven off the Lands" (House of Lords 1847:17). One month later, the Clerk of Quit Rents informed the Ballykilcline tenants that they were required to pay their rent arrears in Strokestown, the nearest market town, on May 31. The tenants dutifully appeared on the appointed day, but only one of them paid the required amount. The others refused to pay, "saying they had not the Money, and that the Rent fixed upon their Lands was too much and more than they could pay" (House of Lords 1847, 18). The tenants then made a formal petition to the commissioners, asking for forgiveness of their rent debt and arguing that they had been victimized by "high, enormous Rents." As a further show of strength, they appended a bold assertion to the end of their petition: If the commissioners did not agree to forgive their arrears payments, they would be forced to send a petition directly to "Her most Gracious and Illustrious Majesty, tending to the Fraud and Imposition they are subjected to" (House of Lords 1847:20).

Instead of accepting the terms of the petition, the commissioners began to press for a legal solution to the rebellion, and in their official records they began to refer to the tenants as "Intruders on the Crown Lands of Ballykilcline." The tenants, however, continued their open resistance, even with the real threat of eviction hanging over them. In a letter dated April 8, 1843, the sub-sheriff of County Roscommon stated that after he had arrested one of the ringleaders in Strokestown, "The roads on every Side of me were surrounded, and the Prisoner would be certainly rescued from me had I not got him into One of the Police Stations along the Road." The tenants attacked the police station, and the only way the sheriff could get his prisoner to the jail in Roscommon town (about twenty-four kilometers south) was to take an indirect route (House of Lords 1847:23). The tenants still refused to pay their rents in 1844, and in May, the bailiffs found the tenants more intractable than ever. In fact, the bailiffs "were attacked by the Tenants, and not having the Protection of the Police were obliged to retreat, after only effecting the Service of Six or Seven of the Notices, and were it not that by chance they met a few Policemen on Duty they would certainly have been killed, as it was the greatest Difficulty and fixed Bayonets that the Police could keep the Mob from them" (House of Lords 1847:50). The tenants were "armed with Sticks, Stones, and Shovels" and used "threatening Language" against the bailiffs. The exasperated agent then sought permission to evict the tenants and either to lock or to "throw down the Houses of the refractory Tenants . . . [to] make an Example among them" (House of Lords 1847:53).

Faced with the reality that the tenants were in a state of overt, protracted rebellion, the commissioners decided that full-scale eviction was the ultimate solution to the Crown's problem. The tenants of Ballykilcline must have realized that they were out of options, because on May 12, 1846, they sent a petition to the commissioners describing themselves as "459 Individuals of moral industrious Habits, exemplary, obedient, and implicit to their Landlady or Landlord, which is the Cause of bringing them into Contempt, but are penitent and regretful for any Misunderstanding which has occurred in the Event of the Case in question" (House of Lords 1847:73). By this date, however, the potato blight had reached County Roscommon, and it was virtually impossible for the tenants of Ballykilcline, like thousands of others across the island, to pay the required rents or even to feed themselves. The tenants were thus evicted from their homes, and many of them eventually emigrated to the United States (Scally 1995:166–229).

The history of the Ballykilcline rent strike, though barely a footnote in Irish history, is almost as meaningful to the townland's descendants as the history of Palmares has been to many African Brazilians. In fact, it was largely because of this turbulent past, as recounted in a published account of the townland's history (Scally 1995), that in the early 1990s a group of descendants of the Ballykilcline evictees formed the Ballykilcline Society. The objectives of the society are to gather information about the history of the townland's families and to hold annual reunions to celebrate their survival and perseverance. The first reunion was held in Ireland in August 1999, with more than one hundred men and women, mostly Americans, attending. That year marked the second season of archaeological research at Ballykilcline, and most of the reunion attendees expressed great interest in the excavation.

Negotiating Ballykilcline

While giving the society's members a tour of the excavation, I realized that these descendant North Americans considered the townland to be their ancestral home. Many openly expressed awe at having the opportunity to walk on the same land as their ancestors. They cared deeply about the archaeological findings, and many viewed the artifacts with an almost mystical fascination, recognizing that their long-removed ancestors had once used the broken ceramics, the tarnished brass buttons, and the shattered glass bottles. The members of the society were also intensely curious about the interpretations we would offer.

The entangled interaction between our archaeological findings and the attitudes and understandings of our Irish and Irish American audiences can be illustrated by specific reference to the excavated ceramic collection. Five years of excavation (1998–2002) at two house sites have revealed that the residents obtained and used both Irish-made coarse earthenwares and English-made refined earthenwares. The Irish specimens were red- and buff-bodied wares typically glazed on the interior with earth tones, whereas the English ceramics were white-bodied wares decorated with the brightly colored transfer-printed, hand-painted, cut-sponge, and sponge/spatter decorations common during the early nineteenth century.

A detailed plat mandated by the Crown and drafted by Dublin surveyors Brassington and Gale in 1836 shows that the two excavated house sites at Ballykilcline were inhabited by the Nary family: "Mark Nary & Sons, Luke, James, & Edward." The houses also appear, in the same positions, on the government-sponsored Ordnance Survey map drawn in 1837 (fig. 10.2). One of the houses is shown to have been larger than the other, and excavations revealed that they were about fifty meters apart. The smaller of the two was situated only about ten meters from an early medieval ring fort. The purposeful destruction of the houses upon eviction, as noted in the historical record,

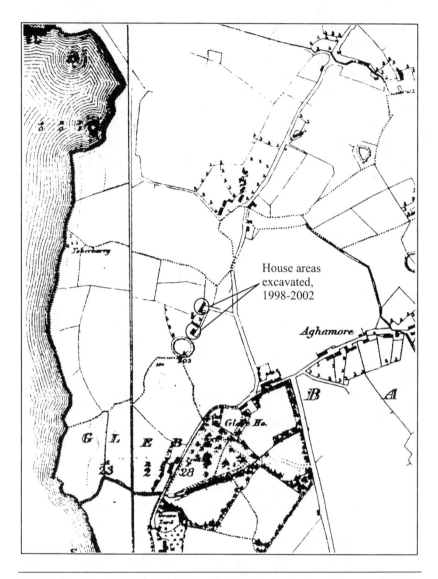

Fig. 10.2 A section of the 1837 Ordnance Survey plat showing the location of the two excavated Nary houses.

precluded the delineation of the precise design of the foundations, although we did discover floor cobbling and wall debris in each spatially discrete area.

The cultural history of coarse earthenware production in late eighteenth- and early nineteenth-century Ireland is still being written, and a great deal still must be accomplished before a thorough understanding of this important craft industry is gained. At present, however, two aspects of the industry are clear: (1) this folk tradition likely has medieval roots; and (2) during the late eighteenth and early nineteenth centuries, traditional Irish potters made mostly utilitarian (kitchen and dairy) vessels (Orser 1997, 2000, 2001).

The English earthenwares, on the other hand, were produced in highly standardized pottery factories in Staffordshire (see Shaw 1829; Thomas 1971; Weatherill 1971, 1986). The mass production of white-bodied ceramic vessels began in earnest in the late eighteenth century, and the industry grew to global proportions during the final decades of tenant life at Ballykilcline. By the time the last tenants were removed from the townland, the English ceramics trade dominated the world market. Ireland had a small fine earthenware industry in the late eighteenth century, located mostly in Dublin and Belfast, but neither even came close to eclipsing the English potteries, and most ceased operation shortly after their creation (see Dunlevy 1988; Francis 2000, 2001; Westropp 1913).

Student excavators at the two Nary house sites at Ballykilcline collected 10,341 artifacts during the five seasons of research. Of this number, 3,262 sherds (or 31.5 percent) were English-made refined earthenwares, and 3,083 sherds (or 29.8 percent) were Irish-made coarse earthenwares. Vessel reconstruction reveals a minimum of 127 refined earthenware vessels and 45 coarse earthenware vessels in the collection. The most prevalent vessel forms for the coarse earthenwares are pancheons (milk pans) (40.0 percent of coarse earthenwares), storage jars/crocks (28.9 percent), and pitchers/jugs (26.7 percent). Teacups (27.6 percent), plates (24.4 percent), and saucers (18.9 percent) are the most common refined earthenware vessel forms.

Even the application of such crude descriptive measures of these wares' presence at the Nary house sites foregrounds an important question that resonated with members of the Ballykilcline Society: How did the residents of Ballykilcline obtain their many vessels? The resolution of this seemingly straightforward academic question has profound significance to the members of the Ballykilcline Society specifically, and to members of the diasporic Irish community in general.

To provide direction for addressing this question, we can use similar research conducted years ago in relation to enslaved African Americans (for example, Otto 1977). An Irish–African American analogy is reasonable for at least three reasons: (1) African-American slaves and Irish tenant farmers were contemporaneous; (2) both groups were enmeshed within an oppressive agricultural system that was structured to keep them powerless and generally destitute; and (3) both groups were perceived in generally similar racial terms designed to restrict them to inferior social positions (Allen

1994; Curtis 1984; Curtis 1971; Ignatiev 1995; Lebow 1976; Lentin and McVeigh 2002; Roediger 1991; Rolston and Shannon 2002). Using this analogy, we can construct three interpretations to account for the presence of English ceramics at the Nary houses: (1) that the tenants purchased the ceramics with the rent monies they withheld from the Crown; (2) that they stole the vessels from the nearby Glebe House (the house and land given to a Protestant minister in a predominantly Catholic area); or (3) that they received them as gifts from the Glebe's residents.

Each option is entirely possible, as are various combinations, but I tend to favor the first option because historical information increases its plausibility. We know, for example, that in the early nineteenth century Strokestown was the site of a weekly market that was "very numerously attended" (Lewis 1837:581). In addition, the head of the Royal Canal from Dublin was only 11.3 kilometers away, and itinerant peddlers are known to have traveled widely throughout Ireland (Ó Ciosáin 1997:59–67). Pictorial information also indicates that peddlers trafficked in English ceramics. Before 1820 inventive retailers even began to establish ceramic outlet centers throughout the island. The establishment of these stores would have meant that tenants did not have to purchase refined earthenware ceramics only at markets and periodic fairs (Thomas 1971:103–16). Wedgwood opened two outlets in Dublin, one in 1772 and another in 1808 (Dunlevy 1988:22–23), and a survey of three commercial directories for Ireland (Pigot 1823, 1824; Slater 1846) shows that the number of outlets selling English-made refined earthenwares increased by more than 550 percent from 1822 to 1846 (from 23 outlets to 151).

We can thus assume that imported, refined earthenware was available to the Ballykilcline tenants if they could afford to purchase it. Because history indicates that they withheld their rent payments, is it possible that they used their funds to purchase English-made dishes? Is it possible that they used the widespread English perception that the rural Irish were racially inferior to help them feign poverty? A brief historical reference does in fact add credence to the tenants' thoughtful manipulation of the racial hierarchy. In the midst of the rent strike, the Ballykilcline agent warned the Crown's representatives that the tenants were not as poor as they portrayed themselves to be, and that some of them were worth as much as £100 (House of Lords 1847:76). The racialist attitudes of the Crown's agents, however, still made it impossible for them to accept the agent's plea and to imagine that Irish peasants could so adroitly manipulate the system. These same royal functionaries may have found it implausible that rural Irish men and women would do anything to improve their standard of living.

The above tenant-as-consumer interpretation has a ring of truth to American audiences because it speaks directly to the native intelligence and tenacity of the Irish and because it acknowledges that the rural Irish of Ballykilcline had good economic sense. The economic abilities of Irish newcomers to North America is so well known that some of their names are synonymous with immense wealth and international power (see Birmingham 1973).

Not everyone, however, is completely comfortable with this interpretation. For example, an older resident of the Ballykilcline area told me that I was wrong to think that the tenant farmers bought their own ceramics. It made considerably more sense to him—because the tenants were ground down into abject poverty by British domination—that the only way they could have obtained the imported dishes was through theft. He believed that theft was a more honorable and overtly defiant way of ensuring the family's security from utter destitution than was simple purchase. Another elderly Irish gentleman asked me why I had so openly accepted the British travelers' accounts of the Irish in the first place. Why had I been surprised, he asked, to discover that Irish tenant farmers were not as barbaric or backward as foreign visitors claimed? In other words, why shouldn't Irish tenant farmers have had imported dishes? His penetrating questions forced me to contemplate how an archaeologist's interpretive thought processes can be subtly manipulated by observations made in the past. Is it more realistic to imagine the men and women of Ballykilcline as shrewd manipulators of the harsh and unfair system they found constructed over them, or is it more reasonable to envision them as debased into an enforced poverty? Was their rent strike an example of resistance or merely the expression of their economic condition? Were the men and women of Ballykilcline intent on maintaining their Irishness by open resistance, or were they seeking a more nuanced Britishness through their acquisition of English ceramics? Without interaction with both members of the diasporic community and residents of its homeland, such questions would have been much more difficult to frame, let alone to address.

Conclusion

The situation at Ballykilcline, both in the past and in the present, makes it extremely difficult to answer the above questions with any certainty. It is not even clear that an entirely unambiguous resolution can ever be presented, even with further research. Of course, as committed archaeologists we hope that we can provide reasonable interpretations that will illuminate such tough questions, but we also realize that several interpretations may be possible and perhaps even inevitable. At a minimum, the very act of asking such pointed questions further demonstrates the challenges of attempting to conduct socially responsible—and at the same time intellectually satisfying—research.

Given Ireland's history, and in some cases present circumstances, it is perhaps understandable that the archaeology of modern Ireland will be fraught with interpretive complexities and possibly even dilemmas. The island has been the site of long-term colonialist intervention, and the landscape has been contested for generations. Early nineteenth-century Ireland, along with its thousands of rural tenant farmers, was on the front lines of the ever-expanding British global marketplace, and thousands of its citizens were either encouraged or forced to flee as exiles to foreign lands. The archaeology of modern Ireland, rather than constituting a straightforward study of peasant agrarian life, provides myriad avenues into many of the topics that are most pertinent to contemporary archaeological research, including race, resistance, and ethnogenesis.

Ballykilcline presents an excellent arena for analysis because its residents paradoxically resisted British domination at the same time that they entered the English marketplace. Archaeology at this contested townland provides testimony to the reality that today's archaeologists must acknowledge the central role of the Irish diaspora in modern Irish history and cultural life, and so must be prepared to incorporate views from both Ireland and elsewhere into their multilayered interpretations. The interpretive process offers many significant challenges, to be sure. The current political situation in Ireland—which as of this writing is still unsettled—impacts archaeological research because of the colonial nature of that past. This past, though distant, is no less forgotten than are the glories of Palmares and its leader Zumbi. The interpretive situation in Ireland, as in northeast Brazil, is made exceedingly complex because of the many constituencies who perceive the past as directly relevant to explaining their place in today's world.

Notes

Many of the ideas presented here have taken shape in discussions with the three Ballykilcline field directors, Katherine Hull, David Ryder, and Stephen Brighton. I have also benefited from numerous discussions with John Waddell and Janice Orser, who have helped me to refine my approach. The field research at Ballykilcline was supported by grants from the Irish Heritage Council, the Committee for Archaeology, and Illinois State University. Thanks must also be extended to the landowners of the Nary sites and to the Ballykilcline Society.

1. This is not always true, of course. In my own case, for instance, I am a member of the truly dispossessed Irish. My father, whose surname at birth was Terrell—a common County Westmeath name—was adopted by an American farm family who desired a resident field hand. His mother was an Irish immigrant to Canada, who gave birth in far northern Maine. My father only learned of his own history when, during World War II, an official with the state of Maine mistakenly sent him a certificate of adoption instead of the required birth certificate. Without this clerical error, my true ancestry would have remained hidden forever.

2. An Irish townland was the smallest unit of administration beneath the parish (see McErlean 1983). Nineteenth-century farm families typically identified with the townland of their birth. Most rural people in Ireland today still make this identification, as do many diasporic Irish men and women.

3. The monarchy of Great Britain changed during the post-Mahon history of Ballykilcline. William IV was king until 1837, when Victoria ascended to the throne. She remained queen throughout the remainder of the townland's habitation.

References Cited

Akenson, D. H. (2000). "Irish Migration to North America, 1800–1920." In *The Irish Diaspora*, ed. A. Bielenberg, pp. 111–38. Harlow: Pearson Education.

Allen, T. W. (1994). *The Invention of the White Race: Volume I, Racial Oppression and Social Control*. London: Verso.

Anderson, R. N. (1996). "The Quilombo of Palmares: A New Overview of a Maroon State in Seventeenth-Century Brazil." *Journal of Latin American Studies* 28:545–66.

Bielenberg, A., ed. (2000). *The Irish Diaspora*. Harlow: Pearson Education.

Biolsi, T., and L. Zimmerman, eds. (1997). *Indians and Anthropologists: Vine Deloria Jr. and the Critique of Anthropology*. Tucson: University of Arizona Press.

Birmingham, S. (1973). *Real Lace: America's Rich Irish*. New York: Harper and Row.

Bourke, A. (1993). "*The Visitation of God*"? *The Potato and the Great Irish Famine*, ed. Hill and C. Ó Gráda. Dublin: Lilliput.

Brah, A. (1996). *Cartographies of Diaspora: Contesting Identities*. London: Routledge.

Campbell, S. J. (1994). *The Great Irish Famine: Words and Images from the Famine Museum, Strokestown Park, County Roscommon*. Strokestown: The Famine Museum.

Coleman, A. (1999). *Riotous Roscommon: Social Unrest in the 1840s*. Dublin: Irish Academic Press.

Collins, K. (1990). *The Cultural Conquest of Ireland*. Cork: Mercier.

Cornwell, G. H., and E. W. Stoddard, eds. (2001). *Global Multiculturalism: Comparative Perspectives on Ethnicity, Race, and Nation*. Lanham, Md.: Rowman and Littlefield.

Cullen, L. M. (2001). "The Politics of the Famine and of Famine Historiography." In *The Famine Lectures: Léachtaí an Gorta*, ed. B. Ó Conaire, pp. 166–88. Roscommon: Roscommon County Council.

Curtis, L. (1984). *Nothing but the Same Old Story: The Roots of Anti-Irish Racism*. London: Information on Ireland.

Curtis, L. P., Jr. (1971). *Apes and Angels: The Irishman in Victorian Caricature*. Washington, D.C.: Smithsonian Institution Press.

Custer, J. F. (2001). "Working Together: Who Cares?" *The Society for American Archaeology Archaeological Record* 1, no. 4:21–22.

Daly, M. (1996). "Revisionism and Irish History: The Great Famine." In *The Making of Modern Irish History: Revisionism and the Revisionist Controversy*, ed. D. G. Boyce and A. O'Day, pp. 71–89. London: Routledge.

Danaher, K. (1972). *The Year in Ireland: Irish Calendar Customs*. Cork: Mercier.

Davis, G. (1997). "The Historiography of the Irish Famine." In *The Meaning of the Famine*, ed. P. O'Sullivan, pp. 15–39. London: Leicester University Press.

Dunlevy, M. (1988). *Ceramics in Ireland*. Dublin: National Museum of Ireland.

Ellis, P. B. (1988). *Hell or Connaught! The Cromwellian Colonisation of Ireland, 1652–1660*. Belfast: Blackstaff.

Francis, P. (2000). *Irish Delftware: An Illustrated History*. London: Jonathan Horne.

———. (2001). *A Pottery by the Lagan: Irish Creamware from the Downshire Pottery, Belfast, 1787–c. 1806*. Belfast: Institute of Irish Studies.

Funari, P. A. A. (1999). "Maroon, Race, and Gender: Palmares Material Culture and Social Relations in a Runaway Settlement." In *Historical Archaeology: Back from the Edge*, ed. P. P. A. Funari, M. Hall, and S. Jones, pp. 308–27. London: Routledge.

Garvin, T. (1982). "Defenders, Ribbonmen, and Others: Underground Political Networks in Pre-Famine Ireland." *Past and Present* 96:133–55.

Grant, E. (1991). *The Highland Lady in Ireland: Journals, 1840–50*, ed. P. Pelly and A. Tod. Edinburgh: Canongate.

Gray, P. (1995). *The Irish Famine*. New York: Harry N. Abrams.

Hanley, G. (1961). "Nicholas Mahon and 17th Century Roscommon." *The Irish Genealogist* 3:228–35.

Harrington, S. P. M. (1993). "Bones and Bureaucrats: New York's Great Cemetery Imbroglio." *Archaeology* 46, no. 2:28–38.

Heaney, S. (1980). *Preoccupations: Selected Prose, 1968–1978.* London: Faber and Faber.

House of Lords. (1847). *Lands of Ballykilcline, County Roscommon: Returns to Orders of the House of Lords, Dated 16th and 19th February 1847.* London: Her Majesty's Stationery Office.

Howe, S. (2000). *Ireland and Empire: Colonial Legacies in Irish History and Culture.* Oxford: Oxford University Press.

Ignatiev, N. (1995). *How the Irish Became White.* New York: Routledge.

Keating, J. (1996). *Irish Famine Facts.* Dublin: Teagasc.

Kinealy, C. (1995). *This Great Calamity: The Irish Famine, 1845–52.* Dublin: Gill and Macmillan.

———. (1997). "Food Exports from Ireland, 1846–47." *History Ireland* 5, no. 1:32–36.

Klesert, A. L., and A. S. Downer, eds. (1990). *Preservation on the Reservation: Native Americans, Native American Lands, and Archaeology.* Window Rock, Ariz.: Navajo Nation Preservation Department.

LaRoche, C. J., and M. L. Blakey. (1997). "Seizing Intellectual Power: The Dialogue at the New York African Burial Ground." In *In the Realm of Politics: Prospects for Public Participation in African-American Archaeology,* special issue of *Historical Archaeology* 31, no. 3:84–106.

Lebow, R. N. (1976). *White Britain and Black Ireland: The Influence of Stereotypes on Colonial Policy.* Philadelphia: Institute for the Study of Human Issues.

Leed, E. J. (1991). *The Mind of the Traveler: From Gilgamesh to Global Tourism.* New York: Basic Books.

Lewis, S. (1837). *A Topographical Dictionary of Ireland, Volume II,* reprinted 1995. Baltimore, Md.: Genealogical Publishing.

Lentin, R. and R. McVeigh, eds. (2002). *Racism and Anti-Racism in Ireland.* Belfast: Beyond the Pale.

MacDonagh, O. (1989). "The Economy and Society, 1830–45." In *A New History of Ireland, V: Ireland Under the Union I, 1801–70,* ed. W. E. Vaughan, pp. 218–41. Oxford: Clarendon.

McDonald, J. D., et al. (1991). "The Northern Cheyenne Outbreak of 1879: Using Oral History and Archaeology as Tools of Resistance." In *The Archaeology of Inequality,* ed. R. H. McGuire and R. Payner, pp. 64–78. Oxford: Blackwell.

McErlean, T. (1983). "The Irish Townland System of Landscape Organisation." In *Landscape Archaeology in Ireland,* ed. T. Reeves-Smyth and F. Hamond, pp. 315–39. Oxford: British Archaeological Reports.

Metress, S. P., and R. A. Rajner. (1996). *The Great Starvation (1845–1852): An Irish Holocaust.* Stony Point, N.Y.: American Ireland Education Foundation.

Miller, K. A. (1985). *Emigrants and Exiles: Ireland and the Irish Exodus to North America.* New York: Oxford University Press.

Mitchel, J. (1868). *The History of Ireland from the Treaty of Limerick to the Present Time.* New York: D. and J. Sadlier.

Mokyr, J. (1985). *Why Ireland Starved: A Quantitative and Analytical History of the Irish Economy, 1800–1850.* London: George Allen and Unwin.

Morash, C., and R. Hayes, eds. (1996). *Fearful Realities: New Perspectives on the Famine.* Dublin: Irish Academic Press.

O'Brien, B. (1999). *The Long War: The IRA and Sinn Féin.* Dublin: O'Brien Press.

O'Brien, G. (1972). *The Economic History of Ireland from the Union to the Famine.* Clifton, N.J.: Augustus M. Kelley.

O'Callaghan, S. (2000). *To Hell or Barbados: The Ethnic Cleansing of Ireland.* Dingle: Brandon.

Ó Cerallaigh, D., ed. (1998). *New Perspectives on Ireland: Colonialism and Identity.* Dublin: Léirmheas.

Ó Ciosáin, N. (1997). *Print and Popular Culture in Ireland, 1750–1850.* New York: St. Martin's Press.

O'Conor, K. D. (2001). "The Morphology of Gaelic Lordly Sites in North Connacht." In *Gaelic Ireland: Land, Lordship, and Settlement, c. 1250–c. 1650,* ed. P. J. Duffy, D. Edwards, and E. Fitz-Patrick, pp. 329–45. Dublin: Four Courts Press.

O'Donovan, J. (1927). *Letters Containing Information Relative to the Antiquities of the County of Roscommon, Collected During the Progress of the Ordnance Survey in 1837, Volume II.* Bray: no publisher.

O'Dowd, A. (1981). *Meitheal: A Study of Co-operative Labour in Rural Ireland.* Dublin: Comhairle Bhéaloideas Éireann.

Ó Gráda, C. (1989). *The Great Irish Famine.* Dublin: Gill and Macmillan.

Ó hAllmhuráin, G. (1999). "*Amhrán an Ghorta*: The Great Famine and Irish Traditional Music." *New Hibernia Review* 3 19–44.

Orser, C. E., Jr. (1996a). *A Historical Archaeology of the Modern World.* New York, Plenum.

———. (1996b). "Can There Be an Archaeology of the Great Famine?" In *Fearful Realities: New Perspectives on the Famine*, edited by C. Morash and R. Hayes, pp. 77–89. Dublin: Irish Academic Press.

———. (1997). "Of Dishes and Drains: An Archaeological Perspective on Irish Rural Life in the Great Famine Era." *New Hibernia Review* 1:120–35.

———. (2000). "In Praise of Early Nineteenth-Century Coarse Earthenware." *Archaeology Ireland* 14, no. 4:8–11.

———. (2001). "Vessels of Honor and Dishonor: The Symbolic Character of Irish Earthenware." *New Hibernia Review* 5:83–100.

Orser, C. E., Jr., and P. P. A Funari. (2001). "Archaeology and Slave Resistance and Rebellion." *World Archaeology* 33:61–72.

O'Toole, F. (1999). *The Lie of the Land: Irish Identities.* London: Verso.

Otto, J. S. (1977). "Artifacts and Status Differences: A Comparison of Ceramics from Planter, Overseer, and Slave Sites on an Antebellum Plantation." In *Research Strategies in Historical Archaeology*, ed. S. South, pp. 91–118. New York: Academic Press.

Pigot. (1823). *The Commercial Directory for Ireland, Scotland, &c. 1820, 1821, 1822.* London: Pigot and Company.

Pigot. (1824). *Pigot and Co.'s City of Dublin and Hibernia Provincial Directory.* London: Pigot and Company.

Pim, J. (1848). *The Condition and Prospects of Ireland, and the Evils Arising from the Present Distribution of Landed Property: With Suggestions for a Remedy.* Dublin: Hodges and Smith.

Pomfret, J. E. (1969). *The Struggle for Land in Ireland, 1800–1923.* New York: Russell and Russell.

Roediger, D. R. (1991). *The Wages of Whiteness: Race and the Making of the American Working Class.* London: Verso.

Rolston, B., and M. Shannon. (2002). *Encounters: How Racism Came to Ireland.* Belfast: Beyond the Pale.

Salaman, R. N. (1949). *The History and Social Influence of the Potato*, ed. J. G. Hawkes, 1985. Cambridge: Cambridge University Press.

Scally, R. J. (1995). *The End of Hidden Ireland: Rebellion, Famine, and Emigration.* New York: Oxford University Press.

Schwartz, S. B. (1992). *Slaves, Peasants, and Rebels: Reconsidering Brazilian Slavery.* Urbana: University of Illinois Press.

Shaw, S. (1829). *History of the Staffordshire Potteries*, reprinted 1970. New York: Praeger.

Sigerson, G. (1871). *History of the Land Tenures and Land Classes of Ireland.* London: Longmans, Green, Reader, and Dyer.

Slater, I. (1846). *I. Slater's National Commercial Directory of Ireland.* Manchester: I. Slater.

Spillman, W. J. (1919). "The Agricultural Ladder." In *American Association for Agricultural Legislation, Bulletin 2*, pp. 29–38. Madison: University of Wisconsin.

Swidler, N. et al., eds. (1997). *Native Americans and Archaeologists: Stepping Stones to Common Ground.* Walnut Creek, Calif.: Altamira.

Thomas, D. H. (2000). *Skull Wars: Kennewick Man, Archaeology, and the Battle for Native American Identity.* New York: Basic Books.

Thomas, J. (1971). *The Rise of the Staffordshire Potteries.* New York: Augustus M. Kelley.

Wakefield, E. (1812). *An Account of Ireland, Statistical and Political.* London: Longman, Hurst, Rees, Orme, and Brown.

Walter, B. (2001). *Outsiders Inside: Whiteness, Place, and Irish Women.* London: Routledge.

Watkins, J. (2000). *Indigenous Archaeology: American Indian Values and Scientific Practice.* Walnut Creek, Calif.: Altamira.

Weatherill, L. (1971). *The Pottery Trade and North Staffordshire, 1660–1760.* New York: Augustus M. Kelley.

———, (1986). *The Growth of the Pottery Industry in England, 1660–1815.* New York: Garland.

Weld, I. (1832). *Statistical Survey of the County of Roscommon, Drawn Up Under the Direction of the Royal Dublin Society.* Dublin: R. Graisberry.

Westropp, M. S. D. (1913). "Notes on the Pottery Manufacture in Ireland." *Proceedings of the Royal Irish Academy* 32, C:1–27.

Whelan, K. (1993). "Ireland in the World-System, 1600–1800." In *The Early-Modern World-System in Geographical Perspective*, ed. H-J. Nitz, pp. 204–18. Stuttgart: Franz Steiner Verlag.

Young, A. (1780). *A Tour of Ireland with General Observations on the Present State of That Kingdom Made in the Years 1776, 1777, and 1778.* London: Cadell and Dodsley.

Epilogue
Archaeology, Heritage, and Public Endeavor

ERVE CHAMBERS

In this conclusion to the volume, Erve Chambers suggests that many aspects of archaeology are becoming increasingly dependent on working with a variety of public and private interests. While applied archaeology emerged largely as an effort to advance the particular interests and resources of the archaeological profession, a more truly public phase of the endeavors of archaeology is beginning, and archaeologists might now need to pay more attention to the concerns and well-being of other stakeholders, including those associated with the localities in which they work.

Introduction

Although I am not an archaeologist, I have a number of friends and colleagues who are. What is more, I have been involved with archaeology in one way or another for quite a while, in relation to departmental administration, teaching responsibilities, and in promoting the idea of archaeology as a distinct approach to applied anthropology. In 1978, for example, when I had the opportunity to help establish the Society for Applied Anthropology (SfAA) publication *Practicing Anthropology*, I tried to ensure that archaeology was well represented. It was not an easy task. For their part, archaeologists seemed reluctant to contribute to a publication that was not dedicated solely to their particular interests, at least as they perceived those interests. Neither did *Practicing Anthropology*'s usual readership appear to be convinced. I recall that a past president of the SfAA criticized my inclusion of archaeologists, arguing that the society was "for cultural anthropologists." That was news to me. It also struck me as an incredibly short-sighted notion. To my mind, what had begun to occur during the late 1970s was a new focus on resource management and practice outside academia that had the potential to draw the interests of archaeologists and cultural anthropologists much closer together.

Both archaeology and the SfAA have changed considerably since 1978. Still, I am not sure we have made much progress in terms of thinking of archaeology as a kind of applied anthropology. When Paul Shackel and I started to talk about preparing this volume, some of my own concerns were very practical. I teach an applied anthropology course for our graduate students at the University of Maryland; this course includes students who have declared a specialization in archaeology. It relies heavily on case study material related to the practice of anthropology, and while there is plenty of such material available in respect to applied cultural anthropology, there are very few corresponding case studies for applied archaeology. The obvious conclusion is that, although archaeologists are now clearly and deeply involved in applied work, they have not been encouraged to discuss and critically reflect upon their experiences in the same way as cultural anthropologists commonly do in their field, where case studies of practice form a distinct genre. The significance of this is much greater than my own need for classroom material. Without the discussions that are implied by studies of practice, there is no way for any of us to even begin to reflect on the effectiveness of the applied activities of archaeologists—or, to put it somewhat more dramatically, there is no reasonably balanced way for us to determine whether or not archaeology is actually useful for any purpose.[1]

Definitions of applied anthropology vary, and in some definitions even a relatively distant association with matters of public interest might be sufficient to claim status as an "applied anthropologist." My definition is a bit more demanding. Applied anthropology (and, consequently, applied archaeology) is directed toward helping people make decisions. In this respect, there must be a deliberate act involving the transfer of knowledge or skills from the realm of anthropology to another realm(s) of interest. In most of the instances discussed in this volume, what is being transferred relates to the uses and management of heritage resources. What is important to recognize here is that what makes this work *applied* is not the knowledge itself, which certainly might be "relevant" to the interests of others, but the act of engagement with others who are trying to make decisions related to particular heritage resources.

There are two major points I want to explore in this concluding chapter. The first is to briefly discuss some of the issues that I think are pertinent to the development of our understanding of applied archaeology. In this respect, I believe that the way some archaeologists think of themselves as being applied has begun to shift in recent years, partly in response to changing ideas concerning the relationship of archaeology to public endeavors, and also as a result of new career opportunities. My second aim is to point out how I feel that the practical experience and scholarly traditions of applied cultural anthropology might help advance our understanding of applied archaeology. I do this as more of an insider who has been long interested and deeply involved in the development of applied anthropology as a distinct kind of practice and scholarship.

We should keep in mind that the place of applied anthropology in relation to our four major subdisciplines remains a controversial issue. There are still many anthropologists who seem to feel that the actual act of applying anthropology is relatively unproblematic. For these persons the only real issue is that one is competent to do good anthropology—the usefulness of that anthropology should then be apparent. But there are others, myself included, who advocate for applied anthropology to be considered a distinct subdiscipline in its own right (Chambers 1985). Our view is that it requires knowledge of a special kind to be an effective applied anthropologist. This is not just practical knowledge, such as how to do budgets or hold public meetings, but also knowledge based on sustained critical inquiry into what happens when anthropology leaves the academy and begins to muddle around in the ideas and affairs of others. Quite obviously, the remarks that follow are colored by my commitment to the idea of applied anthropology as a distinct field of knowledge that is worthy of our most careful scholarship.

Two Stages of Applied Archaeology

Archaeology has developed rapidly as an applied field. I attended graduate school in the early 1970s, and I cannot recall from that time many discussions that would foretell what was about to unfold. Most people were still talking about archaeology as a subdiscipline that was almost exclusively defined by its academic surroundings and basic scientific mission. And yet today the field is at least as much defined by practices outside of academic settings as it is by academic practice, although there remains considerable resistance to accepting the idea that this realignment might have as much to do with the scholarly construction of the field as it does to a simple expansion of employment possibilities—a form of resistance to practice outside of academia that is, by the way, also common in cultural anthropology.

I think there are two clear stages to the recent emergence of a sense of applied archaeology. The first is what I am going to identify as the *enabling stage*. This is the stage that follows passage of the National Historic Preservation Act (1966), the National Environmental Protection Act (1969), and several other enabling acts of legislation and regulation at federal, state, and local levels. These new rules and regulations greatly expanded the public role of archaeology, and they changed the employment opportunities of archaeologists in dramatic ways. I actually recall this stage with a sense of envy. During the 1960s and 1970s archaeologists were much more active and effective than were cultural anthropologists in encouraging legislation and rule making that would ensure their participation in identifying and managing the nation's historic and cultural resources. They also had reference to and rigorously defended a public identity that translated into job titles and contracts that were theirs alone. This is the golden age of contract archaeology and cultural resource management (CRM), supported by new and sometimes still controversial opportunities that have helped transform the subdiscipline. It is during this time that *contract* and *CRM archaeology* became an important part of the subdiscipline's lexicon. This was also a period during which archaeology became much better established in the public sector, with employment opportunities expanding at all levels of government service. The result of both these changes was a dramatic alteration in the institutional base of archaeology—a shift that has been widely acknowledged but which, I believe, has rarely been discussed in terms of its broader consequences for the intellectual development of the field.

As increasing numbers of archaeologists participated in this stage of development, there was a clear need for adding new skills to the subdiscipline. Most of these were practical skills in areas such as management, budgeting, proposal writing, and salvage archaeology. It is important to note that these skills did not detract from the advantage archaeology has had in maintaining a clear public identity. Archaeologists were doing pretty much what they had always done, and their expertise was (and in this respect still is) broadly recognized. The recognition of the need for expanded skills for new approaches to archaeological practice has resulted in a call for innovations to training future anthropologists (Bender and Smith 2000; Trotter 1988).

The enabling stage described above is not superceded by the next. It remains an important part of applied archaeology. Neither is the second stage without precedence in the past, although I do believe that its importance is just beginning to be felt. I will call this the *public stage* of applied archaeology.[2] This stage has come about as a result of both internal and external factors. Internally, for example, we can note that the enabling stage brought archaeologists into closer relationships with a wider variety of people and public interests. What leads us from these experiences to the public stage is the growing recognition that these new or expanded relationships with others are much richer and sometimes considerably more problematic than we might have imagined. This is due in part to external factors that have encouraged the expression of greater and more diverse public interests related to the management of historic resources. For archaeology, the public stage was brought to the fore most dramatically with the repatriation issue—to my knowledge, the first major occasion on which archaeologists were sometimes placed in positions in which they had to weigh their own interests in heritage resources against the competing concerns of others. The public stage is closely associated with new incentives on the part of varied constituencies and interests to make claims on the significance and ownership of heritage materials and their interpretations. These incentives are in turn exaggerated by a growing tendency to increase the practical value of archaeological resources through such developments as heritage resource management, tourism development, and community revitalization.

Another factor leading to the public stage of applied archaeology is the increased influence of a postprocessual model for archaeological practice—particularly to the extent that the model encourages localized, emic interpretations of significance and at least purports to realign the authority of interpretation to include the perspectives of others. Interestingly, the postprocessual approach has the potential to link the interests of some archaeologists with other heritage professionals (that is, some cultural anthropologists and historians and many folklorists) in ways that have not been apparent in the past, creating yet another nuance to the idea of public involvement in heritage resource issues.

The clearest difference between the enabling and public stages of applied archaeology may well be the increased recognition of heritage both as an important tool in the representation of competing ideologies and as a highly valued commodity for economic development. Prior to the public stage, archaeologists tended to regard heritage as a given, the significance of which was best revealed through properly disciplined scientific inquiry and professional experience. While varied *uses* of the past have long been acknowledged, the distinct role of archaeology in *revealing* the past was rarely challenged, at least within the profession. Whether recent approaches to heritage "development" have significantly changed archaeologists' minds in this regard is an interesting question that I am not prepared to answer. What is clear, however, is that the equations by which the significance of heritage resources might be determined have shifted, to the point that archaeologists can no longer afford to ignore the interests of other stakeholders of both localized and more general interpretations of the past. Indeed, the idea that archaeologists are holders of a particular and negotiable *stake* in the representations and uses of the past is one consequence of this more recent public stage of applied archaeology.

The public stage of applied archaeology still requires attention to traditional skills and knowledge related to the subdiscipline, as well as to the new skills acquired more recently during the enabling stage. To these are added the need for additional knowledge and skills in such areas as heritage resource management and the negotiation of heritage resources, local and regional planning and development, tourism development, advocacy, and public participation and collaboration. I believe that the recent expansion of these areas of endeavor also indicates the emergence of a different and somewhat more perilous identity for archaeologists. This new identity is one in which many archaeologists are not simply called upon to do their usual thing, but are also required to participate directly in activities related to the development, revitalization, and management of heritage resources. These individuals can no longer get by only as archaeologists in any traditional sense. Increasingly, archaeologists are becoming active collaborators and participants in community and regional development and in the public negotiation of heritage and tourism resources. This transition might be marked by new and less-distinct job titles, and it is certainly laden with new responsibilities.

If I am at all correct in my reading of these current events, then another difference between the enabling and public stages of applied archaeology should be acknowledged. One distinct contribution of the enabling stage was to make more explicit the role played by archaeology in historic preservation and cultural resource management, as well as to help establish credentials for professional practice. The new roles and skills implied by the public stage seem to be moving some archaeologists in the opposite direction—into fields of endeavor that are at least partially shared with a variety of other professionals and publics, and which are laden with ambiguities related to the exercise of authority and expertise. I will have a little more to say about this situation in the conclusion to this chapter.

Some Contexts for Applied Archaeology

It is not as easy as it might seem to distinguish basic inquiry from applied activities. We can argue, for example, that the results of basic inquiry in any field are generally considered to be useful: aeronautic science keeps airplanes up in the air, and archaeology helps us relate our present to the past. For many anthropologists, this promise of utility is sufficient. But others, myself included, will contend that application is distinct in its deliberateness, in the sense that applied anthropology (and by extension applied archaeology) is invested in the act of *making* anthropology useful, as well as in endeavoring to understand the results of such acts with the aim of establishing a science of specific utilities. These deliberate acts imply in their own right a special realm of knowledge and experience that is other than that which is required to conduct basic anthropological inquiry.

Archaeology was associated with applied interests well before the emergence of the two stages that I described earlier in this chapter. Certainly the most apparent associations have been with efforts related to the stewardship of relevant material resources and to activities intended to increase public support for archaeology—two aims that reflect justifiable self-interest and that are often viewed as being closely related. What I have identified as the enabling stage of applied archaeology seems to me to be the result of more than a century of advocacy and lobbying; on the national level it resulted in early legislation such as the Antiquities Act (1906) and the Historic Sites Act (1935), and at the local level it resulted in various forms of public outreach. I will stick my ethnographic neck out here and at least speculate that the aims of stewardship and increased public support for archaeology have become a kind of cultural model that broadly informs the way archaeologists approach the idea of application. The efficacy and durability of that model seems apparent. What is less clear is the extent to which the model makes it difficult for archaeologists to fully realize the potential of other, emerging modes of application, particularly those associated with what I have described as the public stage of applied archaeology.

An impressive variety of applied roles that have become available to archaeologists have been described by Christian Downum and Laurie Price (1999), who have included applications related to resource claims (such as land claims and repatriation), contributions to cultural identity and representation, technological applications, public education, cultural resource management, cultural tourism, and environmental and ecosystem applications. In a similar vein, Patrice Jeppson and Carol McDavid (2001) have recently noted the increasing ambiguity of the term *public archaeology*, and at least broached the question of whether expanded opportunities in the public sphere might suggest the formation of distinct areas of expertise in such areas as education, legislative practice, media, museums, and tourism development. In what follows I will attempt to expand on this conversation by focusing on three areas of application that I believe to be especially relevant to future developments in applied archaeology: public education, economic development, and community revitalization and empowerment.

Applied Archaeology and Public Education

The most often offered "value added" justification of archaeology is clearly public education (e.g., Little 2002; McManamon and Hatton 2000). The developers of archaeological sites and digs seek to gain public recognition and support through a variety of public education activities including volunteer fieldwork opportunities, tours for school children and others, interpretation and exhibit management, and direct involvement in the development of cultural and heritage tourism. Site-related public education is frequently linked to issues related to stewardship, following the assumption that a better understanding of the archaeologist's use of heritage resources will discourage such activities as looting and site destruction through development activities (for example, Smith and Ehrenhard 1991). Archaeologists have also explored the ways in which fieldwork experiences can serve to reinforce standard curriculum objectives in the schools, providing students with hands-on opportunities to practice mathematical and technical skills as well as to increase their knowledge in such areas as history, geology, and environmental processes (for example, Smith and Harris 2001).

In considering these laudable objectives, it is worth asking how much we actually know about the extent to which such activities actually do contribute to public education. I mean this in two ways. First, is the message getting across in general? How, for example, do people actually read heritage into a site, and what is the relationship between their readings of heritage and the intentions of archaeologists? Second, is the message getting across in specific cases? How effective, for example, is a particular educational strategy, or how well do different kinds of sites fulfill their educational and outreach missions? Much is assumed in terms of the educational mission of public archaeology, but I think we know very little in this regard. In my admittedly narrow range of experience, it appears that the evaluation of archaeological public education activities is often limited (if it occurs at all) to relatively simple surveys designed to collect visitor demographics and gauge first impressions related to site specifics and the valuation of archaeological inquiry. That such evaluative efforts are often associated with attempts to justify or seek additional support for archaeological work makes their scientific usefulness suspect.

There are some promising exceptions. One of these is what seems to be an increasing tendency for archaeologists to collaborate with other professionals (as distinct from local or community collaborations, which will be discussed later in this chapter). There have, for example, been interesting collaborations between archaeologists and cultural anthropologists (see McDavid's and Warner and Baldwin's articles in this volume) and between archaeologists and educators (see Wall, Rothschild, Copeland, and Seignoret's article in this volume). Patrice Jeppson's (2000) convincing discussion of the collaboration between herself and an educator in the introduction of archaeology into the Baltimore County public school system is another case in point. Jeppson attributes much of the success of the project to her educator colleague's professional knowledge of curriculum development and his understanding of practices related to the transfer of knowledge within this specific educational setting. She notes further that the collaboration helped her better understand the extent to which most public education efforts are based foremost on meeting archaeology's needs, and she advocates a shift to a perspective that is more focused on identifying and meeting the needs of the public.

Jeanne Moe (2000) has noted that the evaluation of archaeological public education efforts has several dimensions. Many such efforts do provide information regarding the kinds of knowledge and understanding gained through public education. However, it has proven more difficult to measure changes in attitudes and values or, even more importantly, to obtain information as to whether increased knowledge actually results in desired behavioral objectives, which might, for example, include encouraging people not to harm heritage resources. In comparing two public education projects, Moe also suggests that the success of public education activities can vary from one place to another. Her example refers to regional differences in beliefs related to the ownership of heritage resources and to private landowner rights. A similar case might be made for differences related to class, ethnicity, and many other factors. In other words, there appears to be a need for a more contextualized approach to the evaluation of public education in archaeology and for a recognition that public programs need to be designed in relation to their intended audiences.

Applied Archaeology and Economic Development

My second issue relates to the increasing role of archaeology in matters related to economic development. Largely through the popularity of cultural and heritage tourism, archaeology is sometimes justified as contributing to the economic development of a locality or region. This assumption is rarely challenged, and again I mean this in two ways. In the first instance, we need to recognize that the actual economic benefits of tourism are difficult to determine and often contestable (Chambers 2000). Although economic benefit is almost always the primary justification offered for tourism development, its unspoken motivation might have more to do with issues of representation: Who will have the right to determine how a locality is represented, to manage access to its resources, and so on? Secondly, the distribution of economic benefits through activities like tourism is complex, and, as I see it, it is rarely equitable. My point is this: As archaeological sites and activities increasingly become *attractions*, and as more become tourism destinations in their own right, there is an obligation to better understand the economic implications of involvement in this rapidly growing industry (Pyburn and Wilk 1995). Currently, the association between archaeology and commercial enterprise might be more apparent to some outsiders than it has been to many archaeologists. It seems no accident, for example, that many state and local archaeology programs are housed within departments of community and economic development. To my knowledge the consequences of this relationship for the ways in which public archaeology regards its objects remain largely unexplored.

Katherine Slick (2002) has discussed archaeology's increasing involvement with tourism initiatives as a result of increased commercial and public interest in environmental and cultural tourism. She also refers to the National Trust for Historic Preservation's guidelines for effective tourism collaboration, which include paying attention to community needs, establishing partnerships, and developing marketing strategies. While archaeologists might be tempted to leave such issues to tourism and economic development professionals, Slick argues that they can no longer afford to distance themselves from either the skills or implications of tourism promotion. It might be noted that there are both practical and ethical concerns to be considered in this respect. On the practical side, archaeology is becoming increasingly dependent upon tourism, and in some instances archaeologists have been primary actors in the development of tourism in association with sites they have helped establish. Just as a couple of decades ago archaeologists who had begun working with CRM firms pointed to the need for new skills in such areas as proposal writing and budget maintenance, future archaeologists might well be indicating the need for skills development related to such things as determining tourism carrying capacity, environmental mediation, planning and project development, and the marketing of heritage resources.

On the ethical side, it is hard to miss the fact that tourism occurs in communities whose members might well reap some benefits as well as pay significant costs related to its development. As archaeologists come to represent and support tourism development as a means of furthering their profession, they certainly need to recognize that they incur responsibilities to the communities in which they become engaged. In this respect it is important to recognize that the tourism industry as a whole does not have a good reputation for either admitting the existence of or attempting to mitigate local costs associated with tourism. The assurance of economic benefit (based on a kind of "trickle-down" formula often expressed in terms of the "multiplier effect") is seldom challenged, even though it has become apparent that in many instances promised economic returns are never realized on the community level, or, where they are realized, they often serve to relegate locals to low-paying, dead-end employment "opportunities" in the service sector.

Neither has the industry at large been very good at assessing or acknowledging the community costs of some kinds of tourism development, such as gentrification, increased prices for basic goods and services, lessened access to public resources, and environmental degradation.[3]

Archaeologists need to become more aware of these issues, as well as better schooled in efforts to adopt more sustainable and community-based approaches to tourism development. Increased awareness could also help sensitize archaeologists to new issues. For example, to what extent might their longstanding commitment to stewardship and the promotion of the archaeological profession encourage them in some cases to unwittingly act in ways that are not in the best interests of the communities in which they work? The value of tourism development can, for example, be assessed in relation to opportunity costs: What is the value of one kind of investment of public funds as opposed to another? This issue has been of little significance to archaeologists because they are inclined to see economic development as a means to their particular ends of protecting heritage resources and furthering their profession. What, on the other hand, might be the consequences of viewing a community's economic well-being as the end, and archaeology as but one possible (and in some cases perhaps not the best) means to that end? At the very least, this would require archaeologists to be able to demonstrate in specific terms the economic and developmental consequences of their activities, rather than simply assume that communities will somehow benefit.

Applied Archaeology and Community Revitalization and Empowerment

Related in many ways to both education and economic development is my third issue, which pertains to community revitalization and empowerment. Archaeology is increasingly seen as having the potential to contribute to the communal identity of localities and to the empowerment of their citizens. There are a lot of intangibles here. Archaeology can contribute to a community's understanding and valuation of its past, thereby increasing public spirit and hopefully encouraging residents to aid in the protection of historic resources. Once again, much is claimed in this regard, and little is known. Archaeologists might be faced with a particular problem in regard to this issue. They are quite rightfully regarded as heritage experts, and they are thereby increasingly called upon to identify heritage resources. What this can mean is that those resources that become recognized by archaeologists as being emblematic of heritage (or, to put it another way, those aspects of heritage that most interest archaeologists) are becoming powerful determinants of what heritage is actually taken to be. However, such determinations rarely involve much consideration of how local communities actually identify their heritage, which is a complex issue in its own right. It seems to me that even where archaeologists and other heritage professionals have attempted to encourage local participation in decisions related to the management of heritage resources, the range of options is often predetermined by the interests of the professionals. Rarely, it seems, is there any attempt to start from the ground up and determine the markers and substances of heritage from grassroots priorities and values.

I want to stress that this problem is not limited to archaeology; it also accompanies the work of other kinds of heritage professionals. As heritage becomes an important strategy for community revitalization and development, and outside experts enjoy increasing opportunities to work with communities in this respect, it is not stretching the case to suggest that a good part of what becomes identified as a locality's heritage depends on what variety of professional becomes involved. The markers of heritage can be different for archaeologists, folklorists, historic building preservationists, arts advocates, or tourism developers; they might vary even further within groups, as they often do between prehistoric and historic archaeologists. There are also currents in heritage development that can cross professional boundaries and have a large influence on how local heritage is defined. I am thinking, for example, of increased interest in landscapes as having heritage value and in recently established national priorities that identify routes (such as waterways, trails, and historic roadways) as important indicators of heritage.

The efforts of heritage professionals are often associated with an intent to revive local interest in heritage, and, supportable as that goal might be, many of these efforts can be more accurately phrased as a desire to interest communities in *some particular aspects* of their heritage. Unfortunately, it seems rare in such work that a community's prior sense of their heritage is fully acknowledged. Yet it is quite possible that a community will have a much more comprehensive and integrated sense of the connections between their past and present than can be discerned by the rather more narrow interests of heritage professionals. Let me share an example with which I am familiar. My colleague Michael Paolisso and I have been working for a couple of years in a waterman community on Maryland's Eastern Shore.[4] We are not the only ones who have become interested in the watermen; indeed, through the efforts of folklorists, popular writers, tourism professionals, and a variety of others, they have become a prevailing symbol of the Chesapeake Bay region, presented largely as a distinct and vanishing way of life. When *we* look at the ways in which waterman heritage has been presented to the public, with a view to including our own primary interests in the subject, we see a preponderant focus upon the *craft* of being a waterman. This includes occupation-related lore and practices, material culture associated with the industry, and an appreciation of the environmental consequences of fishing. These are all important aspects of waterman traditions and are recognized as such in the communities in which they occur. Still, as we become more familiar with the watermen, it becomes increasingly clear that such an emphasis does not provide a complete or accurate view of how they approach their own heritage. One vital component that is missing is the importance of locally established religious practices. The waterman communities of Maryland's Eastern Shore view the traditions associated with their craft through the equally rich, prevailing traditions of their established faith-based practices. The secularization of the waterman industry through the efforts of heritage professionals and others might well represent an association with some generic sense of heritage, but it is not an accurate representation of how the watermen realize the relationships between their past and present lives.

This distinction is not only important in regard to issues of fairness in representation, or of accuracy in describing heritage, but also relates to a couple of the aforementioned goals of heritage development, which are to revive local interest in heritage and to encourage communities to assume responsibility for the preservation of their past. Both goals are difficult to achieve in cases in which local conceptualizations of heritage are not recognized, or where there is a significant disparity between the views and priorities of heritage professionals and those of community members.[5]

As archaeologists have become increasingly involved with some of the issues discussed in this chapter, they have recognized the need to pay more attention to the ways in which their activities impinge upon the interests of others. This has resulted in experimentation with a variety of collaborative and participatory approaches. The word *variety* is key here. Different kinds of archaeological projects will suggest varied approaches to involving others. A distinction can be made, for example, between *collaborative* and *participatory* models. In general, a participatory approach implies that the major aims of a project have been developed from the outside: defined, for example, by the archaeologist or by a client outside the community. Such an approach might be most practical where the aims of a project are relatively uncontroversial and do not appear to compete significantly with other local interests. The methods of a participatory approach might include informing community members of a project, soliciting their support, and perhaps inviting them to actually participate in some aspects of the work, as exemplified by the cases provided in many of the chapters in this volume. A collaborative approach, on the other hand, suggests that the archaeologist and some other party or parties of interest develop the goals and objectives of a project jointly. Collaborative work often implies that both project design and interpretation are shared activities, or that an activity is designed in such a way that the heritage conclusions of both the archaeologist and the local community are represented. In some instances the archaeologist might not be the initiating or even the most powerful partner in a collaborative exchange, as exemplified by Jeffrey Hartman's article in this volume.

A Few Conclusions

The most obvious observation I have made in this chapter is that the ways in which archaeologists work appear to be changing once again. This does not mean that earlier models associated with academically based scholarship and an enabling stage of cultural resource management are being diminished, but that new opportunities have emerged alongside them. This new sense of doing archaeology not only *in* public but also *with* the public appears to have increased the responsibilities associated with doing archaeological work and to have made the role of the professional archaeologist somewhat less distinct from that of other heritage professionals. I have also suggested that archaeologists have traditionally framed their applied activities as being motivated primarily by their desire to protect heritage resources and increase public recognition of their field of study. These are worthwhile goals, but the kinds of involvement I have discussed suggest that archaeologists, along with other anthropologists, are being presented with occasions to contribute in other ways that are related to public education, economic development, and community revitalization. This implies that archaeologists need to be increasingly aware of the relationships between their special interests and those of other professionals as well as the communities in which they work. On occasion they might have to make hard decisions between their roles as advocates for archaeology and heritage resources and their responsibilities to the localities of their endeavors.

Throughout this chapter I have used the term *heritage resources* in preference to two common alternatives. The reason that I avoid the term *archaeological resources* should be obvious. I am, on the other hand, appreciative of the argument Frank McManamon and Alf Hatton (2000:2–4) have made in favor of employing the term *cultural resources*, at least in respect to the volume of work they were introducing. My choice of *heritage resources* for the issues discussed in this chapter is based on some of the very reasons that McManamon shies away from the term—because it involves the work of a wide and ambiguous variety of professionals and is easily associated with a "heritage industry" that is sometimes more concerned with the desire for favorable and commercially successful representations of the past than it is with accuracy and authenticity (or, depending on your view of the interpretative aims of archaeology, at least with equitable representations of the past). Such conflicts and concerns associated with heritage are, to my mind, at the heart of what applied archaeologists face as they situate their work ever more deeply into an arena of public interests.

As I mentioned at the beginning of this chapter, the present volume results in part from recognition of the need for more and better case material related to the applications of archaeology. The individual chapters represent a variety of conditions and approaches that I trust will advance our knowledge of their field as well as place these efforts within the larger context of applied anthropology. To my mind, they are steps along the way to a more reflexive and critical understanding of applied anthropology as a distinct subfield of our discipline. They could be improved in one respect. There is as yet no standard or even clear means for placing such case material within the context of similar efforts. What I mean by this should be apparent if we think of the way we typically write basic (that is, nonapplied) research. It would be difficult to get any such material past an editor or peer reviewer without providing a fairly comprehensive review of how the research fits within the context of earlier inquiries. By the same token, applied work could be presented within a context of similar initiatives—comparing, for example how an archaeologist's approach to collaboration relates to other collaborative efforts, or how the preservation successes associated with one project advance or reflect on other similar efforts. The lack of such an invaluable context for individual applied efforts is due in no small part to the small number of cases available for comparison, making the need for additional case material all that more apparent.

I have written this chapter from the perspective of an applied anthropologist whose training has been in cultural anthropology. There is a smidgen of self-interest on my part in suggesting that the kinds of career opportunities and challenges that many archaeologists now face might require new skills and areas of specialization, some of which can be provided by their cultural colleagues. By the same token, as applied cultural anthropologists find themselves increasingly involved in issues related to heritage development and resource management, the need for additional preparation in archaeology seems equally apparent. I am not unhappy that such circumstances seem to bring both the basic and applied interests of archaeologists and cultural anthropologists much closer together. That is as it once was, I am told, and it is certainly as I believe it should be.

Notes

1. This is not to say that cultural anthropologists have fully mastered the art of effective case studies related to their applied practices. While case studies abound, they tend to be limited in two respects: (1) little attention has been paid to the long-term consequences of applied work; and (2) there have been few attempts to compare studies in order to generalize practice from one setting to another.

2. I am aware that the term *public archaeology* has been used for some time, most generally in association with efforts to educate or involve the public in archaeological work. What I have in mind here is a broader usage, in which the *public* can be seen as having come to play important roles in determining the nature of archaeological practice in various contexts of heritage resource decision making.

3. Gentrification is, for example, an issue that needs to be addressed by archaeologists involved in historic preservation efforts, where the "good" of preservation seems so apparent that the potential for displacement of low-income families and loss of community resources that specifically serve ethnic and low-income populations is not fully considered.
4. The watermen (and women) are involved in local crab and oyster fisheries and have enjoyed a way of life that is currently threatened by declining stocks and competition with other resource uses. My colleague Michael Paolisso at the University of Maryland has been the principal investigator in this research.
5. This problem becomes even more complex when we recognize that communities rarely share a single sense of their heritage. Where heritage professionals do connect with local perceptions of heritage, it is often with those segments of a community whose views correspond most closely to theirs. In traditional communities such as the watermen enjoy, these linkages are frequently made with relative newcomers to the community, retirees, or other often privileged immigrants whose backgrounds are often more similar to those of the heritage professionals than they are to the experiences of the more longstanding community members.

References

Bender, Susan J., and George S. Smith, eds. (2000). *Teaching Archaeology in the Twenty-First Century.* Washington, D.C.: Society for American Archaeology.
Chambers, Erve. (1985). *Applied Anthropology: A Practical Guide.* Prospect Heights, Illinois: Waveland Press.
———. (2000). *Native Tours: The Anthropology of Travel and Tourism.* Prospect Heights, Illinois: Waveland Press.
Downum, Christian E., and Laurie J. Price. (1999). "Applied Archaeology." *Human Organization* 58, no. 3:226–39.
Jeppson, Patrice L. (2000). "An Archaeologist/Educator Collaboration: Lessons Learned during a Year of Archaeology in the Baltimore County Public Schools." Paper presented at the meeting of the Society for Historical and Underwater Archaeology Conference, Quebec City, Canada. http://www.p-j.net/pjeppson/AAA2000/Papers/shaJeppson1.htm. Accessed August 10, 2003.
Jeppson, Patrice L., Carol McDavid, and Linda Derry. (2001). Abstract for "Public Archaeology: International Perspectives, Debate, and Critique (Part One)." Session presented at the meeting of the Society for Historical and Underwater Archaeology Conference, Long Beach, California. http://www.p-j.net/pjeppson/SHA2001/SHA2001.htm. Accessed August 8, 2003.
Little, Barbara J., ed. (2002). *Public Benefits of Archaeology.* Gainesville: University of Florida Press.
McManamon, Francis P., and Alf Hatton, eds. (2000). *Cultural Resource Management in Contemporary Society: Perspectives on Managing and Presenting the Past.* New York: Routledge.
Moe, Jeanne M. (2000). "America's Archaeological Heritage: Protection through Education." In *Cultural Resource Management in Contemporary Society: Perspectives on Managing and Presenting the Past,* ed. Francis P. McManamon and Alf Hatton, pp. 276–87. New York: Routledge.
Pyburn, Anne K., and Richard R. Wilk. (1995). "Responsible Archaeology Is Applied Anthropology." In *Ethics in American Archaeology: Challenges for the 1990s,* ed. Mark K. Lynott and Alison White, pp. 71–76. Washington, D.C.: Society for American Archaeology.
Slick, Katherine. (2002). "Archaeology and the Tourism Train." In *Public Benefits of Archaeology,* ed. Barbara J. Little, pp. 219–27. Gainesville: University of Florida Press.
Smith, Charlotte A., and Jennifer Freer Harris. (2001). "Why Is Archaeology Important? Global Perspectives, Local Concerns." *Early Georgia* 29, no. 1:27–33.
Smith, George S., and John E. Ehrenhard, eds. (1991). *Protecting the Past.* Boca Raton, Fla.: CRC Press.
Trotter II, Robert T., ed. (1988). *Anthropology for Tomorrow: Creating Practitioner-Oriented Applied Anthropology Programs.* Washington, D.C.: American Anthropological Association.

Notes on Contributors

Daryl Baldwin is an enrolled member of the Miami Tribe of Oklahoma. He graduated in 1999 from the University of Montana with a Masters in Arts with emphasis in Native American linguistics. Over the last 10 years he has worked with the Miami People developing culture-and language-based educational materials and programs. He is currently the Director of the Myaamia Project at Miami University in Oxford, Ohio. The Myaamia Project is a joint venture between the Miami tribe of Oklahoma and Miami University. Its mission is to preserve, promote, and research Miami Nation history, culture, and language.

Peter J. Birt is a Ph.D. candidate at Flinders University, Adelaide, Australia. He has recently published "The Burra, Archaeological Insights and Future Directions" in *Proceedings of the Third National Archaeology Students Conference* (2002).

Erve Chambers is Professor and Chair of Anthropology at the University of Maryland. He has been an active member of the Society for Applied Anthropology for more than two decades, and served as the international organization's president from 1987 through 1989. He is founding editor of the publication *Practicing Anthropology* and author of numerous publications, including *Native Tours: The Anthropology of Travel and Tourism*, 2000; *Tourism and Culture: An Applied Perspective* (edited volume, 1997); *Housing, Culture, and Design: A Comparative Perspective* (edited volume with Setha M. Low, 1989); and *Applied Anthropology: A Practical Guide*, (1985).

Cynthia Copeland is an educator with the Seneca Village Project, New York City. She is co-author of *Seneca Village: A Teacher's Guide to Using Primary Sources in the Classroom*, (with Stewart Desmond, Nancy Katzoff, L. J. Krizner, Lisa M. Sita, and Grady T. Turner, 1999).

Jeffrey L. Hantman is an Associate Professor of Anthropology and Director of the Archaeology Interdisciplinary Program, in the Department of Anthropology, University of Virginia. He serves as an advisor and collaborator with Monacan Tribe of Virginia on issues relating to the Monacan Ancestral Museum, repatriation and reburial, and federal recognition efforts. Hantman is author of "Writing Collaborative History," *Archaeology*, October, 2000 (co-author with Karenne Wood and Diane Shields, 2000); "Collective Burial in Late Prehistoric Virginia: Excavation and Analysis of the Rapidan Mound," *American Antiquity*, 2003 (co-author); "Monacan Archaeology of the Virginia Interior, A.D. 1400–1700," in *Societies in Eclipse: Archaeology of the Eastern Woodland Indians*, 2001.

Michael T. Lucas is the Assistant Archaeology Program Manager for the Maryland-National Capital Park and Planning Commission. His articles include "A la Russe, à la Pell-Mell, or à la Practical: Ideology and Compromise at the Late Nineteenth-Century Dinner Table," *Historical Archaeology* 1994; and "Changing Social and Material Routine in Nineteenth-Century Harpers Ferry," *Historical Archaeology*, 1994 (co-author with Paul Shackel).

Carol McDavid is a Board Member and Public Archaeologist for The Levi Jordan Plantation Historical Society and the Site Director, Public Archaeology for Rutherford B.H. Yates Museum. Some of her publications include "Descendants, Decisions, and Power: The Public Interpretation of the Archaeology of the Levi Jordan Plantation" in "In the Realm of Politics: Prospects for Public Participation in African-American Archaeology," *Historical Archaeology*, 1997; and "Archaeologies that Hurt; Descendents that Matter: A Pragmatic Approach to Collaboration in the Public Interpretation of African-American Archaeology," *World Archaeology*, 2002.

Teresa S. Moyer has been working on various museum and public education projects for the National Park Services. She is currently working for the National Park Services and is co-author of *Administrative History of Harpers Ferry National Historical Park*, (co-author with Kim Wallace and Paul Shackel).

Paul R. Mullins is an Assistant Professor in the Department of Anthropology, Indiana University-Purdue University, Indianapolis. He is author of

Race and Affluence: An Archaeology of African America and Consumer Culture, 1999. He is a co-editor of *Annapolis Pasts: Contributions from Archaeology in Annapolis*, (Paul Shackel and Mark Warner, 1998).

Charles E. Orser, Jr. is a Distinguished Professor of Anthropology at Illinois State University. He is author of *A Historical Archaeology of the Modern World*, 1996; *Race and the Archaeology of Identity* (ed.), University of Utah Press, Salt Lake City, 2001; *Encyclopedia of Historical Archaeology* (ed.), 2002; and *Race and Practice in Archaeological Interpretation*, 2003.

Matthew B. Reeves is the Director of Archaeology, Montpelier Foundation. He is author of *Dropped and Fired: Archaeological Patterns of Militaria from two Civil War Battles, Manassas National Battlefield Park*. Occasional Report No. 15, 2001; and "Reinterpreting Manassas: The 19th Century African-American Community at Manassas National Battlefield Park," *Historical Archaeology*, 2003.

Nan A. Rothschild is the Ann Whitley Olin Professor at Barnard College, Columbia University. She co-director of the Seneca Village project and has worked extensively in New York City. Rothschild is author of *New York City Neighborhoods: The 18th Century*, 1990; "Social and Spatial Proximity in Early New York City," *Journal of Anthropological Archaeology*, 1992; *Shared Spaces, Separate Lives: Colonial Encounters in North America*, 2003.

Herbert Seignoret is Research Assistant in Mathematics at the City College of New York. He is responsible for "Privy to History," an exhibit on 19th-century domestic life in an Irish home in New York, with C.C.N.Y, 1996; "City College Digs New York," an exhibit on 19th-century domestic life in an Irish home in New York, with C.C.N.Y. undergraduates, using artifacts from field school excavations, 1996. Presented papers include Seneca Village: Archaeology in Community Context (with Nan Rothschild, Cynthia Copeland, Roelof Versteeg, and Diana Wall), 2001; The Seneca Village Project: A Unique Partnership (with Cynthia Copeland, Nan Rothschild, and Diana Wall), 2001; and The Seneca Village Project: Outreach and Education in the Study of an African-American and Irish Immigrant Community, 2001.

Paul A. Shackel is Professor of Anthropology, University of Maryland. He also serves as the Director, Center for Heritage Resource Studies. Shackel is author of *Archaeology and Created Memory: Public History in a National Park*, 2000; *Myth, Memory and The Making of The American Landscape*, 2001; *Memory in Black and White: Race, Commemoration, and the Post-Bellum Landscape*, 2003.

Mark S. Warner is an assistant professor of anthropology at the University of Idaho. He is a historical archaeologist whose research interests include issues of minority group identity and zooarchaeology. He is a co-editor of *Annapolis Pasts: Contributions From Archaeology in Annapolis* (Paul Shackel and Paul Mullins, 1998) and has recently published "Ham Hocks on Your Cornflakes: Examining the Role of Food in African American Identity" in *Archaeology*, 2001.

Diana diZerega Wall is an Associate Professor of Anthropology at City College of New York. She is co-director of the Seneca Village project. Wall is author of *The Archaeology of New York City*, (with Anne-Marie Cantwell, 2001); and *The Archaeology of Gender: Separating the Spheres in Urban America*, 1994.

Index

community based archaeology programs
(*continued*)
African Jamaicans and, 71–81
American Indians and, 19–33; 137–151
an overview, 199–201
Australia and 153–169
the Irish Diasporic community and,
171–191
nontraditional communities and, 6–10,
85–100
community revitalization and applied
archeology, 203–206
contextual approach, 41–43, 47
Cornish system, 155
Crispus Attuck High School, 58
cultural resources, 206
cultural resource management, 196

D
Digging the Past Program. *See* Mount
Calvert

E
economic development and applied
archaeology, 201–203
empowerment, archaeology and, 50
enabling stage of archaeology, 195–197

F
Flinders Art Museum, 165
Fragments of the Past Program, 165
Frog Manor Plantation, 40

G
Gilmore family. *See* Montpelier
Great Famine, 12, 175
Ballykilcline and the, 177–183
school curriculum and teaching of, 176
Great Hunger, the. *See* Great Famine
Great Potato Famine. *See* Great Famine
Great Starvation. *See* Great Hunger

H
heritage development and archaeology,
10–12,137–192
heritage resources, 193–207

I
Indiana African-American Genealogy
Group, 62
Indianapolis Urban League, 58

interactive interpretation, 42, 46–47
Irish Holocaust, the. *See* Great Famine
Irish Potato Famine. *See* Great Famine

K
Ku Klux Klan 60–61

L
Levi Jordan Plantation, 5, 35–56, 80
Public Archaeology project at; 38–41
post processual approaches at, 41–48;
Also see multicultural expressions
Levi Jordan Plantation Historical Society
(LJPHS), 39–56
Lowell National Historical Park. See
multicultural expressions
Lower East Side Tenement Museum, 93. *See
also* multicultural expressions

M
Manassas National Battlefield Park, 6,
75–77; *See also* Sudley, Virginia
Maryland Historical Trust. *See* Mount
Calvert.
Maryland-National Capital Park and
Planning Commission (M-NCPPC),
120–134; applied archaeology at,
120–121;
memory and racism, 76–77
Miami tribe, 137–151
collaborative research and, 144–148
history of, 139–142
preservation and the, 137–138
tribal infrastructure of, 142–143
Mid-North Regional Development Board,
159, 165
"Milk Cap Day." *See* Riverside Amusement
Park
Monacan Heritage Museum, 23, 31
Monacan Tribe, 5, 19–33
archaeology and the, 23–25
collaborative approaches and the, 25–29
tourism and identity and, 21–23
tribal recognition and, 23–25. *See Also*
multicultural expressions
Montpelier, 6, 77–79
Gilmore family at, 77–79
Mount Calvert, 10, 120–134
Archaeological Society of Maryland at,
125–126
Charles Town also known as, 122